Anonymous

Louisville of Today

Anonymous

Louisville of Today

ISBN/EAN: 9783743345126

Manufactured in Europe, USA, Canada, Australia, Japa

Cover: Foto ©ninafisch / pixelio.de

Manufactured and distributed by brebook publishing software (www.brebook.com)

Anonymous

Louisville of Today

Richly Endowed by Nature as a Manufacturing and Jobbing Centre and a Place of Residence.

A GLANCE AT HER HISTORY, A REVIEW OF HER COMMERCE, AND A DESCRIPTION OF HER LEADING BUSINESS ENTERPRISES; WITH ILLUSTRATIONS OF HER PUBLIC AND COMMERCIAL BUILDINGS AND PLACES OF INTEREST.

(A SOUVENIR OF THE CITY FOR DISTRIBUTION DURING THE G. A. R. ENCAMPMENT.)

ISSUED BY THE
CONSOLIDATED ILLUSTRATING COMPANY,
LOUISVILLE, KY.

COPYRIGHT BY
CONSOLIDATED ILLUSTRATING COMPANY,
1895.

General Index.

	PAGE
Acme Brick Co.	125
Adams, Geo. E., Exchange, Groceries and Liquors	193
Ahlers, Geo. L., Partner Hoffman, Ahlers & Co.	100
Alberding, G., Cigars and Tobacco.	172
Allison, G. M. & Co., Remington Standard Typewriter and Columbia Cycles.	140
American Grocery Co., Incorporated	114
American Corporate Agency.	108
American Restaurant, J. Mivelaz, Proprietor.	89
Amphitheatre Auditorium, Daniel Quilp, Proprietor.	87
Armstrong, W T., Furniture, Carpets, etc.	102
Armstrong, J. A., Pres. The Louisville Chair Co.	81
Armstrong Lumber Co.	125
Atherton, J. M. & Co., Distillers.	80
Ausbeck, Gus, Grocer.	160
Badgley & Hoenter Co., The (Inc.), Photographic Materials and Supplies	154
Baker & Smith Co., Heating and Ventilating Apparatus and Power Plants	96
Bald Bros., Harness, Saddles and Fine Turf Goods.	128
Baldwin, D. H. & Co., Pianos and Organs	134
Ball, Adam, Groceries, Meats and Vegetables.	173
Bannon, Thos., Groceries.	199
Bannon, P., Proprietor Louisville Sewer Pipe Works	131
Barbaroux, E., Pres. American Corporate Agency	108
Barbaroux, Lewis, Sec'y American Corporate Agency	108
Bartman, John & Sons, Lumber.	158
Barbee, Jno. T. & Co., Whiskies.	162
Barnes, C. P. & Brother, Jewelers and Opticians.	165
Barnett, J. T., Livery and Sale Stables.	182
Baron, Frank P., Jr., Harness, Saddles, Bridles, Collars, Whips, etc.	94

	PAGE
Barth, A., Tanner and Currier	86
Bartley, David, Treas. Belle of Nelson Distillery Co.	150
Bates & Sons Co., The (Incorporated), Contractors for Roofing, Asphalt, Granitoid Paving, etc.	173
Bassett, E. R., Paper Hangings	199
Bascom, L. B., House Painter and Decorator.	177
Bauer, Frederick A., Wholesale and Retail Candies	127
Bauer, Samuel M., Jobber of Drugs, Chemicals, etc.	194
Bauer, John, Proprietor Preston Street Pottery	111
Bauer, Fred., Manufacturer and Dealer in Stoves, Tin, Copper and Sheet Iron Work	144
Beatty, Ed. D., Tin Roofing, etc.	168
Beck, Martin, Pork, Lard and Sausage.	170
Becker, C. G. & Son, Grocers.	115
Beckman, Joseph, Manufacturer of Shears, Scissors, etc.	143
Belle of Nelson Distilling Co.	150
Bender, F., Druggist.	155
Bergen & Meehan Co., The, Staves, Headings and Cooperage	188
Berle, P. G., Dealer in Boots and Shoes	99
Bernheim Bros., Whiskies.	110
Besten & Langen, Cloaks, Furs, Suits, etc.	195
Bethel, J. C., Pres. Carter Dry Goods Co.	95
Bickel, Geo., Groceries, Produce, Fuel, etc.	189
Bitzer, Peter, Groceries and Feed.	164
Block, J., Vice-Pres. J. J. Douglas Co.	151
Blue Grass Exchange, Mike Shea, Proprietor	198
Bockee, Garth & Schroder, Leaf Tobacco.	174
Boenwald, C., Groceries and Provisions	199
Bohhnen, A., Groceries and Meats.	160
Bohn, George P., Tin, Copper, and Sheet Iron Ware	193
Booker, Samuel & Co., Mammoth Stables.	169
Bonkofsky, P. E., Importer of Millinery	173

viii   GENERAL INDEX.

	PAGE
Bonnie Bros., Distillers and Wholesale Liquor Merchants	151
Bosquet, Silberg & Co., Wholesale Grocers	97
Bosse Bros. & Son, Funeral Directors	112
Bourbon Exchange, Jacob Henry, Proprietor, Wines, Liquors, etc.	143
Brackett, C. H., Mgr. Empire Drill Co.	117
Bradbury, W. H., Sec'y Carter Dry Goods Co.	95
Bradley Carriage Co., J. J. Burkholder, Proprietor	185
Braun Brothers, Wooden and Willow Ware	160
Brecher, Phil., Vice-Pres. The Fischer-Leaf Co.	84
Brinke & Punst, Groceries, Meats, etc.	106
Brinke, Fred., Staple and Fancy Groceries	168
Brocar, F. E., House Painter	137
Browning, Pete, Proprietor The Gladiator's Place	188
Bruns, S., Boots and Shoes	198
Bruner, H. C. & Son, Produce Commission Merchant	170
Bryant & Stratton Business College	93
Burford, E. A. & Co., Manufacturers Agents and Commission Merchants	107
Burghard, J. T. Co., The, Wholesale and Retail Dealers in Carpets, Lace Curtains, etc	142
Byrne & Speed, Wholesale and Retail Coal Dealers	107
Burrell, Frank R., Mgr. N. A. Walker Sewer Pipe Co.	112
CALIFORNIA FIG SYRUP CO.	130
Callaway, James F., Leaf Tobacco Broker	197
Carr, J. S., Sec'y and Treas. Tapp, Leathers & Co.	100
Carter Dry Goods Company	95
Chess, Wymond & Co., Cooperage	121
Chickering, A. A., Coal, Groceries, etc.	112
Clark, James A. & Co., Whiskies	145
Clark, J. M. Pickle Co., The	132
Clark, J. M., Pres. Kis-Me Gum Co.	148
Clark, E. B., 2d Vice-Pres. Carter Dry Goods Co.	95
Clegg, Fred. A., Mgr. Baker & Smith Co.	96
Club, Miss E., Millinery	155
Cochran, John & Co. (Incorporated), Distillers	136
Coddeway, A. F., Pres. The Western Ins. Co. of Louisville, Ky.	105
Cole, W. F. & Co., Manufacturers, Agents and Jobbers	172
Coleman, T. C., Steam and Street Railway Supplies	128
Coker, P. G., Importer of Millinery	91
Collins, Hilton, Manufacturer of Single and Doubletrees, Neckyokes, etc.	184
Comstock, C. J., Lumber Dealer	161
Cooper & Clark, Electrical Specialties	121

	PAGE
Corbin, Geo. W., Sign Writer	165
Coyne, Joseph, Railroad Contractor	133
Cox, Charles A., Secretary and Manager Louisville Cold Storage Co.	
Crush, Charles, Tailor and Clothier	177
Crutcher Brother Co., The, (Inc.), Dealers in Coal	123
Curran, F. & Co. Wholesale Liquors	143
DAUTRICH, Jacob, Cigar Box Manufacturer	144
Davis, Vincent, Mgr. Eclipse Vinegar Works	174
Dawers, C. H., Tailor	116
Day, Albert, Pres. Turner, Day & Woodworth Manufacturing Co.	84
Deckel, Charles, Grocer	169
Deering Harvester Co., Harvesting Machinery and Binder Twine	150
Dehler, Jr., Geo., Hardware and Cutlery	167
Densmore, The Joseph Fruit Co., Importers and Jobbers of Foreign and Domestic Fruits and Nuts	94
Dickson, F. C., Mgr. The Kentucky Public Elevator Co.	88
Diebold, John & Sons, Dealers in Stone	139
Disston, Henry & Sons (Inc.), Prop. Keystone Saw, Tool and Steel Works	130
Doerr, J. Henry, Photographer	108
Dohn, F. J., Groceries and Produce	146
Dolfinger, J. & Co., Importers and Dealers in Queensware	166
Doll, D. B., Woolen Mills Agent	198
Dorn, K. H., Malt, Hops and Distillers' Supplies	135
Dow Wire Works Co.	187
Douglas, J. J. Co., The, Distillers	151
Drach, Thomas & Bohne, Architects	81
Drew Brothers, Groceries, Wines and Liquors	180
Duckwall, E. G., Commission Merchant	154
Dudley, H. A., Pres. Pearl Laundry Co.	137
Dumesnil, H., Treas. Carter Dry Goods Co.	95
Durrett, R. T., Vice-Pres. Kentucky Title Co	109
EAGLE BRASS WORKS	102
Early Times Distillery Co.	197
Eclipse Vinegar Works	174
Edelmuth, M., Cigars and Tobacco	147
Eggers, Chas., Merchant Tailor	164
Eisenman, Shallcross & Co., Produce Commission Merchants	119
Eitel & Cassebohm, Manufacturers of High Grade Cigars	97
Elliott, C. I., General Agent and Manager D. M. Osborne & Co.	109
Ellwanger, Peter, Raiser and Shipper of Early Vegetables	148
Liwang, A. W., Secretary and Treasurer, J. T. Burghard Co.	142

GENERAL INDEX.

	PAGE
Emker, A. M., Wholesale Produce and Commission Merchant	152
Empire Drill Co.	117
Ewing, D. H. & Sons Creamery	103
Excelsior Novelty Works, Electric Works of all Kinds	144
FALLS CITY BUGGY TOP CO.	127
Falls City Manufacturing Co., Manufacturers of Pants	92
Falls City Planing Mill	102
Falls City Stables	111
Falls City Wine Works	185
Ferguson, Thomas, Foundry Machine and Pattern Works	174
Fibe, Joseph, Groceries, Provisions, Etc.	198
Fink & Feldhaus, Wholesale Saddlery	186
Fischer Leaf Co., The, Mantles, Grates, Tiles, etc.	83-84
Fisher, Wm. H., Hardware and Butcher Supplies	181
Fitzelton, N. L., Prop. Falls City Manufacturing Co.	92
Fleischaker, Louis, Drygoods, etc.	140
Fowler & Constantine, Druggists	112
Fowler, John, Prop. Eagle Brass Works	101
Frankel, N. A. & Co., Commission Merchants and Wholesale Liquor Dealers	191
Frazer, L. M., Clothing, Shoes, etc.	104
Frese, R., Sec'y The Western Insurance Co. of Louisville, Ky.	105
Fruechtenicht, H. & Son, Flour and Feed	170
GATCHEL, W. D. & Sons, Photo. Goods and Picture Frames	155
Gates, Chas. D., Sec'y Turner, Day & Woolworth Mfg. Co.	84
Gaumann, Fred., Groceries, Drygoods and Notions	149
Gatus, Henry, Pharmacist	142
Gazzola, Frank E., Manager Pabst Brewing Co.	129
Georgel, C., Treas. and Gen. Mgr. Louisville Silvering and Beveling Co.	82
Germantown Brewery	149
Gerst, A., Drygoods and Notions	156
Glass, L. B., Manager Pearl Laundry Co.	137
Goan, William, Groceries, Provisions and Feed	145
Goff & Co., Makers of Fine Cigars	114
Golden Rule Store, The, C. E. Overstreet & Co., Drygoods, etc.	158
Gorman, D. A., Vice-Pres. Southern Heating Co.	163
Gottbrath, H., Groceries, Liquors and Tobacco	198
Gould, Frank E., Manager Henry Disston & Sons' (Inc.)	130
Graft, B. C., Secretary and Treasurer H. W. Werst **Plumbing Co.**	97
Graham, S. P., Lumber and Shingles	146
Gray **Street Market**, Philipp Ziegler, Prop.	176

	PAGE
Green, Theodore, Manufacturer of Pianos	177
Green, John W. & D. S., Stock and Bond Brokers	135
Griffin, Wm., Vice-Pres. H. W. Werst Plumbing Co.	97
HARLEM, L. E., Groceries and Produce	139
Haggard, B. S. & Co., Wholesale Commission Merchants	199
Hallenberg, Adolph, Architect	147
Harris, H. E., Sec. Swann Abraham Hat Co.	172
Harthill, Alex., Tobacco Buyer	88
Healme, F. J., Prop. Falls City Manufacturing Co.	92
Heath-Morris Co., Bexry Boxes and Baskets	118
Heck, Frank, Grocery and Saloon	175
Hedden Drygoods Co.	184
Hegewald, Chas. Co., Founders and Machinists	190
Heing & Co., Metal Novelties	122
Henning's, J. W. Sons, Real Estate and Insurance	191
Henry's, Frank, Exchange, Wines, Liquors, etc.	171
Hess, Geo. & Bro., Undertakers	172
Hikes, G. A. & Brother, Meat and Vegetables	160
Hillerich, J. F. & Son, Wood Turners, Band and Scroll Sawing, etc.	92
Hoerter, J. A., Treas. Badgley and Hoerter Co.	134
Hoffman, Ahlers & Co., Distillery and Brewery Coppersmiths	100
Holmes, D. W., Prop. Falls City Stables	111
Home Laundry Co.	189
Hotel Victoria	178
Houston, A. P., Sec. and Treas., The Louisville Chair Co.	82
Huber, G., Brewer of the Celebrated Cream Beer	173
Husemann, E. H., Groceries, Liquor and Tobacco	145
Hudson, P. S., Vice-President Baker & Smith Co.	96
Hyland, Patrick, Grocer	153
JACKE, WILLIAM, Grocery and Saloon	182
Jackman, J. R., Treas. Excelsior Novelty Works	144
Jefferson, T. L., Sec. and Treas. Kiss-Me Gum Co.	128
Jetter, Wm., Manufacturer and Dealer in Boots and Shoes	165
Johanbocke, F. W. & Sons, Wholesale Hats, Caps, etc.	164
Jones, Gabe A., & Son, Livery and Sale Stables	136
Justi, John, Wall Paper	186
KELLER, WM. F., Groceries	184
Kelly, Wm., Groceries, Wines, **Liquors**, etc.	126
Kentucky Jeans Clothing Co.	113
Kentucky Planing Mill	129
Kentucky Public Elevator **Co., The**	120

GENERAL INDEX.

	PAGE
Kentucky Title Co.	129
Kentucky Wall Plaster Co. (Inc.)	180
Kemper, W. D., Grocer	189
Kettmann, Geo. H. & Co., Importers and Jobbers of Watch Materials, etc.	166
Kice & Co., Real Estate	191
Kiefer, John, Meats, Groceries, etc.	110
Killgore & Stoltz, Mfrs. of Platform and Elliptic Spring Wagons	198
King, J. C., Undertaking Co.	96
King, R. E., Sec. & Treas. The J. M. Clark Pickle Co.	132
Kiss-Me Gum Co.	148
Klauber, Edward, Photographer	192
Klee, Coleman & Co., The Mineral Waters, &c.	150
Klein, William & Son, Confectioners	104
Knadler Pickling and Preserving Co, The	173
Koch, Ernst H., Boots & Shoes	106
Koelliker, L., Practical Plumber, Gas and Steamfitter	179
Koestner & Borkel, Cafe, Billiard and Pool Room	168
Kopp, William, Mfr. Wardrobes, Safes, etc.	128
Korb, Louis, Wall Paper and Window Shades	198
Krack, Dr. J. A., Druggist	123
Kraemer, Christ, Restaurant, Bakery and Confectionery	136
Kraft, Geo. C., Beef, Mutton, Lamb, etc	176
Kraft, H. A., Dealer in Meats	182
Kraushaar, Val., Grocery and Saloon	164
Kremelberg & Co., Buyers of Leaf Tobacco	160
Kuhn, John H., Mfg. of Riding Saddles	99
Laufberg & Macke, Altar Builders	128
Layer, G., Fresh Meats	142
Leahy & Scanlon, Coal	132
Lechleiter, Robert, Feed and Fresh Meat	143
Leisman, J. C., Groceries, Provision, etc	185
Lemont, S. M., Pres. Louisville Cold Storage Co.	98
Leonhardt, Albert H., Groceries and Produce	150
Lewman, M. T. & Co., Contractors and Builders	93
Lindsay, Chas. M., Atty. Kentucky Title Co.	129
Long, F. E., Prop. Tenth Street Planing Mill	156
Loomis, Geo., Mfr. of Fine Carriages	171
Louisville Bryant & Stratton Business College	95
Louisville Chair Co., The	81
Louisville Coffin Co.	198
Louisville Cold Storage Co.	98
Louisville Electro-Plating Co.	181

	PAGE
Louisville Electrical Works	177
Louisville Girth and Blanket Mills	162
Louisville Grain and Feed Co.	197
Louisville Silvering and Beveling Co.	82
Louisville Sewer Pipe Works	135
Louisville Steam Forge Co.	124
Louisville Transfer Co.	196
Lyons, W. L. & Co., Stock and Bond Brokers, etc.	134
Lyons, W. L., Vice-Pres. Louisville Silvering and Beveling Co.	82
McAtee, A. H. & Co., Insurance	134
Macfarlane & Co., Iron and Coke	187
Mann, Wm., Florist	179
Mansfeld & Son, Mfrs. Bank Fixtures	206
Markendorf, Martin, Pharmacist	135
Marret, Joseph E., Florist	190
Martin, F. P., Commission Merchant, Lumber, etc	199
Mayer, Jacob H. & Son, Collar Mfr.	112
Meier, Wm. G. & Co, Leaf Tobacco	115
Mellinger, W. E., Pres. Southern Heating Co.	163
Mendel, Chas., Vice-Pres. Kentucky Jeans Clothing Co	113
Mengel, C. C. Jr. & Co., Logs and Lumber	88
Merrick Brothers, Tin, Iron and Slate Roofers	139
Merwin, S. M., Treas. Oneil Coal and Coke Co.	132
Mestemacher, Henry, Locksmith and Bellhanger	185
Mettler, Frank, Watchmaker and Jeweler	109
Meyer, A. W., Vice-Pres. J. T. Burghard Co	141
Meyer, Edmond L., Boots and Shoes	164
Minor, J. S., & Sons, Contractors	126
Miller, J. Wm., Groceries and Produce	160
Miller, Wallace G., Vice-Pres. The J. M. Clark Pickle Co	132
Mills, D. S. & Co., Commission Merchants	161
Mitchell, John & Co., Mfs. Boilers, Tanks, etc.	102
Montenegro, Dr. A. C., Vice-Pres. Kis-Me Gum Co	148
Moody, G. E. & Co., Proprs. Kentucky Planing Mill	118
Moosmann, R., Merchant Tailor	189
Moses, L. & Co., Whol. Clothing Mfgs.	105
Mutual Life Insurance Company of Kentucky	124
Myers, Alex., Broker	168
Nagel, Geo. & Son, Groceries, Produce, etc.	133
Nalley, C. C., Livery and Sale Stables	178
Nanz & Neuner, Florists	116
Neff, Paul A., Grocer	161

GENERAL INDEX.

	PAGE
New Albany Mfg. Co., Quarry Machinery	89
Newman, H. W., Plumber, Gas and Steamfitter	188
Newman, G. A., Gen. Agent of Eastern Department California Fig Syrup Co.	150
Nicholas, St., Hotel and Restaurant	109
Nilest, Martin & Co., Clothing, Shoes and Furnishing Goods	104
Nones, W. C. & S. M., Wholesale and Retail Dealers in Vehicles	165
Norman Lumber Co., The (Inc.)	181
Nugent, E. B., Dry Goods	118
O'Brien, Edward J. & Co., Leaf Tobacco Brokers	115
O'Connor, James, Pres. Oneil Coal and Coke Co	152
Ohmann Bros., Staple and Fancy Groceries	199
Oneil Coal and Coke Co	152
Opdebeeck, C., Leaf Tobacco Broker	141
Osborne, D. M. & Co., Mfrs. Harvesting Machinery	109
Overbecker-Gilmore Co., The, Wholesale Grocers	135
Pabst Brewing Co.	129
Parker, J. C., Whol. Paper and Twine	113
Payne, J. H. & Co., Builders and Contractors	120
Paxton & Thorne, Merchant Tailors	170
Peace, P. P., Gen'l Mgr. The Louisville Chair Co.	82
Pearl Laundry Co	137
Pearson, L. D. & Son, Funeral Directors	133
Pfaffinger & Co., Pork and Beef Packers	138
Pfeiffer, Chas., Pres. The Fischer-Leaf Co.	84
Pfeifer, J. N. & Co., Hatters and Clothiers	193
Phingst, H. Adolph, Apothecary	103
Phister, L., Stoves and Tinware	157
Phelps, Laban, Sec'y Louisville Silvering and Beveling Co.	83
Porter, G. F., Pres Excelsior Novelty Works	144
Precht, A. & Son, Dealers in Boots and Shoes	199
Preston Street Pottery	111
Price & Lucas Cider and Vinegar Co.	119
Priest, W. C., Appraiser for Kentucky Title Co.	129
Queen, R. E., Pres. California Fig Syrup Co	150
Raible, Smith & Co., Sheet Metal Goods	199
Ramsey, A. M., Plumber	170
Ramser, Chas., Dealer in Stoves, Tinware and Hardware	161
Ramser, Geo., Stoves and Tinware	168
Rapp, Jr., Mike, Grocer	174

	PAGE
Reccius, J. W., Sporting Goods	154
Rectanus, Theo., Druggist and Chemist	148
Rectanus & Schilling, Druggists	183
Reiling, W. D., Prop. Louisville Girth and Blanket Mills	162
Reis, S., Wholesale Horse Collar Manufacturer	165
Richardson, H. W. & Co., Distillers and Wholesale Dealers in Kentucky Whiskies	130
Riedling, J. & Son, Flour, Hay, Grain, etc	138
Rietze, Gus. C., Hatter	184
Roberts, S. & Co., Coal	116
Roche's Photographic Studio	179
Rogers, Chas. A., Catholic Books, Etc	186
Roney, Geo. W., Prop. Falls City Mfg. Co.	92
Rowell, Robert, Printers Warehouse, Electrotyping, etc.	183
Rowland, D. G. & Co., Seeds, Agricultural Implements, etc	140
Rowland, Edward, First V.-P. Carter Dry Goods Co.	95
Rubel, Robt. O. & Thomas H., Prop'rs Falls City Buggy Top Co.	127
Rufer's Hotel	104
Rufer, John C., Mgr. Rufer's Hotel	104
Rudolph & Bauer, Candies	127
Ruth Brothers, Furniture Mfrs.	157
Sacksteder, John & Son, Props. of the Mt. Eden Vineyard	139
Sandfort, H., Groceries, etc.	141
Schaich, F., Bakery and Confectionery	126
Schanzenbacker, Peter, Lead Tobacco	144
Scheffer, E., Chemist	186
Schieman, Edw. B., Pharmacist	183
Schimpeler, F. X. & Sons, Distillers and Jobbers of Kentucky Whiskies	149
Schneider, J., Harness, Saddles and Collars	137
Schooving & Mattmiller, Merchant Tailors	108
Schuster, G. A. & Sons, Grocers	169
Schwarzwalder, J. & Sons, Beer Casks, Kegs and Tanks	152
Scott, C., Prop. Louisville Electrical Works	177
Scott & Snyder, Interior Decorators	145
Seebold, John F., Wholesale and Retail Pittsburg Coal	125
Seibert, Jacob, Wall Paper, Window Shades, etc.	131
Seekamp, Henry, Prop. St. Nicholas Hotel and Restaurant	109
Seekamp, A., Wines and Liquors	169
Seelbach's European Hotel and Restaurant	191
Seng Bros., Diamonds, Jewelry, **etc.**,	108
Shanahan, D., Sons & Co., **Railroad** Contractors and Bridge Builders	140

GENERAL INDEX

	PAGE
Sheehan, M., Grocer	141
Sheppard, S. C., Steam, Forge and Machine Works	119
Shippen Brothers, Wholesale and Retail Lumber	108
Sloan & Dawers, Tailors	126
Smith, Geo. L. Mantel Co.	130
Smith, Gran W. & Son, Funeral Directors and Embalmers	98
Smith, J. J., Pres. Baker & Smith Co.	96
Southern Chair Manufactory, Fred Weikel, Propr	123
Southern Heating Co.	163
Southern Oil Tank Line, The, Manufacturer of Petroleum and Its Products	93
Springer, Chas. W., Mineral Spring Waters	96
Sparrier's Sons, A. J., House and Decorative Painters	165
Staab, J. L. & Co., Produce Commission Merchants	164
Starke, Ed., Baker	184
Stinger, J. P. B., Mgr. Excelsior Novelty Works	144
Stickler, John B. & Son, Gas Fitting and Plumbing	141
Stilz, William, Dealer in Seeds, Produce, etc.	171
Stitzel Brothers Co., Distillers of Fine Kentucky Whisky	82
St. Nicholas Hotel and Restaurant	109
Stoker, Ed., Tin Roofing, etc.	181
Streng & Thalheimer, Boots and Shoes	195
Strohmeier, Julius, Baker and Confectioner	177
Sues, Julius, Toys, Rubber Goods, etc.	199
Sullivan, J. T. & Co., Wholesale Produce	157
Sulzer-Vogt Machine Co., Ice and Refrigerating Machinery	122
Swann-Abraham Hat Co.	172
Swearingen, E. L., Pres. Kentucky Title Co.	120
Symmes, H. H. & Co., Contractors for Asphalt, Asbestos and Granitoid Work	157
Tafel, Alb. C., Surgical Instruments	117
Tapp, P. H., Pres. Tapp, Leathers & Co.	100
Taylor, T. P. & Co., Druggists	110
Tellman, Charles, Grocer	156
Thierman, The H. A. Co., Distillers and Wholesale Liquor Dealers	118
Thompson & Co., Wholesale Produce	159
Thomson, A. V., President Kentucky Jeans Clothing Co.	113
Thomson, W. A. & Co., Receivers and Shippers of Grain	180
Tilford, R. J., Pres. Belle of Nelson Distillery Co.	150
Tingley, Wm., Wagon Builder	199
Toewater, F. R., Representing Liggett & Myers Tobacco Co.	101
Trost & Spahn, Horse Shoers, Blacksmiths and Wagon Builders	153
Trost Brothers, Distillers and Wholesale Liquor Dealers	149
Truman, T. G., Partner D. G. Rowland & Co.	140

	PAGE
Trumbo, W. B. Co. (Incorporated), Furniture, Carpets and Oil Cloths	102
Turner, C. C., Sec'y and Treas. Baker & Smith Co.	96
Turner, H. C., Vice-Pres., Tapp, Leathers & Co.	100
Turner, Day & Woolworth Mfg. Co., Manufacturers of Handles	83
Tyler, Owen, Building Material and Supplies	135
Uhrig, Valentine, Bungs	140
Union Mills, Flour and Mill Feed	187
Vaughan, G. & Co., Dealers in Leaf Tobacco and Strips	140
Villier, Chas. A., Sec'y and Treas. The Kentucky Public Elevator Co	88
Vogt, Adam, Sec'y and Treas. Sulzer-Vogt Machine Co	122
Vogt, Henry, Pres. Sulzer-Vogt Machine Co.	122
Vogt, F. Wm., Pres. Louisville Silvering and Beveling Co.	85
Wagner, Paul, Hardware	128
Walker, J. S. & Co., Manufacturers Burlap Bags, etc.	135
Walker, N. U., Sewer Pipe Co.	112
Walter, John E. and Frank, Proprietors Clay Street Brewery	86
Watkins & Cowles, Coal, Pig Iron, etc.	129
Weber, Chas. A., Fancy Groceries, etc.	163
Weber, Valentine, Grocer	151
Weirich, H., Manufacturer Boots and Shoes	127
Weller, W. L. & Sons, Wholesale Liquor Dealers	100
Weller, Ben S., Boots and Shoes	201
Werst, H. W., Plumbing Co.	97
West Louisville Brewery	109
Western Insurance Co. of Louisville, Ky., The	105
Whitehead & Co., Groceries, etc.	158
Wiest, Nick, Baker and Confectioner	107
Will, J. P. Co., Proprietors Falls City Planing Mills	106
Wilson, Hardin, Sec'y and Treas. Kentucky Jeans Clothing Co.	113
Wilson Ear Drum Co.	166
Witherspoon, R. S., Manufacturer of Women's and Misses' Shoes	175
Wolf, Henry H. & Co., Wholesale Manufacturing Clothiers	98
Woolworth, James, Vice-Pres. Turner, Day & Woolworth Mfg. Co.	84
Wright & Taylor, Distillers and Wholesale Dealers in Fine Kentucky Whiskies	85
Wunderlich, The F. Co., Wholesale Liquor Dealers	192
Zoeller, Edward, Band and Orchestral Instruments	153
Zollars, J. W., Representative Deering Harvester Co.	156
Zorn, S. & Co., Grain Shippers	130

LOUISVILLE
OF TO-DAY.

THE history of the city of Louisville, its foundation a little over a century ago as a trading post, its marvelous growth as a commercial and manufacturing centre, and its development into one of the greatest and finest of American cities, is the history of the settlement of the West and fertile prairies of the great Southwest. It has been the scene of fierce struggles between the advance guard of civilization and the barbarous tribes of aborigines; it has witnessed the cabals and intrigues of Englishmen eager to secure for their king and country the advantages that they knew must result from the possession of this, the key to the immense territory which extended in unbroken solitude throughout the valleys of the Ohio and the Mississippi; it has seen its inhabitants involved in the throes of deadly civil war, and it has emerged from all those ordeals mighty and prosperous, the peerless Queen City of the South, a great and powerful commercial metropolis, foremost in the arts of trade, of commerce, of industry, and of transportation, one of the brightest gems in the diadem that encircles the brow of fair Columbia.

It is not the object of this work to elaborately record all the facts that go to make up the early history of Louisville, but rather to present in a succinct and comprehensive form the historical growth and development of those factors which have resulted in the Louisville of to-day. But in order to better and more clearly understand how a mighty city has been carved out of the wilderness, it will be necessary to briefly narrate such early facts as led to the establishment of the trading post on the bank of the Ohio, and to follow up the various steps that have led on to the evolution of our present great metropolis.

EARLY YEARS OF LOUISVILLE.

Many years before the British made any settlements in this section of the country or the Ohio valley, the territory was claimed by France, but the capture of Quebec brought with it the cession of the country we now live in. Louisville is situated at the point where the navigation of the Ohio is obstructed by the rapids, and for six miles above the city the river stretches out into a broad, smooth sheet of water a mile in width almost without a current, forming a safe and beautiful harbor.

In 1766 Captain H. Gordon, a British engineer, came and passed the rapids, as he terms the falls, on July 23d of that year.

LOUISVILLE OF TO-DAY.

The superior attractions of the present site of Louisville could not long go unheeded and eventually in 1770 parties came from Fort Pitt, now Pittsburg, and surveyed the tract adjacent to the falls with a view of distributing them as bounty lands.

In 1773, Captain Thos. Bullitt was commissioned by Lord Dunmore to proceed to the Ohio and make in its vicinity surveys for the location of several land warrants granted by the government in pursuance of the law, assigning bounty land to be located on the western waters for the soldiers of Virginia in the French and Indian war. Even previous to the arrival of Captain Bullitt these lands had been patented by John Campbell and Dr. John Connolly. After Bullitt's expedition the falls were visited only by a few hunters and traders until 1778 when a new attempt at a permanent settlement on this site was made, by the gallant Colonel George Rogers Clark, whose name is famous in the early history of Kentucky. He was a surveyor, like George Washington, and was a man of superior talents and ability, and when twenty-six years old held the commission of captain, having been engaged in Lord Dunmore's wars against the French, Canadian and Northern Indians. Captain Clark declined a commission in the British army on the close of hostilities against the French, and in 1775 visited the infant settlements in Kentucky, and was afterwards commissioned major, with authority to command the militia of the settlement.

The Revolutionary war had now begun and Major Clark being an ardent patriot saw that from the northwestern posts garrisoned by British troops extensive supplies of arms and ammunition were given to the Indians who infested Kentucky, and formed the bold project of stopping these evils. He obtained a few state troops from Virginia and descended the Ohio with one hundred and fifty men and thirteen families and reached the falls May 29th, 1778, and from that day the foundation of Louisville properly dates. He landed his forces on Corn Island, then a little below the old mouth of Beargrass, not far from the foot of Fourth Street, an island about four-fifths of a mile long and about five hundred yards at its greatest breadth lying near the Kentucky shore. Having built some cabins surrounded with palisades, so as to make them defensible against an attack of Indians, he proceeded with his forces on his successful expedition against Kaskaskia. Though these pioneers were now four hundred miles distant from the nearest settlements they went to work planting corn on their little island, the rifle in one hand and agricultural implements in the other, and Corn Island derives its name from the first crop of corn grown on it in this region. Of the earliest settlers only a few names have been preserved, viz: those of Captain James Patton, who piloted the first boat over the falls; Richard Chenoweth, John Tuel, William Faith and John McManus. The woods of Kentucky luckily abounded with game so that at first the chief subsistence of the pioneers was obtained from the products of the chase.

In 1779, having built a fort on the eastern side of the large ravine, which formerly entered the river at the present terminus of Twelfth Street, they emigrated thither and thus laid the first permanent foundation of Louisville, named in honor of Louis XVI. of France in recognition of his assistance tendered the colonies in their struggle for liberty. At the termination of the war of the Revolution, in 1783, immigration rapidly increased.

In December, 1790, President Washington strongly recommended

CHARLES D. JACOB,
Ex-Mayor of Louisville.

LOUISVILLE OF TO-DAY.

the admission of Kentucky into the Union, and an act looking to that effect passed the National Legislature, 1791. It was adopted by the people, state officers were elected, and in June, 1792, the state was admitted into the Union.

The first newspaper, known as the Farmers' Library, was published in Louisville in 1801, and was followed the next year by the Louisville Gazette. Whether these newspapers succeeded is not known, but it speaks well for the intelligence and progress of the place that in two successive years two public journals were hopefully started.

In 1808 a theatre was erected in the city on the north side of Jefferson Street between Third and Fourth Streets and was destroyed by fire in 1843.

The river history begins in 1811, and Fulton's steamboat, the "New Orleans," left Pittsburg to run from New Orleans to Natchez, but was delayed by the falls, and during her detention made several trips to and from Cincinnati. However, in November she was enabled to pass and reached Natchez on the 1st of January, 1812. Violent earthquakes were experienced in the city in 1812, so that the houses were hung with some suspended object, which acting as a pendulum determined by its motion the probable amount of danger, and when it began to vibrate freely, the building was instantly deserted.

A Methodist church was built in 1808, on the north side of Market Street between Seventh and Eighth Streets, and was followed by a Catholic chapel, which was erected by the Reverend Father Badin in 1811.

In 1816, the First Presbyterian church was founded, the building being erected at the northwest corner of the alley, between Market and Jefferson Streets on the west side of Fourth Street. It was destroyed by fire in 1836.

In May 1825, LaFayette visited Louisville, receiving an enthusiastic reception, indeed his whole tour throughout the United States was distinguished by splendid festivities and rejoicings.

The city was incorporated February 13, 1828, and its progress since has only been interrupted by an occasional crisis in financial affairs or some other calamity uncontrollable by man.

Louisville was the first city in Kentucky lighted by gas; this was done by a corporate company in 1838, and during this year the conflagration known as the great fire of Louisville took place. Thirty buildings were consumed, and the loss amounted to over $300,000, which was a vast sum in those days.

The Louisville and Portland canal was completed December, 1829, and the general government is now the owner of the entire stock having taken possession in 1872 by virtue of an act of the Kentucky Legislature. Before the canal was enlarged sufficiently to fully accommodate the commerce of the river, the rapid growth of the railroad system of the city and country had deprived river commerce of its supremacy. The canal is one and nine-tenth miles in length, and sixty-four feet wide, extending from opposite the foot of Sixth Street to Twenty-eighth Street. To the date of its being made a free water way over $6,000,000 had been collected for toll and the cost has been about $5,000,000. The improvements just completed will make the canal two hundred and fifty feet wide at the upper end, which width will extend three hundred and fifty feet below the railroad bridge, and increase its width to one hundred and twenty-five feet below the locks at the lower end.

HENRY WATTERSON.

COURT HOUSE.

GEOGRAPHICAL ADVANTAGES.

Geographical position and manufacturing advantages are necessarily so homogeneous in the progress as well as in the birth of a great manufacturing community, that in the subject-matter of this volume these two requisites are combined in their exposition as they naturally are in their power. Louisville combines more geographical advantages of position than almost any city in the Union, bearing the same commercial relation to the new South as Chicago does to the new Northwest, with this important difference, viz: in addition to her extensive railroad connections she has an advantage that cannot be overestimated in the noble river that,

J. H. HANCOCK,
Treasurer.

HENRY S. TYLER,
Mayor.

flowing at her feet and capable of bearing the traffic of a nation, mingles its water with those of the majestic Mississippi, and thus through that great artery and its tributaries, brings to our doors the rich products of the vast regions that border the Upper and Lower Mississippi, the St. Francis, the White, Black, Arkansas, Yazoo, Ouachita, Red, and many other navigable water-courses. Can there, therefore, be any doubt of the future of the Falls City as a commercial and shipping as well as a manufacturing point? The contemplated improvement of the rivers may for a brief time be delayed, but the very necessities of the country will force the expenditure of the ready money requisite to render this great highway of transportation all that it can be made, and which its location to producing and consuming populations of the country indicate it must be. Not only will the increasing wants of the people for cheap transportation require this, but the steadily growing bulks requiring transportation will render it necessary, and such improvements of the navigation of all connecting rivers, as will make most available to those points this system of inland navigation, without a parallel in any nation or any country. Again, for the carrying on of manufactures of great magnitude and variety Louisville is not excelled in natural advantages, and in the means for building up large and successful establish-

CHARLES P. WEAVER,
Postmaster.

ments by any of the most favored of the other cities of the continent. It would not be possible within the limits of a single volume to give in detail all the facts in connection with the manufacturing operations conducted in Louisville. Suffice it to say whiskey and tobacco are the leading products of Louisville; yet vast quantities of agricultural implements, vehicles of all kinds, leather, textile fabrics, boots and shoes, cements, steam-engines, machinery, architectural iron-work, stoves, tin and sheet-iron ware, sash, furniture, doors and blinds, cooperage, etc., add to the volume of her industries. To put the matter briefly, it may be tersely stated that Louisville is the largest tobacco market in the world; it makes and ships more cement than any city in the United States; it makes more oak-tanned leather than any city in the United States; it makes more plows than any city in the world; it makes more jeans than any other city; and last, but not least, it handles more fine whiskey than any other market in the United States.

THE TORNADO OF 1890.

This great calamity, which visited Louisville on the evening of March 27th, 1890, is of historical importance. A heavy rain-storm began before eight o'clock, followed by hail and severe lightning. The wind then rose and at 8:30 P. M. the tornado struck the city, ploughed its way through in a few minutes, and in its brief time wrought terrible havoc and disaster. The storm approached Louisville from a southwesterly direction, severely

CITY HALL.

LOUISVILLE OF TO-DAY.

damaging the suburban town of Parkland, and struck the city at its southwestern point, passing through northeasterly to the river at the foot of Seventh Street, thence crossing to Jeffersonville, damaging the front of that city greatly; thence recrossing the river and destroying the standpipe of the water-works, about three miles east of where it first struck the river. The path of the storm through the portion of the city visited was from six hundred to eight hundred yards wide, and in its passage it killed outright seventy-six persons, and injured over two hundred more. It destroyed partially, and in some cases totally, five churches, one railroad depot (Union), two public halls, three school buildings, two hundred and sixty-six stores, thirty-two manufacturing establishments, ten tobacco warehouses, and five hundred and thirty-two residences. The pecuniary loss by storm was, after careful calculation, estimated at $2,150,000. The calamity aroused the

CUSTOM HOUSE AND POST OFFICE.

sympathy of the country, and pecuniary assistances for the relief of the suffering it caused was freely tendered; but Louisville felt able to attend to her own stricken ones, and the offers were thankfully and gratefully declined. Something over $15,000 was sent in a way that could not be refused, but that amount and about $1,000 more was spent in relieving suffering outside the territory of the city. The citizens contributed over $115,000, besides clothing, bedding, and food, and with these means, through the admirable system pursued by the Board of Trade Relief Committee, food, shelter, medical attention and burial expenses were promptly provided and distress from want prevented, and the losses of the poor, including the rebuilding of three hundred and eleven homes and their wreckage of furniture, made good. The faithful and successful work of this committee of relief is worthy of, and has justly received, the highest praise. The destruction of the stand-pipe at the water-

LOUISVILLE OF TO-DAY.

works threatened a water famine, which would have caused many factories to shut down work and thrown many people out of employment, and seriously affected the health of the city, but this danger was happily averted by the energy of the Water Company and the skill of its engineer. For a month or more a large number of her pushing business men were occupied with relieving the distress, removing the wreck, and rebuilding necessitated by the tornado, and consequently in some departments the business of the city was neglected and fell off.

LOUISVILLE OF TO-DAY.

The situation of Louisville on the Ohio, one of the chief tributaries of the greatest river system in the world, and in immediate touch with a vast area of country in the heart of the continent, whose natural resources and capacity to sustain an immense population are still not fully recognized is absolutely unrivalled. Our city is also situated almost exactly in the centre of the population of the United States, as nearly as possible, equal numbers of people being found on the east and on the west as well as on the north and south. This central position affords singular advantages for the distribution of goods of every description, and in this respect the pushing houses of the city, especially in the wholesale and jobbing lines, have displayed marked enterprise in extending their influence and occupying new fields, with the result of successfully competing with many centres much older commercially, but whose methods are those of the past. Apart from natural advantages, however, Louisville may justly be regarded as one of the wonders of modern times in point of human achievement and effort. Extensive river improvements, the construction of the great bridge over the Ohio, and many other notable accomplishments, together with the enormous growth of manufacturing and mercantile interests have combined to place the Falls City" among the mightiest in the central states, who are dependent upon their own resources for advancement. The development of the city to such extensive proportions is an achievement of human skill and industry that may well awaken a feeling of pride in every citizen's breast, and cause us to look with complacency upon the results attained in government, art, science, culture, commerce and general advancement. Louisville has no natural barriers to retard its growth and the extension of its area, as so

many others have, in all sections of the country. On the other hand attractive residence sites are to be had in almost every direction in abundance, manufacturing establishments can choose from dozens of suitable locations, where railroads are ready to provide them with switches, or where boats can tie up and unload their cargoes, and become again burdened with the products we supply, and ample room exist for decades of growth in area and population. From whatever standpoint viewed, Louisville presents all the aspects and elements of metropolitan and twentieth century life. On every hand are to be seen evidences of material wealth and prosperity, irrefutable indications of comfort and luxury, of taste, culture and refinement, while on the main shopping thoroughfares, in the leading manufacturing sections, along the railroads, quays, and in every avenue of commerce, the features of a metropolis are still more apparent. A notable feature respecting the more recent advances made by the city, is the steady increase in population observable, even during the times of monetary stringency, when the former immense immigration to this country has fallen off to such insignificant figures. The United States census of 1890 showed a population of 161,129 for the city. In 1895 the number of names upon the directory was 90,208. Using the universal multiplier of two and one quarter, this gives a population at the present time of 202,968, an increase for the year of 1,569, and for the five years since 1890, of 41,839. The next official census will be a real surprise to many of our citizens, and, when comparisons are made with other centres at that time, the enormous advances made by our city will be brought vividly home to the whole country, and our bright future as a capital of the southern states, as a mart for goods of every description and as a distributing point for thriving towns and villages, and a rich country, will be acknowledged on all hands. It is surprising in times like these how much additional capital is being invested in industries of every description. This displays the undisturbed confidence felt by our business men and those who are about to originate new enterprises, in the speedy return of prosperity to the southern states, and the rapid recovery that all lines will experience in the near future. We are preparing for fresh advances, and wherever it is possible to increase the advantages to be derived from trade in any particular line, these improvements will be made, until Louisville will offer her vast con-

LOUISVILLE OF TO-DAY.

course of customers a market for their productions which cannot be excelled in any important particular. The same superiority which constitutes Kentucky's metropolis such an unrivalled point for the distribution of goods also acts in favor of the reverse process, the collection of raw materials for use in our manufactories, the buying up of agricultural products of every description, and the bringing to this market of articles of all kinds which can be grown in the rich country tributary to this city. Our commercial associations and business men of every kind are fully alive to the necessity of facilitating the transaction of industrial and trade operations to the greatest degree that is consistent with legitimate dealing, and never before has there been displayed a more sublime faith in the future which awaits the city of Louisville, when once the highways of development are opened upon modern lines than now. The intimate knowledge of this vast subject in all its bearings, that our leaders in commerce and finance possess, is well illustrated by the wise action of our Board of Trade recently, in the encouragement of immigration to the state of Kentucky. There are few states or territories in the Union that possess greater natural advantages than ours, or that offer a more practical and varied field for the capable agriculturist. Yet each year thousands of the best class of settlers pass our doors on their way to the western prairies, where droughts and scorching winds effect such ruin, and sweep away in a month the profits of years. With the dissemination of more accurate knowledge, the channels of immigration will change, and rich sections like Kentucky, now passed by in the feverish desire to get to the much belauded prairie states, will receive the attention they deserve. Upon this solid basis of a prosperous and steadily growing agricultural community will be built the extensions and additions to our already great commercial structure, and Louisville, with its exceptional natural advantages and enterprising merchants and manufacturers, will then take its rightful place as the peer in every respect of the best interior marts of trade.

TRANSPORTATION FACILITIES.

In the matter of railroads Louisville is especially favored, having quick, easy and cheap communication with all important points on the continent, while new lines are steadily pushing towards her gates, each opening up new avenues for her enterprises. Whatever the Falls City has gained in the past from her unrivalled water highways, and however much she may hope to acquire in the future under a comprehensive system of river improvements by the national government, her present and future prosperity is largely influenced by the facilities for railway transportation, which the city may possess. The location of Louisville is that of a natural geographical centre. Such a position in this era of railroads is of greater or less importance in proportion to its railway facilities.

Ability to receive and distribute quickly and cheaply all kinds of freight and produce is an all important factor in estimating the value of a location as a point for profitable business investment, and as also indicating the possibilities of progress.

As the leading factor in the new life of the city—one that has more than any other contributed to her prosperity and advancement—the Louisville and Nashville Railroad demands first place in consideration because of its importance. This railroad was chartered March 2, 1850, and the first through train ran the entire distance to Nashville (185.23 miles) in November, 1859. It was a great triumph, and one of which Louisville, one of the heaviest stockholders, was justly proud. More than twelve thousand men are employed by the company in various capacities, and the payment of wages averages nearly $500,000 per month.

In 1830 the Lexington & Ohio Railroad was chartered. It was the pioneer railway of Kentucky and the first to enter this city.

The road was completed and the first train passed over it on the 29th of February, 1838. The business was profitable from the first, but was strenuously objected to by citizens along the route, especially on Main Street. They procured an injunction against its operation and prolonged litigation was the result. The road was never constructed above Sixth Street, and in 1844 was transferred to the Louisville & Portland Railroad Company by the State.

To the Louisville & Frankfort Railroad Company, which was incorporated in 1847, was transferred by the State so much of the last mentioned road as lay between Louisville and Frankfort. About the same time the division between Frankfort and Lexington was also transferred by the State to a new company which was chartered in 1848 under the name of

COLUMBIA BUILDING.

LOUISVILLE OF TO-DAY.

the Lexington & Frankfort Railroad Company. The Lexington division was completed in 1849 and the Louisville division was finished by the new organization in 1851, and then for the first time traffic by rail passed through from Louisville to Lexington. In 1856 the legislature authorized both roads to consolidate, and in 1866 and 1867, the Short Line having been built, the whole consolidated under the name of the Louisville, Cincinnati & Lexington Railroad Company.

The Jeffersonville, Madison & Indianapolis Railroad Company is a consolidation of two roads, the Jeffersonville, and the Madison & Indianapolis Railroad Companies. The former was originally the Ohio & Indianapolis Railroad which was chartered by the Indiana legislature in 1846. It went into full operation in 1853. The Madison & Indianapolis road was chartered in 1842 and set in operation in 1847. In May, 1866, both companies merged their lines into a single one, and in 1873 the whole was leased to the Pennsylvania Railroad Company which now operates it.

The Chesapeake & Ohio road traverses the entire State of Kentucky from east to west. It was formed in 1868 by a consolidation of the Virginia Central and the Covington & Ohio railroads. The road with its leased lines extends from Newport News to Louisville and from Louisville to Memphis, via Paducah, and to other points intermediate.

The Louisville Southern Railroad, the picturesque route to Lexington through the centre of the Bluegrass region, was originally chartered as the Louisville, Harrodsburg & Virginian Railroad Company, on March 5, 1868. Its name was changed by an act of the Kentucky legislature in 1884, to the Louisville Southern Railroad. The main line was completed and opened May 16, 1888. The Lexington branch was opened August 24, 1889.

The Louisville, St. Louis & Texas road, called "the Texas road" is completed to Henderson, Ky. The road follows the south of the Ohio River.

The Louisville, New Albany & Chicago Railroad, the direct route to Chicago, is the only line running dining cars between Louisville and Chicago. There is not a line or road in the United States in better condition, more popular or under better management than this one, and whose office is on the northeast corner of Fourth Avenue and Market Street.

The Louisville, Evansville and St. Louis Consolidated railroad. This road, better known in Louisville and vicinity as the "Louisville & St. Louis Air Line," is of much importance to the commercial interests of the Falls City, giving to merchants a territory fully one hundred miles in length and fifty miles in breadth, offering not only a competing line, but the shortest line from Louisville to St. Louis, Mo., and all points West and Southwest; to Rockport and Evansville, Ind., Owensboro and Henderson, Ky., to Vincennes and Terre Haute, Ind., via Princeton and the Evansville & Terre Haute Railroad; to Cairo and points in Southern Illinois via Mt. Carmel and the Cleveland, Cincinnati, Chicago & St. Louis Railroad. At Browns, the Peoria, Decatur & Evansville Railway gives a valuable and direct line to Peoria, Decatur and Mattoon, Ill. Of the other many railways entering and connecting with this centre space will not permit of mention. Suffice it to say that Louisville's advantages for receiving raw material and distributing freight are well-nigh unsurpassed. Indeed, marching with rapid steps to the position of a metropolitan manufacturing centre, Louisville has at her command a railway system equal to her demand for supplies of whatever nature, and to her distribution requirements, whatever may be the magnitude of her productions.

BRIDGES.

There are three substantial bridges across the Ohio river. The first of these was built by the Louisville Bridge Company, and crosses the river at Fourteenth Street. It was begun in 1867, and the first train passed over as a formal opening of the bridge for business on July 18, 1870. It cost in round numbers one and a half million of dollars. It is 5,294 feet in length, or one mile and fourteen feet. Over the Indiana channel it is 101½ feet above low-water mark, and in the centre ninety-five feet above.

Louisville and Jefferson bridge. The piers for this bridge cross the Ohio river opposite Campbell Street to Jeffersonville, Ind. The bridge with its approaches, is one and three-quarter miles in length—the bridge proper being 2,545 feet long; the Louisville approach 2,586 feet, and the Jeffersonville approach 4,863 feet in length. Over the centre of the river it is ninety-eight feet above low-water mark and fifty-three feet above high-water mark. A double track is run over the Jeffersonville approach up to the first pier of the bridge, a single track being used across.

The Kentucky and Indiana bridge. This bridge crosses the Ohio river at Thirty-second Street and was built by the Kentucky and Indiana Bridge Company at a cost of $1,700,000 including approaches, and was opened for business in October, 1886. The bridge has a driveway for wagons on either side of the railroad track, and is throughout a splendid specimen of bridge architecture. The bridge proper is half a mile long, and with its approaches measures about one mile.

MUNICIPAL.

The municipality is governed by a Mayor and a legislative body composed of a Board of Councilmen, two of whom are chosen from each of the twelve wards of the city and a Board of Aldermen consisting of one representative from each ward, chosen by vote of the citizens.

FIRE DEPARTMENT.

For many years as in all other cities of the United States, the protection of property from the ravages of fire was entrusted entirely to the efficiency of volunteer organizations, and the history of their gallant conduct is a bright page in local annals.

The department now possesses all the latest improved apparatus and appliances for the extinguishment of fire, and no expense has been spared by the city to provide every modern requisite, that will in any way conduce to the rapid and effectual work of the firemen.

The fire alarm telegraph in use in the city is that known as the "Central Station System" and is operated by alarm boxes, the location of which are denoted by serial numbers.

A Salvage Corps, which is supported by the insurance companies, also acts in conjunction with the department, equipped with Babcock's extinguishers and modern apparatus, its object being to save property from damage by water, etc., and taken altogether Louisville is admirably protected by all that human skill and ability can accomplish.

THE POLICE DEPARTMENT.

The city is divided into Eastern and Western divisions for police patrol purposes, and these two divisions are divided into two sections each.

Each division has a station house, while the third station is the central one located in the basement of the City Hall.

The officers and men are highly trained and most efficient, and compare favorably with any other city in the country.

The department is provided with patrol wagons and ambulances and the good order that prevails throughout the city and the promptness with which law-breakers are brought before the courts, reflect the greatest credit on the force.

THE CITY WATER SUPPLY.

Louisville is supplied with water by the Louisville Water Company, which, though distinct from the municipal corporation, is almost a city department, Louisville owning $1,274,600 of stock, the total stock amounting to $1,275,100, consequently the officers are answerable to the city as the principal stockholder. The water is obtained from the Ohio four miles above the city, and pumped into two reservoirs, having a capacity of 100,000,000 gallons, 179 feet above the low-water mark of the river. The works were completed in 1879 and have cost altogether about $6,000,000, the annual receipts for water supply amounting to about $230,000, while the expenses for conducting the works aggregate $70,000 yearly.

BANKING AND FINANCE.

Louisville stands out in strong contrast to other Western and Southern cities, as regards all matters connected with modern banking and finance, and no city in the United States can point to such an unabated and uniform prosperity as the banking institutions of the Falls City during the present generation. A large part of the South is entirely dependent upon her for banking facilities, and during the financial crisis of the past few years, merchants, manufacturers and financiers have not relied on Louisville in vain. Managed with rare fidelity and sagacity, no spirit of speculation has shaken her banks and no defalcation has gutted their vaults.

Louisville, as is well known, is a great centre for loaning money to outside corporations, and few cities in the West or South have so much of their capital invested in property beyond their limits as ours.

AMERICAN NATIONAL BANK BUILDING.

LOUISVILLE TRUST COMPANY'S BUILDING.

THE COMMERCIAL CLUB.

The Commercial Club was organized in 1887 and has a membership of over thirteen hundred, representative business and professional men. It is not a social organization but a large mercantile army, that has for its object the advancement of the city's financial, commercial and manufacturing prosperity.

The Club is made up of the younger business element of the city, and has achieved great success by bringing Louisville and Kentucky before the notice of the world by special undertakings and the dissemination of interesting and valuable printed matter, which has advertised the city and attracted large capital and business here.

Its various committees are constantly introducing projects for the good of the city and its citizens in a business way, and endeavor by entertainments and correspondence to attract new enterprises and thus further the prosperity and commerce of the city. The Club has spacious quarters in the Board of Trade Building.

THE BOARD OF TRADE.

One of the most important organizations in Louisville is the Board of Trade, which was duly incorporated by the Legislature in 1873, and has ever aimed to assist not only the merchants and manufacturers of our city, but also the people of the city and state in all matters relating to business prosperity. Its policy has always been to advertise the advantages of Louisville as a trading point and aid our merchants in extending their business. The Board often brings to the city excursions of merchants from some locality, where our merchants have customers. It receives and entertains them at its own expense affording them every opportunity for seeing that it would be advantageous for them to trade with us. It has a membership of over five hundred members, consisting of the leading wholesale and retail merchants, manufacturers and many belonging to the professions.

In addition to the issuing, etc., of daily market prices, both local and at large, the care of transportation interests and other matters usual in Boards of Trade, it has a first-class reference and statistical Library, which is extremely valuable to members and citizens. The Board occupies offices in its own spacious building at Third and Main Streets, where its large Trade Hall, having a seating capacity of six hundred and also the committee rooms are located.

LEADING MANUFACTURES AND RESOURCES.

We have already alluded, under the caption of "Geographical Advantages" in a cursory manner, to the direction these advantages are utilized in the matter of production, and while in a measure the succeeding remarks may be more or less of a reiteration, we still deem the subject worthy of a slightly more extended review, while much further information will be found in the concluding pages of this work, where reference is made to the leading corporations and firms engaged in the variety of manufactures carried on in this prolific city.

Tobacco.—From its very infancy, one might truly say, Kentucky has been noted throughout the world for her successful cultivation of leaf tobacco, and while other sections are learning the secret of the successful growth of this profitable product, the Blue Grass State has never lost her pre-eminence. Her soil gains rather than loses in fertility, and if the farmer is satisfied with less return than the former almost fabulous profits of twice the value of his land from a single year's crop, the interest continues to be such a vast and important one as to exercise most marked influence on the business life of Louisville, which is the greatest central receiving depot for the leaf tobacco trade on the face of the globe. Her most formidable and energetic competitor for supremacy in this interest, Cincinnati, has without doubt succeeded in making serious inroads on the Falls City's territory, and has diverted from her a considerable share of the annual crop. This was effected chiefly through the agency of the Cincinnati Southern Railroad, which, penetrating the heart of the best tobacco-growing counties, offered extraordinary inducements to shippers in the matter of freight rates, etc., while the Cincinnati Tobacco Association, composed chiefly of Kentuckians, has left no stone unturned to draw to their market as much as possible of this great staple. They have been met, however, with equally vigorous methods: the construction of new railroads, liberal concessions in freight rates, commissions, storage, etc., until, as the figures for the past year show, Louisville has more than regained her former ascendancy. The great importance of the

58 LOUISVILLE OF TO-DAY.

Louisville tobacco market is in its universal character, being the only city in the United States where all grades can be obtained; while Cincinnati, St. Louis, Paducah, and other tobacco centres, though controlling a large market, simply handle certain classes of this staple. There are many warehouses, rehandling establishments, and manufactories of smoking and chewing tobaccos and cigar manufactories, and a large contingent of tobacco brokers, agents, and others who cannot be classified conveniently, who employ millions of capital and upwards of five thousand workmen.

The Whiskey Interest.—When the statement is made that the revenue taxes on whiskey paid monthly into the office of the collector in this city aggregate from a million and a quarter to a million and a half of dollars, some criterion may be formed of the vast importance of the trade in this class of goods. The registry records for the collection district of which the Falls City is the centre, show no less than one hundred grain distilleries, with a conjoint producing capacity well approaching one hundred thousand gallons per diem. There are required to barrel the product about one hundred and fifty thousand casks, and the capital invested in the distilleries is approximated at $5,000,000. The purity and general excellence of the whiskies here produced are acknowledged the world over, rendering them adaptable alike for medicinal and stimulative purposes. The two foregoing interests may be emphatically mentioned as the leading manufactures of Louisville; yet again, the following facts elucidate the announcement that the Falls City rivals and excels her sisters in several other important lines.

Kentucky Jeans.—In the production of jeans and jean clothing Louisville is the largest market in the Union, the trade of the world being supplied with these goods, the output of her large mills engaged in this industry aggregating annually nearly eight million yards of cloth, amounting in value to some two million and a half of dollars.

Gas and Water Pipe, etc.—Prominent among the branches of iron manufacture in this city may be mentioned that of gas and water pipe, here being located the largest establishment of this type on the Western Continent, supplying a trade which extends from the Atlantic to the Pacific. A large number of prosperous establishments are likewise engaged in the production of stoves, architectural iron work, galvanized iron cornices, and other metal work, the consumption of iron reaching over one hundred thousand tons annually.

Plows.—Louisville has built up a truly world-wide reputation as a centre for the production of plows, having located here the largest plow manufactory in either hemisphere, the productions of which are in use in every quarter of the globe where modern agricultural farming is in vogue.

Cement.—The enormous quantities of cement here produced (nearly one million barrels annually) may perhaps be attributed to the favorable mineralogical conditions which prevail as to the formation of the bed of the Ohio River; nevertheless, the stupendous proportions to which its production and preparation for the market is increasing must stand as a highly commendatory feature in listing the city's leading manufacturing industries.

Tanning.—Tanning is one of the original industries in every new country, and all the old records of Louisville's varied resources and industries note the establishment here and operation of leather-making enterprises. Although many of the domestic uses of leather have passed away, new and much more varied demands for it have arisen; and while there have been consolidation and concentration in vast establishments, Louisville has retained her tanning interests; and here, located about the falls, her business men have equipped themselves with such modern methods in tanning as to excite the envy and curiosity of the old-time European houses. Confining themselves chiefly to fine sole and harness leather, they make from oak bark a superior grade, the extent of their operations being deductible from the statement that nearly one thousand operatives here find constant employment.

Wood-Working.—Large areas of the original forests of the Ohio Valley, of which Louisville may be regarded the metropolis, were early cleared by the axe of the pioneer. More gradually but surely of late years the increasing value of cleared lands has greatly reduced the timber-covered acreage, but the remaining local supply of hard woods and the advantage of locating here have maintained a variety of planing and saw-mills, turning, bending, and other wood-working establishments in Louisville. The mechanical industry of cabinet-making is carried on generally in connection with the trade in furniture; but in this branch of industry, which since the recent development of household art-decoration

BULL BLOCK.

LEVY S BUILDING

has been revolutionized, Louisville furnishes workmen of the highest integrity and skill; and the furniture establishments of the city, while dealing largely in manufactured wares, have factories in which the handiwork of the best artisans turn out an annual product valued at nearly $2,000,000.

Carriages and Wagons.—The demands of a thickly-populated, highly-cultivated and prosperous section, and of a city where fine turnouts on the road are such a common sight, would alone furnish trade for a very extensive industry in the manufacture of carriages and wagons; but such has been the special development of this interest, and so widespread is the fame of Louisville mechanics in this line, that the carriage and wagon-making establishments of the city turn out vast quantities of work for distant markets.

Horses and Mules.—Louisville is unquestionably the leading mule and horse mart in the Union. The trade in fine and higher grades of stock, especially in good driving horses, is very considerable. Numerous stock and exchange stables afford facilities to buyers and sellers, and many noted horsemen make Louisville their headquarters for selecting, training, raising or matching the finest carriage horses, trotters, teams and racers. Many of the Eastern horse-fanciers depend largely on the judgment of Louisville dealers, and all the interests of the turf find patronage and active support here. The sale of mules alone reaches twenty thousand annually.

The Fuel Trade.—Louisville is a great distributing point for south-bound coal, both river and rail providing cheap transportation. Upwards of $3,000,000 of Pittsburg coal is handled in the Louisville harbor annually, of which probably two-thirds goes on down stream. The capacity of coal tow-boats between here and Pittsburg is four to ten thousand tons; between here and New Orleans from fifteen to twenty-five thousand tons. This coal is distributed all along the Ohio River and the upper and lower Mississippi, over ten million tons annually reaching New Orleans and the lower coast. Both rail and water rates are comparatively low, and with good coal at moderate prices, there is reason to anticipate a vast growth of trade.

REAL ESTATE.

In many cities in the United States the rise in real estate values is not indicative of increased prosperity, but merely of a somewhat greater inflation. This is not the case in Louisville, where values rise and fall according to the legitimate demand, and these consequently present a true index of the conditions prevailing at the moment. There are few centres if any in which the real estate business has resisted the great tendency to "boom," in the usual unhealthy manner, so effectively. Everything has remained upon a sound basis, and purchasers and investors outside of the city buy and sell through reliable agents here with the same facility as if personally conducting their operations. Those who purchase real estate in Louisville do so almost invariably with the intention of building, and they are therefore at once interested in the city's well being, and take their place among our most public spirited citizens. Perhaps there never was a time when greater opportunities were offered to all classes of investors than at present. Now is the time to acquire Louisville real estate, whether the object be speculation or investment. Many instances could be adduced of moderate fortunes having been made in a few years, by judicious purchases of well located lots. It is hardly possible to make a mistake, excepting that of dealing with an unreliable agent, and luckily there are few of those here. During 1893, the banks holding real estate paper required additional payments to be made upon property, before such paper would be renewed. When the necessary assessments were levied, it was astonishing how promptly they were met. Now paper of this description is freely accepted, and renewed without question, thus indicating clearly the real value of these securities, as judged by the best authorities upon such a subject.

The splendid street car system now in operation has greatly enhanced the values of residence property in the suburbs, and enables even the small salaried and working classes to possess their own homes, far from the noise and dust and smoke of a great city, while within easy reach of its stores and marts. The tendency is also toward expansion, additional electric lines being continually projected, and new stretches of beautiful country being made available for the erection of comfortable and handsome residences.

One notable feature of the dealings in Louisville real estate, is the number of sales that are made to persons of the middle class. Our city has more taxpayers in proportion to the population than any other in the country. It is becoming more and more every year a city

LOUISVILLE ATHLETIC CLUB.

PENDENNIS CLUB

of homes, where the working and salaried classes own the property they occupy. One can not but regard this tendency with gratification, as it means steady prosperity without extremes of wealth and want, and it is the best possible preventive against those unreasonable panics which in other cities deserve as much condemnation as their opposites, the periods of undue inflation.

Building associations are most important accessories to transactions in suburban realty, and as now developed are unquestionably destined to affect Louisville in the near future, as powerfully as they have in Philadelphia in the past. There is great need of more conservatism in the management of these concerns, nothing being so fatal to their success as even a breath of suspicion regarding their solidity. Stringent laws concerning them are necessary, so that the savings of the people may be safeguarded as effectually as if they had been placed in a bank, and then, under able management, with men of high standing directly responsible, the power of these associations to lift the masses into comfort and a better position will be exerted to the utmost, and the best modern agency for the solution of the most pressing of social questions, will be in active operation.

PROMINENT BUILDINGS.

The erection of large buildings of every description is continually going on in Louisville, and from present prospects seems to be destined to be as actively pushed in the future, as in the past.

Prior to the year 1885, there was considerable opposition to the new style of structures called "sky scrapers," but with the spread of more general information regarding the thoroughly fire proof manner in which they were built throughout, and the increased strength which was obtained by the use of iron and steel, this soon disappeared. Louisville today contains many fine examples of many-storied buildings, and as excessive height has never been attempted, the architectural effect is much enhanced.

PUBLIC BUILDINGS, ETC.

The Falls City has a number of buildings devoted to the uses of the municipality and the various public institutions, prominent among which is the new Customhouse, erected at a cost of two and a half millions of dollars, at the corner of Fourth and Chestnut Streets. The County Courthouse, which occupies the half-square bounded by Fifth and Sixth Streets, Jefferson Street and Court Place; a massive and perfect structure of Corinthian architecture, adjacent to which is the City Hall, built at an immense outlay. The Board of Trade, the City Workhouse, the Almshouse, the School for the Blind, the City Hospital, the University buildings, and the numerous extensive charities present architectural attractions that serve to ornament every part of the city. Among what might be termed semi-public buildings might be mentioned also the hotels, theatres, concert halls, leading business houses, churches, colleges, hospitals, etc., of which Louisville boasts a large number of very fine ones. Galt House, Louisville Hotel, Courier-Journal building, Public Library building, and others, some of which are illustrated in these pages, present some of the most attractive features of the Falls City, and support her claim to a high place among those communities which entertain a proper estimate of, and render a due regard to taste and talent as exemplified in the arts and progressive tendencies of the times.

PLACES OF AMUSEMENT.

Louisville, which has for years had the reputation among theatrical managers of being an A1 "show town," supports a number of well-equipped, first-class theatres and amusement halls, and they are largely patronized by the best class of people, citizens and strangers. The plays presented in the theatres are generally of a high order of merit, and the prices of admission are reasonable. Each has a history of success or failure peculiarly its own; and upon the boards of these houses of entertainment the greatest actors of the past and present both of our own country and of Europe, have delighted thousands by their faithful representations of the different phases of human life.

LOUISVILLE AN EDUCATIONAL CENTRE.

This position claimed for Louisville will be admitted by all. From the lowest step in the ladder to the highest, no city can boast of equal advantages in the shape of education. The public school system has been brought to a state of perfection perhaps unequalled in the Union.

Framed on all the systems in every other state, it combines the best features of all, and improvements on most. Rising in the scale, it will be found that no educational want has been left unsupplied; whatever the pursuit or profession the student may intend to follow through life, he will find a school, academy or college in which he will have full scope for his ambition. It has been stated on the reliable authority of the Committee on Industrial and Commercial Improvement of the Board of Trade, in reports issued by that body, that "Louisville was one of the first cities to provide a practical business course of training for the boys and girls of the public schools whose aims and circumstances did not require or ask a classical finish." This is, indeed, a move in the right direction in this age of commercial progressiveness. Again we quote from their exhaustive report, and for which we here wish to accord them the credit so eminently due them on this and many other interesting statistics from which we have taken excerpts: "The high schools now admit of a business course in which bookkeeping and business usages are taught. The female high school has introduced the teaching of stenography and typewriting, and girls who must rely on their own exertions for support will have an opportunity, free of cost, to prepare themselves for those positions which so many of the sex have been taking during the past ten years." There are forty-four public schools in Louisville, classified as follows: One male high school, one female high school, thirty-three white ward schools, and nine colored schools. Higher education is represented by the Louisville Presbyterian and Southern Baptist Theological Seminaries and State University, the University of Louisville, the Louisville Medical College, the Hospital College of Medicine, the Louisville Law School, the Louisville College of Dentistry, the Kentucky School of Medicine, the Louisville College of Pharmacy, the Louisville Educational Association, all of which are widely recognized institutions in their particular branches of tuition. Special mention should be made, too, of the Kentucky Institute of the Blind. The Polytechnic school and library likewise take rank as one of the most invaluable educational institutions, and its methods and objects are so unique that the organization stands without a peer among the homes of learning in the Southern States. The curriculum of study covers medicine, surgery, geology, law, etc., the library containing a collection of nearly fifty thousand volumes. A number of private schools, mostly for the primary education of either sex, combine to complete the unsurpassed educational resources of the city.

RESIDENTIAL LOUISVILLE.

If Louisville possesses, as she certainly does, all the advantages to which reference has been made, it will perforce be admitted that no element in the constitution of a great city is wanting. The capitalist who would invest money to advantage can here find a promising field for enterprise. There is also plenty of room for more manufacturing industries. The man of leisure, with fixed income, may find in the Falls City, too, a delightful home, and live just as his means may allow, even to the enjoyment of luxury. The mechanic and tradesman can, by industry and economy, secure a comfortable domicile on easy terms, and in Louisville every reasonable wish may be gratified, and the new settler find a welcome to any class of society which may be congenial to his taste. The great problem of how and where to live never agitated so many minds as now. The pressure of a high civilization, the requirements of life under conditions of tense strain, the increasing impracticability, with rich and poor alike, of making both ends meet in what seem inevitable responsibilities and importunate demands, all combine to render the question a vital one. Many perplex themselves a while and then give up the conundrum. The capable workman drifts into swarming tenement-houses. The well-to-do organizers of business interests drop into boarding houses or hotels. The wealthy emigrate to Europe on indefinite tours and errands to escape the annoyance of unfaithful servants and the care of establishments. Young men take a practical view of the matter and omit to marry. Young women take advantage of the dilemma, educate themselves for doctors, teachers, lawyers, etc., and very sensibly make royal and hospitable homes for themselves, welcoming whom and when they choose. But the little children of native-born American citizens become fewer and fewer, and children of the emigrant and alien outnumber the infant home-born sons and daughters of the Republic. In considering how and where to live, there are growing indications that the native citizen is just perching like an uncertain bird of passage on the wing, or losing individuality in tenement-house herds, hotel hives, and pleasure

GATE HOUSE AT WATER-WORKS.

GATEWAY TO CAVE HILL.

haunts. Growing more slowly and clinging more to traditions, Louisville enjoys many remarkable advantages as a residence city for all classes, not the least of which is the taste, that has been characteristic from the first, in the beautifying and building of homes. The business quarter has always been plain, though the buildings have been equal to all the demands of an active commerce; while all who could build houses have made them as handsome as their means permitted. The great plain upon which the city was built, covering seventy square miles, and extending back six miles to the river, to a group of picturesque knolls or hills, has afforded every facility for the economical gratification of taste. Ground being plentiful and level, distance was not difficult to overcome; and so, instead of being crowded into restricted limits set up by natural barriers, the city has spread at her own pleasure. The streets are broad, well-paved, drained, and beautified with a profusion of fine shade trees. There are few cities in the world with such finely shaded streets as Louisville possesses, and none where the streets are wider. The residences are, as a rule, provided with spacious yards and gardens, and in the spring of the year a drive over the city past the miles of great enclosures filled with flowers and shrubbery, and under the shade of trees rich with foliage and blossoms, is like a trip to fairyland. It is simply the *pride* of home, united with good taste and a constant study of the most effective architecture, that has thus produced in Louisville a city of remarkable residential attractions. The resident, be he workman with hands or brain, may have his own home, made attainable by the large industries which are glad to exchange just coin for fair service, and truly has it been remarked by the talented authoress of "Home and Home Influences": "To the hard-worked man nothing affords greater relief, gives greater strength for the daily struggle, than the ability in one moment to turn his back on the din and turmoil, and dust and confusion—the inevitable concomitants of busy quarters—and from his own hillside cottage breathe the pure air of heaven." This acquisition is easily and economically attainable, even by the subordinate artisan, in this same city of Louisville. And thus the man of wealth, the manufacturer and capitalist, seeking a home in the City of the Falls, finds his interests and the well-being and safety of society resting upon a sound, secure basis of well-conditioned labor. This, indeed, is Louisville's strong point, that her citizens, employer and employed, form a homogeneous household, depending upon each other, and each controlling their own affairs. The people who make up this community are best estimated through the important public works, large and liberal charities, superior system of public schools they have so long fostered with especial solicitude, the inestimable benefits of the religious privileges afforded by the many churches, the advantages of free libraries, art galleries, the most charming social circles—all these advantages in a setting of beautiful climate and sanitary local influences, together with the oft-quoted business prospects and opportunities of the city, make, as it were, a medley of substantial attractions as a residence suited to the varied requirements of the multitudinous types of men and women in whose lives and business schemes there is ever an undertone of "Donum, dulce donum."

STREET TRAFFIC.

In every city there is some street which is the special resort of ladies for promenading and shopping. Here strangers and visitors first receive their impressions of the wealth and taste of the citizens, and in reporting their opinions to their friends the effect will be favorable or otherwise, just as they are struck with the elegance of the stores and the richness of the goods displayed. Fourth Street, Louisville, has long been known to travelers as the centre of attraction, but the tourist of 1885, in describing the splendid plate-glass fronted emporiums, especially in the dry goods trade, would completely cast in the shade all previous descriptions. The "parade" on Saturday is a characteristic sight. There are few shoppers that are not on foot, and the promenade is occupied by an apparently endless stream of ladies. This street is lined with many handsome structures and is rapidly extending itself. The southern end is a favorite and beautiful residence section, though metropolitan necessities have long since developed many rival streets and built them up with residences that are equalled in beauty and taste by but few cities. Main Street, again, may be regarded as the great wholesale and tobacco street of the Falls City; and being the first thoroughfare next to the river settlement, naturally contains many evidences of the original character of the city. Many of the business houses are old-fashioned, plain and small, while interspersed among these are some of the handsomest and most costly

UNION STATION.

modern structures. There are few streets where the increasing traffic of heavy business may be seen in such volume as here. During the busy seasons the roar and noise of vans and wagons are deafening. Where Ninth Street intersects begins the "tobacco district," where are conducted the great sales, and where are situated the great warehouses capable of handling one hundred and fifty thousand hogsheads annually. Turning again to another branch of what, after all, may rightly be regarded as street traffic; no thoughtful person can walk down any of the leading thoroughfares in the morning, or at six o'clock in the evening, without being struck with the well-dressed crowds of men and women, all tending toward or returning from the scene of their daily labors; and he must indeed be void of patriotism whose feelings are not thrilled by the sight of so much enterprise and industry, making our streets vie with those of New York or Philadelphia. Nor is there any reason to doubt that, before long, we may see the numbers greatly increased. While the extension of manufactures may embrace those not so cleanly, no one would object to see the linen overalls and clumsy footwear, which in other cities, although corresponding with the work of the operatives during the week, are often replaced by silk and patent leather on Sundays and holidays.

THE LOUISVILLE PRESS.

The papers and periodicals of Louisville have always been distinguished by characteristics that have commended them to the thinking portion of the community. There has been an utter absence of that continual straining after effect, which mars so many of our newspapers, and disgusts those who desire to ascertain the actual events of the world, without being compelled to view them through a distorting medium. Reliability, perspicacity, comprehensiveness, variety, and high quality, have been the chief features of our prominent representatives of the press, and nowhere in the country are the people more thoroughly posted in the affairs of the world, than in Louisville. The subjoined sketches have been prepared from such scanty information as could be obtained, and for the rest the mere mention of the names of the publications is all we can offer. The *Louisville Evening Post*, our most successful evening paper was first established in the spring of 1878. It has ever been honest, independent and fearless in its treatment of affairs at home and abroad, supporting the cause of the people against corrupt politicians and greedy corporations and protecting in every way the poor against the oppression of the wealthy. It is the most popular paper with the people of the Falls City to-day, and is noted for preferring accuracy to sensationalism, while it has ever stood out for honest legislation, honest government and the honest enforcement of the laws. It reaches more homes in the three Falls Cities, than any other daily newspaper, its patronage being the result of recognized merit, not the chimerical prosperity of catch-penny gift enterprises. The *Louisville Courier-Journal*. This fine newspaper is the result of the consolidation of the old *Courier* and the *Journal* and together with the *Commercial* it monopolizes the English morning field in the city, while it also has great influence in the Ohio Valley and the entire South. It is Democratic in politics, and its editorial chair is brilliantly filled by Henry Watterson, who gives the "bull mark," so to speak, to its intellectuality. He is ably supported by W. N. Haldeman, president of the *Louisville Courier-Journal* Company, a talented writer, politician and business man, thus furnishing an ample guarantee that in intelligent management this legitimate offspring of a union of the two ante-bellum leaders of Kentucky journalism will continue to be in the future, as in the past, a book, pulpit and platform all in one. The appointments of the *Courier-Journal* Company's building, corner Fourth Avenue and Green Street, are of a very superior character, the structure being an honorable monument to the progressiveness of the press apart from ornate adornment to the city. The *Louisville Commercial* was first published December 30th, 1869. It is Republican in politics and was the first Republican paper established south of the Ohio River. It has a wide influence throughout the South and is a vigorous and able exponent of protection and sound currency. This paper represents one of those indomitable instances of journalism as far as its management is concerned, which through stress of circumstances have retired for a time from the field of letters (to quote from the late Lord Beaconsfield) "without dishonor," only to return to the combat with renewed vigor and to be crowned with success, so eminently due such energy. It is now published by the Louisville Press Company and to-day fills an important niche in the city's newspaper interests. The *Louisville Times* was

LOUISVILLE OF TO-DAY.

founded in 1884 and is an evening paper. It is ably edited and enjoys a large circulation in the city and county. The *Louisville Anzeiger*, as voicing the sentiments of the Teutonic element, and is the most influential paper published in the German language in Louisville and south of the Ohio River, and it goes without saying the *Anzeiger* has proved a great journalistic success. The *Critic* is an independent Sunday paper, being always reliable, clean, bright and fearless and extremely prosperous. *Truth* is the leading society journal of the South. It has a large clientele, and is recognized as one of the most effective advertising mediums in the city.

THE NUMEROUS CHURCHES.

In no city in the Union are churches more numerous, or the congregations larger in proportion to the population; and it is safe to say that in this respect the church accommodation is larger than in any other city. Taking the average capacity to be one thousand, and the number of churches in Louisville and suburbs at about two hundred, the entire population, if present at one time, could nearly be accommodated; and this cannot be said of any other city. Although this can never happen, and is a mere hypothetical case, it is evident the average attendance must be very large and the accommodation abundant. It is safe to say, that in few cities elsewhere can such a sight be witnessed on a fine Sunday evening, within the same limits, as in Louisville, when the churches are emptied of the crowd of worshippers, and the sidewalks are blocked with the throngs returning to their homes. The writer, having spent Sundays in every large church-going city on both sides of the Atlantic, can make this statement without fear of successful contradiction; nor is there anywhere to be seen better dressed or more respectable looking congregations than worship in the Falls City churches. What the feelings must be of those who absent themselves from Louisville churches on Sunday the writer cannot imagine, never having had such an experience; but it seems as if that very absence would preach a sermon which, to every freethinker or agnostic, would be as powerful in favor of Christianity as if a sermon were listened to inside the walls of a church. The ringing of the bells is at an end, the rumbling of the carriage has ceased, the pattering of the feet is heard no more, the flocks are folded in the numerous churches. For a time everything is hushed, but soon is heard the deep, pervading sound of the organ, rolling and vibrating through the buildings and out into the streets; and the sweet chanting of the choirs make them resound with melody and praise, while it is poured forth like a river of joy through the recesses of the city, elevating and bearing the soul on a tide of triumphant harmony to heaven. Verily, the wanderer about the streets at such a time is not a proper subject for envy. The church buildings of the city are one hundred and eighty odd in number, and the congregations are distributed as follows: Baptist, 21; Christian, 12; Protestant Episcopal, 12; German Evangelical, 7; German Evangelical Reformed, 2; Jewish, 4; Lutheran, 8; Methodist Episcopal South, 14; Methodist Episcopal North, 6; Northern Presbyterian, 9; Southern Presbyterian, 10; Associate Reformed Presbyterian, 2; Unitarian, 1; Spiritual, 3; Catholic, 24; Gospel Missions, 7. Colored Churches—Baptist, 22; Christian, 1; Protestant Episcopal, 1; Methodist Episcopal North, 13. Louisville is the seat of the Protestant Episcopal and the Roman Catholic dioceses. The Catholic Cathedral of Our Lady of the Assumption is one of the finest edifices in the West. The religious establishments comprise monasteries and convents, a Young Men's Christian Association, supplied with libraries, reading rooms and gymnasiums; and two branches, one for German-speaking people, the other for railroad employees. Many of the ecclesiastical edifices listed are worthy of the greatness of this growing city, not only in point of dimensions, but also in point of chaste architectural beauty. The various denominations, in fact, seem to have vied with each other in building churches of striking architecture, and in no direction have the wealth and public spirit of the citizens manifested themselves more efficiently.

LOUISVILLE CHARITIES, ETC.

In her hospitals, dispensaries, asylums, and benevolent associations the Falls City has reason to rejoice. Intelligent, benevolence and well-directed charity are characteristic of her inhabitants, as will be amply evidenced by a perusal of the following items pertaining thereto. There are about forty of these institutions, among which the unfortunate or the erring, from the cradle to the grave, of all religious creeds and all social condi-

LOUISVILLE OF TO-DAY.

UNION DEPOT.

tions, may find refuge. The public almshouse cost over $200,000, and persons who are unable to labor, or are helpless from age, are received here. The city also supports a public hospital, founded in 1817, and which is one of the largest and finest buildings in Louisville. St. John's Eruptive Hospital is also under the control of the Committee of Public Charities. The religious charities and hospitals are upon a very large and generous scale. The Church Home and Infirmary in the Highlands above the city is under the care of the Episcopal churches, and provide a home for aged and helpless and working women, and an infirmary for the sick of either sex. It was founded through the gift of $100,000 from John P. Morton. The John N. Norton Memorial Infirmary, for the nursing of the sick, is situated in the residence district on Third Street, and is also under Episcopal management. These charities occupy magnificent buildings. Sts. Mary and Elizabeth Hospital, for the nursing of sufferers by railway accident; St. Joseph's Infirmary, for nursing desperate cases and strangers; and the Home for the Aged Poor—are a trio of great establishments under the care of the Catholic church. These, and the United States Marine Hospital and a number of private establishments, besides four free public dispensaries, provide for the convenient care of all public sufferers. The defective, dependent and delinquent classes have a smaller ratio in the population of Louisville than in any town of corresponding size in the country. The average of thrift, of intelligence, of industrial activity and social elevation is so high; the distribution of property is so general; the absence of any criminal or squalid quarter in the city so notable; and so conspicuous is the fact that places of comfortable and even elegant residence are confined to no particular section of the city, but are found everywhere within its limits—that the active or stringent suppression of crime has become more or less a dead letter. The city, however, sustains three industrial schools of reform for juvenile delinquents. One is for white boys, another for friendless girls, and the third for colored youth. The buildings are large and costly, and the grounds ornamental. These industrial schools are celebrated among philanthropists and those interested in prison reform. Louisville has eleven orphanages, two homes for friendless women, a home for old ladies, and a central organized charity association. Rivaling and excelling, however, any other eleemosynary institution in the United States ranks the famous Masons' Widows and Orphans' Home, organized, under the terms of its charter, "to provide and sustain a home for destitute widows and orphans of deceased Freemasons of the State of Kentucky, and an infirmary for the afflicted and sick Freemasons and others who may be placed under its charge." The building is the largest in the city, and being the only charity of its unique type in the Union, is regarded with veneration by Masons the world over, and is the subject of pride to the citizens of the entire state.

LOUISVILLE AS A CITY OF CULTURE.

Admitting that the Louisville of to-day is a business place and a place for business in the best and broadest sense, it may be inferred by many who are strangers to the place that the Falls City, like many manufacturing centres in the Union, has, in a measure, neglected, for the accumulation of wealth, the cultivation and fostering of the arts and sciences. But such is not the fact. A consideration of the many institutions of learning here existent ought to prove sufficient to contravene any such sentiment. Indeed, in law, medicine, theology and journalism, the so-called "learned professions," Louisville has always afforded a field for the exercise of the highest talent, and for rise to the rank of widest distinction. From the beginning her Bar has been conspicuous throughout the country for eloquence, ability and success; among the names of the dead shine the names of many who obtained high rank in this forum, and of the members now enrolled on the lists of the legal profession nearly all are in full practice. The courts sitting here are the Federal, the United States Circuit and District Courts, the Jefferson Circuit Court, Court of Common Pleas, County Court, Chancery Court, and City Court. The history of the medical faculty, numerous and distinguished in city and county, has been a very brilliant page in the annals of the profession throughout the country; the kindred profession of dentistry here has been represented by those who have attained national and world-wide distinction in this modern science; while in theology and the history of religion, both city and

KENTON CLUB.

74 — — LOUISVILLE OF TO-DAY. — —

county have, through their variety of denominational life, their large membership and prosperous church communities, maintained a leading place; and this has not been surrendered in any degree. Numerous societies devoted to literary and scientific purposes have at all times flourished in this city; and lyceums, debating societies, and literary and social organizations under various auspices, open their doors to young and old. Again, as in every community in which there is a strong infusion of German life and spirit, a decided musical taste and talent have always asserted themselves in the Falls City. Besides that which finds expression through church, private and social organizations, two notable public societies for musical and social objects—the Liederkranz and Maennerchor—aggregate an immense membership. The charm of elevated social life attracts hither teachers and votaries of musical culture; enterprising dealers in instruments, sheet music, etc., provide for all the wants of the trade; and that side of culture which gratifies its taste or finds expression in music has large opportunities for satisfaction here. The graphic and the plastic arts have due encouragement, and in all the modern branches of painting, crayon-work, and in the highest excellence of photographic skill, Louisville's artists have won wide reputation.

BENEVOLENT ORDERS, CLUBS, ETC.

A populous and progressive city, and a centre of political, commercial and industrial activity, Louisville contains, in the very nature of things, a great number of societies, organizations, etc., devoted to a variety of purposes, beneficent, protective, social, etc. Among such who are established in their halls and hold stated meetings in the Falls City may be mentioned: Freemasons, Odd Fellows, Knights of Pythias, Knights of Honor, Red Men, Ancient Order of United Workmen, Grand Army of the Republic, Sons of Veterans, Good Templars, Foresters; besides college fraternities, the funeral benefit associations, a typographical association, and some representatives of the Knights of Labor. The membership of beneficial orders is very numerous; their financial condition is good. Nearly all (especially the Masonic fraternity) occupy well-furnished halls with fine equipment, and their rank in the respective orders at large is of the highest. There are likewise a number of exclusive social clubs in Louisville of great wealth and influence. Principal among these, and possessing their own establishments, are the Pendennis, the Standard, the Pelham, the Brownson, and the Progress. There are few clubs in the South so splendidly established as the Pendennis and Standard, while to the patron of the turf the famous Louisville Jockey Club affords attractions equal, if not superior, to those provided by any similar organization in the United States. From the standpoints of culture, social life and recreation, as reviewed in the two foregoing sections, it may aptly be said that, indeed, the Falls City is highly favored in all those elements which to the student, the scholar and the man of leisure go to make life worth living.

THE SUBURBS OF LOUISVILLE.

The Falls City is surrounded by many delightful suburbs. These are Parkland to the southwest, Clifton, the Highlands, Anchorage, and Pence Valley to the east. In the eastern end of the city, likewise, the new water reservoir affords handsome park opportunities, and in that direction also is the Cave Hill Cemetery, by natural advantages of location and lavish expenditure for beautifying purposes one of the loveliest cemeteries in America. The two Indiana cities of New Albany and Jeffersonville, with a combined population of about 50,000, are practically a part of Louisville, connected with it by bridges and ferries, and have a common industrial and commercial interest.

HOTELS AND BOARDING HOUSES.

The necessary provision for the wants of the numerous traveling public, as well as the prevailing popular spirit of hospitality, and the cheap and ample market-supplies near at hand, have contributed during all her history to the establishment and support in Louisville of numerous capacious and well-kept hotels, these places of public entertainment having simply grown in number with the gradual development of the city. To mention only the two leading caravansaries—the well-known Galt House and Louisville Hotel—we doubt if, in appointments, they will not bear favorable comparison with any hostelries in the Union. Well-kept boarding houses, likewise, are distributed over the city; the most fastidious can secure elegance and comfort at unusually favorable prices; and for mechanics, workingmen and artisans, clerks, agents and other wage-earners,

LOUISVILLE OF TO-DAY.

Louisville offers inducements to be found nowhere in the country at any centre of population or business. Special arrangements for families, for rent of rooms without board, or board without rooms, can always be effected at prices far below the prevailing rates elsewhere, and which afford the highest inducements to the best class of operatives to remove hither and to stay.

VITAL STATISTICS.

The city, in point of fact, is a remarkably salubrious one, and the public health has for many years been as good as that of any city in the country. In proof of this assertion the mortality tables exhibit the pleasing fact that the Falls City stands first in the list of cities of over 50,000 population in point of light death-rate; Louisville being absolutely free from the epidemics prevalent in more southerly states, the predisposing cause of which may undoubtedly be attributed collectively to the abundance of pure water, pure air, perfect sewerage, and exceptionally good sanitary conditions which prevail in this favored section.

CEMETERIES.

In the olden time each of the churches of earlier erection had adjoining it a "God's Acre," where the dead were decently laid to rest; they are possessed of melancholy interest to the present citizenship, and in the names " carved on the tomb" is lettered much of the history of the city. But the gradually growing needs of Louisville for more commodious places of interment led to the construction of extensive cemeteries in different sections of the city and suburbs. To-day they are twelve in number, as follows: Adas Israel Cemetery—Preston Street road, near toll gate; Cave Hill Cemetery, Baxter Avenue, head of Broadway; St. John's (Catholic)—Duncan, corner of Twenty-sixth Street; National Cemetery—situate in the interior of Cave Hill Cemetery; Old Catholic—South side of Jefferson, between Fifteenth and Eighteenth Streets; St. Louis (R. C.) Cemetery—Barret Avenue, near limits; Portland Cemetery—South side of Bank, between Thirty-fifth and Thirty-sixth Streets; St. Michael's German Catholic Cemetery—Goss Avenue, near limits; Eastern Cemetery—No. 1313 Baxter Avenue, adjoining Cave Hill; Hebrew Cemetery—No. 2118 Preston Street; St. Stephen's Cemetery—Preston Street, beyond limits; Western Cemetery—No. 1532 West Jefferson Street.

CITIZEN SOLDIERY.

Louisville maintains a well-disciplined state militia in the Louisville Legion, Kentucky State Guard. It was organized in 1877, and was the outgrowth of the different militia companies which were mobilized for the assistance of the city and state authorities in keeping order during the labor troubles of that year. The Legion was furnished with the wherewithal to be uniformed by a few liberal and public-spirited citizens. The armory, which is on Seventh Street, between Walnut and Chestnut, is rented and paid for by the city. The arms and equipment are furnished by the state. The term of enlistment is three years. One night in each week is set apart for drill, and the affairs of the Legion are conducted by the commissioned officers who meet monthly. As an additional means of supporting the Legion the legislature passed a bill, approved December 16, 1882, by which the command was authorized to elect thirty honorary members who, on paying one hundred dollars each per annum, should be exempt from active service. This fund defrays the current expenses of the regiment and the armory. In May, 1881, the Louisville Legion was organized into a regiment, and has since kept up its organization to a high degree of efficiency. The Legion is in a good state of organization, and not only have its members done good active service, but the influence of the command in the community has been excellent. It has compelled respect for authority, infused an increased regard for the polite in intercourse, instructed its members in military tactics, improved the physique and personal bearing of many, and cultivated a good fellowship and healthy exercise, which has been promotive of a morale not hitherto existent.

GRAND ARMY ENCAMPMENT.

The National Encampment of the Grand Army of the Republic having selected Louisville as its place of meeting for 1895, great and general interest has been aroused regarding the city, and its capacity to entertain such a host of people as will undoubtedly attend. This interest has been considerably enhanced from several causes, one of the principal of which has been the important part played by the city and state during the Civil War, and the many battlefields within easy reach, this section of country having been the scene of almost continuous warfare, upon a large or small scale, until the close of the struggle. Another reason why the encampment of 1895 commands more than ordinary attention, is, that this is the first occasion upon which it has been held south of the Ohio River, and the extraordinarily hearty invitation extended by the people of Louisville to the Army, has awakened great enthusiasm, and a desire to make this first really Southern meeting a grand success in every particular.

Those at the head of the administration of our city should never forget that every year there are thousands of people entering upon business life of some sort who are utterly uninformed regarding the great advantages to be obtained by choosing such a city as ours for the scene of their operations. These need instruction, and one of the most effective means of preparing their minds for receiving and retaining information regarding Louisville is to have neat and tasty souvenirs of the city, which will be broadly distributed, showing the condition of the city and in connection with such a National event as that of the Grand Army of the Republic is afforded a sure opportunity for the broad circulating of such a work. Louisville wants more able willing hands; Kentucky wants more agriculturists and workers, and these are the classes whose curiosity will naturally be aroused by the occurrence of such an event, and who will retain a deep and lasting impression of the superiority of the resources of Kentucky, and the desirability of its chief city as a field for labor, and as an eligible place in which to invest the surplus proceeds of that labor.

The occasion of this great meeting should also be improved to the utmost in the dissemination of valuable and interesting information to the multitude of visitors who will flock to our city at that time. We have every reason to be proud of the achievements of the past and the position we hold to-day; and while visible evidences abound of our greatness, still many features must pass unnoticed, which will be brought vividly to the mind and permanently recollected, by being elaborated in an interesting manner,

MASONIC TEMPLE.

and used in conjunction with accurate and carefully produced illustrations in our volume of Louisville of to-day.

Many Kentuckians not exceeding thirty-five thousand were in the Confederate Army, and when they returned to their homes their swords were beaten into plowshares, while from that day to the present they have been excellent citizens, many of them rejoicing that the conflict was not irrepressible; and that it terminated in an undivided country.

There are yet living in this community a few hundred of the men who, early in 1861, gathered around the flag held up by the gallant Rousseau, the commander of the Louisville Legion, the nucleus of the Army of the Cumberland. The dash, determination, and bravery of Rousseau at that critical period gave hope and courage to others; the sentiment of loyalty took root, and soon Kentucky threw off the mantle of neutrality and decided that the Union must be saved. In all, the state sent over one hundred thousand men to the field, and there was not a battle west of the Alleghanies or south of the Ohio River in which there were not Kentuckians; they were with Rosecrans at Stone River; with McClellan in West Virginia; with Grant at Vicksburg; with Banks in the Red River campaign; with Buell at Pittsburg Landing; with "Pap" Thomas in Chickamauga and Nashville; and with Sherman "marching through Georgia." The Puritan who touched elbows on the march with the Kentucky soldier never doubted his loyalty or bravery. Louisville annually

makes this sentiment of love of country and admiration for brave men manifest, turning out on Memorial Day and decorating the graves of the four thousand heroes who sleep in the windowless palaces of rest in the National Cemetery.

It is only a few miles from here, about thirty by rail, to the spot where Lincoln was born, and the big-hearted people of that section take pride in giving reminiscences, handed down from father to son, of the family. They will tell of the poverty of the Lincolns when little Abe was in swaddling clothes; show the spot where their log cabin stood, now marked only by the remains of the old-fashioned mud and stone chimney; tell of the death of Nancy Hanks, the modern Mary, who gave the Union its savior, and lastly, of the departure of the Lincolns from the land of bondage to the free soil of the Northwest. The Lincoln farm, situated near Hodgenville, in Larue County, will some day be the Mecca at which patriotism will worship. Kentucky Confederates are not behind the most loyal in expressing admiration for the greatest of Kentuckians, Abraham Lincoln. This is most clearly shown in the splendid lecture on Lincoln now being delivered the country over by that famous adopted son of Kentucky, Henry Watterson.

LOUISVILLE OF TO-DAY.

Not far from the city is Ashland, the home of Henry Clay, the great Commoner, whose remains sleep under a magnificent monument in an adjacent cemetery.

The field of Perryville, where one of the most desperate battles of the war was fought is easily reached, the same is true of the battlefields of Richmond, Munfordville, Bowling Green, Cynthiana and Wild Cap.

The railroads will run excursions to the birthplace of Lincoln, to Mammoth Cave and all the battlefields during the encampment of the **Grand Army**.

The grave of General Zachary Taylor is seven miles east of Louisville, while the bodies of many Kentuckians who were killed fighting under his command **in Mexico**, sleep on "Fame's eternal camping ground" at Frankfort.

Our citizens have subscribed $100,000 to meet the expenses of **the** G. A. R. The committee having charge, headed by that wealthy **and** typical southerner, Colonel Thos. H. Sherley, has been faithful **in its** labors, and the earnestness manifested has created a determination **among** the people to give the Grand Army an old fashioned Kentucky **welcome**. In this work the Ex-Confederate has been as enthusiastic as the "boy in blue."

The comrades of the seven Grand Army Posts of Louisville **rejoice** over this manifestation of patriotism and hospitality, and stand as **they** did in 1861, ready to welcome the defenders of the Union to the soil **of** "the dark and bloody ground."

PROSPECTS.

After carefully considering the past of Louisville and the really wonderful things that have been accomplished, it is difficult to speak of the future with that judicial calmness and freedom from excessive optimism, which is necessary to come to approximately correct conclusions. By some it is thought the Falls City will soon distance St. Louis.

Our citizens at the present day enjoy to the fullest extent the benefits and advantages that have been gained by those who have gone before. Our extensive factories and workshops, with their numerous important industries, tell this story plainly, while our trade and commercial interests as have been already demonstrated have poured **treasures into our** coffers, having reached a high tide of prosperity.

Our city's finances, municipal departments and steady growth in internal improvements, all bespeak in their excellent condition the wisdom and ability of our City Fathers and citizens. Louisville's splendid transportation facilities afford unlimited, rapid and convenient modes of egress for her surplus products, and similarly convenient inlets for **the** handling and disposal of all kinds of produce. The Falls City, in its **picturesque** aspects of location and landscape, leaves nothing to desire. Our splendid business buildings add their majestic effect to the eye, which is also held by the fine shaded streets, the inviting green of the parks, and the vista of ornate residences and stately churches. The city still steadily treads the path of progress in all that relates to manufactures, commerce, education, literature, science, art, religion, morality, and benevolence, **and in** these dominant features is unrivalled by any other community of its size in America or Europe. So much for Louisville's past and present, which excellent record is destined to be dimmed by the still greater triumphs of accomplishment of the future. The next few years must see a great diversion of capital to the southern **states**, whose natural advantages have never been brought out since the war, **and** Louisville will become not only the chief market in America for tobacco and whiskey, as at present, but also for cotton and wool. Here **we take** leave of the Falls City and turn in the following pages to the men of brawn and brain, whose energy and enterprise are well illustrated **in their** brief reviews of their successful records in manufactures, commerce, **art and** the learned professions, and have materially contributed in placing the fame of the Metropolis of Kentucky in its present exalted position.

DUPONT'S RESIDENCE IN CENTRAL PARK.

THE CITY OF LOUISVILLE.

THE city of Louisville occupies a very prominent position among the great centres of trade of this country. The city has a most propitious future before it, and her citizens, if they but exercise that concerted action necessary to secure what is naturally their due, will find that their trade relations, will reach the most satisfactory proportions. In the following pages an effort has been made to review a considerable number of the manufacturing and mercantile interests, and this volume, taken as a whole, will fairly indicate the advantages and resources possessed as a producing and purchasing centre.

J. M. ATHERTON & CO.; Distillers; No. 125 West Main Street.—The distilling interests of our state are of the first magnitude. Large capital and able business management have combined to secure to this industry the highest efficiency, and the marketing of fine Kentucky whiskies, has grown to be one of the principal commercial interests of this city. The leading firm of distillers of natural, high grade Kentucky whiskies is the well-known concern of J. M. Atherton & Co. Mr. J. M. Atherton the proprietor of the vast interests allied under the above name and style, is one of our best known, and most public spirited citizens, whose sound judgment and progressive policy are proverbial, and whose stocks of old and matured whiskies find a ready market throughout the entire United States. The J. M. Atherton Co., was organized in 1881 to acquire and operate the following large distilleries: The Atherton, established in 1867; the Mayfield, established in 1870; and the Windsor, established in 1880. The brands made by these various distilleries were known to the commercial world as "Atherton," "Mayfield," "Windsor," "Clifton," "Howard," "Brownfield," and "Carter" whiskies. Of the Atherton brand both bourbon and rye whiskies are made, and it may not be out of place to state here that Kentucky in the near future bids fair to become a formidable rival of Pennsylvania in the manufacture of fine rye whiskies. Until recent years the distillation of rye whiskies was regarded as rather an incident of the Kentucky whiskey business than as a prominent factor in it, and the impression became general that while Kentucky made the finest bourbons in the United States, and in fact had been granted almost a monopoly of the manufacture of fine bourbons that only in Pennsylvania or Maryland could the highest grades of rye whiskey be made. Mr. Atherton was one of the first Kentucky distillers to give careful attention to the manufacture of rye whiskey, believing as he did that there was no reason why Kentucky could not make rye whiskey as equally fine in quality as her famous bourbons. The Atherton distilleries are now making about from four to five thousand barrels of rye whiskey a year, all of which is made from the highest grade of carefully selected rye grain. Mr. Atherton's skill and ability as a distiller are widely known. He has made a close study of every detail of the industry, and has fully equipped his various plants with the latest improved machinery and appliances. The various distilleries with their local office, warehouses, cattle sheds, machine shops, etc., cover several acres of ground. They are located forty-five miles south of Louisville, near New Haven, Nelson County, Ky., a section which has long been famous for the production of the finest quality of Kentucky whiskies. As the distilleries were located about two miles off the L. & N. R. R., Mr. Atherton in 1879 built a branch road from the L. & N. to the distilleries, which he owns and operates himself. The warehouses are all brick, heated during the winter months by steam, and have a total storage capacity of one hundred and eleven thousand five hundred barrels. Mr. Atherton makes nothing but the highest grades of whiskies, both bourbon and rye, and his brands have become famous strictly on their own merits, as absolutely pure, and wholesome stimulants, equally adapted for fine bar trade, or for medicinal purposes. The annual output of these distilleries is about twenty-five thousand barrels, and the various brands are handled by leading jobbers and dealers everywhere. The office of J. M. Atherton & Co., which firm succeeded the corporation of the J. M. Atherton & Co., on July 1st, 1895, is located No. 125 West Main Street, Louisville, Ky. Mr. J. M. Atherton was a native of LaRue County in this state, but moved to Louisville in 1872, and has since resided here, making this centre his business headquarters. He is a director of the Bank of Kentucky, the Franklin Insurance Co., Louisville Gas Co., and of the Ohio Falls Car Works, located in Jeffersonville, Ind., and is now president of the Pendennis Club, one of the leading social clubs of the city.

LOUISVILLE OF TO-DAY.

THE LOUISVILLE CHAIR COMPANY; Corner Brook Street and Barbee Avenue.—One of the oldest established industries of our city is that of the Louisville Chair Company, which is producing grades and styles of chairs far ahead of any other make in the market, while as to quality of materials used, workmanship and moderate scale of prices, the trade finds this line the most desirable in every way to handle. This industry was founded in 1869 by Mr. H. Buchter. In 1881 the Buchter Chair Company was organized, and in July, 1887, the important interests were incorporated under the laws of this state, with a paid-up capital of $100,000, and the appropriate title of the Louisville Chair Company was adopted, while Mr. J. A. Armstrong assumed the presidency. Five years ago its old premises proving entirely inadequate, the company purchased its present spacious site, and here erected large and substantial buildings, specially designed to meet the requirements of the business. The plant covers an area of four acres, and has perfect transportation facilities, being located on the line of the Louisville and Nashville Railroad. The main factory is an immense structure, of an "L" shape, the dimensions being 50 x 100 and 50x160 feet, while the office and showrooms occupy a very handsome two-story brick building, 50x260 feet in area. All the latest improved machinery and appliances have been introduced here, including many special new machine tools, and the most elaborate work is turned out rapidly and effectively. Upwards of two hundred and twenty-five hands are employed, who turn out three hundred dozen chairs weekly. Full lines of cane, wood seat and upholstered chairs are manufactured, specialties are made of solid walnut cane seat, dining and sitting-rooms and of fancy chairs and rockers in vast variety. Mr. P. P. Peace, the general manager, and Mr. Houston, the secretary and treasurer,

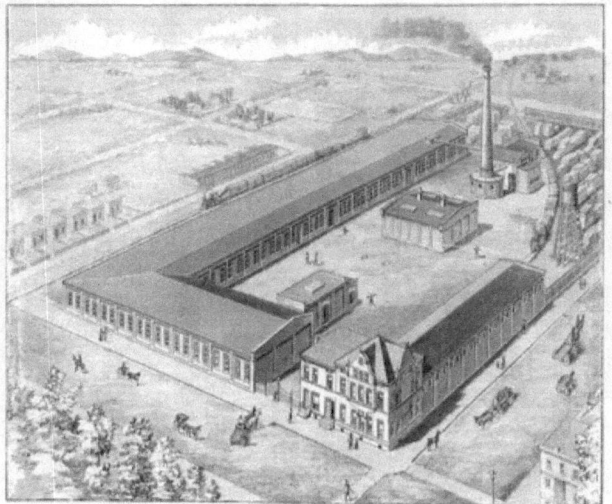

give close supervision to the work in hand. Mr. Peace selecting the lumber with the utmost care, while only the best seasoned wood is made up. In this respect the company has achieved a national reputation, for its chairs cannot be duplicated elsewhere for superiority of materials. In an article, so constantly in use as a chair, and subjected to severe strains, it is a matter of the highest importance to have perfect material and workmanship, and in these respects, the Louisville Chair Company maintains the lead, and its trade extends throughout the United States. Mr. J. A. Armstrong, the president, is a native of this city, and is a prominent capitalist and business man, a director of the Louisville Banking Company and Louisville City National Railroad. Mr. A. P. Houston, secretary and treasurer, is a native of this city and was formerly a member of the Buchter Chair Company, and to his energy is largely due the prosperity of the concern. Mr. P. P. Peace, the general manager, has been identified with the company for the past six years, and is an able business man. Born in Philadelphia, Pa., he has been a resident of this city for the past ten years, and is universally respected.

STITZEL BROTHERS COMPANY; Distillers of Fine Kentucky Whiskey; Twenty-sixth Street and Broadway.—The distilling of pure whiskies has long been one of the chief industries of this section, and the world's supply of high grade, old fashioned bourbon and rye whiskies is very largely shipped from this city. One of the leading representatives of the trade is the Stitzel Brothers Company, whose brands have achieved an international reputation, while their distillery is one of the most perfectly equipped in the business. The firm of Stitzel Brothers was formed in 1876, the co-partners being Messrs. Frederick and Philip Stitzel. They began operations in the present desirable location, the plant having always been known as the Glencoe Distillery. In 1888 the important interests were reorganized and incorporated under the laws of this state, with a paid-up capital of $50,000, the appropriate title of the Stitzel Brothers Company, being adopted. The officers of the company are as follows: Mr. Frederick Stitzel, president; Mr. Philip Stitzel, vice-president, and Mr. Jacob Stitzel, secretary and treasurer. The distillery premises cover an area of fully two and one half acres. Here are a large and splendidly equipped stillhouse, elevator, etc., immense warehouses, cattle sheds, etc. The plant stands second to none as regards modern high-class machinery and appliances, power being supplied by a thirty horse power engine. A specialty is made of the distilling of the highest grade of bourbon whiskies, including such world famous brands as Glencoe, Parkland, Fred Stitzel and Lock Horn, while their Pomona brand of old rye whiskey is equally famous. They select their grain with the utmost care, follow the most approved processes in mashing, fermenting and distilling, use a pure water, and in every way secure to all their goods the highest degree of purity and quality. Their warehouse has a storage capacity of twenty-two thousand barrels, while the distillery has a capacity of six hundred bushels of grain a day, turning out fifty-four barrels of whiskey. All their whiskies are carefully warehoused at an even temperature, and are held until thoroughly aged and mellowed, and their old whiskies are pronounced by experts to be the finest ever passed across a bar, or used for household and medicinal purposes. The company controls a prosperous trade, extending all over the United States to Mexico. The Messrs. Stitzel are natives of Germany, resident in this city since 1853, and are universally respected. There has been no public enterprise of any moment, calculated to advance the prosperity of this section, that they have not supported.

LOUISVILLE SILVERING AND BEVELING COMPANY; Corner Webster and Washington Streets.—The industries of the prosperous Falls City are numerous, and may truly be said to cover every branch of skilled activity, and yet we doubt if there is one of greater importance, or one requiring a higher trained experience and skill, than that of glass cutting and beveling. It is in such connection we make reference in the pages of this statistical review of the enterprise of the Louisville Silvering and Beveling Company, which was incorporated in accordance with the laws of the state of Kentucky, July, 1887, and under able guidance has scored a marked success. The company has a paid-up capital of $50,000, the personnel of the present executive management being as follows: F. Wm. Vogt, president, a native of Louisville and one of the original projectors of the enterprise; W. L. Lyons, vice-president, now connected with the concern since 1891, banker, broker, native of Louisville and prominent Freemason; Laban Phelps, secretary, member of the firm of J. S. Phelps & Co., tobacco warehousemen; C. Georgel, treasurer and general manager, of French nationality, formerly with the Pittsburg Plate Glass Company, in the same capacity, also the originator of this industry. The premises occupied consist of a substantial three-storied brick building, 210x130 feet in dimensions, well sub-divided for the purposes of the business as follows: First floor, office, shipping, packing, receiving, grinding and beveling departments; second floor, polishing department; third floor, silvering department. The machinery equipment is of the latest improved pattern, including patent silvering and beveling devices, etc., operated by a seventy-five horse power steam engine. Here a force of eighty skilled operatives are provided with employment, the output being one thousand feet of finished material per day. The company are direct importers and manufacturers, bevelers and silverers of plate glass and mirror plates. Their products meeting with a large and steadily growing sale, chiefly among furniture dealers and manufacturers throughout the South, West and the Republic of Mexico.

TURNER, DAY & WOOLWORTH MANUFACTURING COMPANY; Manufacturers of Handles; No. 1417 Seventh Street.—There is no more useful industry in this city, than that of the "Turner, Day & Woolworth Manufacturing Company," the world's leading manufacturers of hickory axe, adze, pick and tool handles. The present concern is a consolidation of the factories established by Mr. James Boyce at Norwich, Conn., and Baltimore, Md. in 1854; and by Mr. James Woolworth at Sandusky, Ohio. In 1884 the consolidation was effected, and the present corporation was organized with ample capital, (now amounting to $400,000) and the headquarters and principal works were permanently located in this city. The directorate and officers of the company are as follows: Mr. Albert Day, president; Mr. James Woolworth, vice president; Mr. Charles D. Gates, secretary; Mr. Clarence F. Turner, treasurer. The officers manifest sound judgment and skill in the carrying on of this extensive concern. The factory is a two-story building, 157 1-2 feet by 300 in dimensions, while on the opposite side of the street are the office and yards, the latter covering an area of fully an acre. The latest improved lathes, saws, etc., have been introduced here, power being supplied by a fine two hundred horse power engine. The works are a model in every respect, and embrace all the latest appliances. The company owns and controls large tracts of the choicest hickory timber in this state and in Tennessee, and employs from 400 to 500 men, the works having a capacity of turning out 1500 dozen finished handles daily. These handles are recognized standards with the trade in this country, and they are also exported largely to Central and South America, Mexico, West Indies, Europe, Australia, India, etc. Mr. Albert Day is a native of Hartford, Conn., and has been actively engaged in this branch of industry for upwards of thirty years past, and is one of our most respected business men. Mr. Woolworth is a native of Massachusetts, and resident of Sandusky, previous to its consolidation, and is active in the management of the business. Messrs. Charles D. Gates, and Clarence F. Turner are both natives of Connecticut, resident here since 1884, and give close and faithful attention to the discharge of their duties as secretary and **treasurer** respectively.

THE FISCHER-LEAF COMPANY; Mantels, Grates and Stoves; Nos. 433 and 435 West Jefferson Street.—Prominent among the representative industries of this city is that of the Fischer-Leaf Company, manufacturers of marbleized iron and slate mantels, grates, fireplace trimmings, and the celebrated Arizona stoves and ranges. The business was established in 1866 by the firm of Fischer, Leaf & Co., who early developed a flourishing trade. Repeated enlargements of facilities were necessitated, and in 1885 the important interests were reorganized and incorporated under the present title, with a paid-up capital of $250,000. The foundry and shops, cover an area of ground, 210x230 feet in dimensions and here have been erected spacious buildings for foundry, pattern and machine shops, warehouses, etc. The moulding floor is one of the best arranged in the United States, enabling the company to turn out castings in any quantity and of all sizes. The plant is equipped with the latest improved machinery and appliances, run by heavy steam power and affording employment to upwards of two hundred and fifty in the various departments. The officers, president, Pfeiffer; vice-president, Brecker; secretary and treasurer, Ochsenbirt, are all practical men in this line, devoting close supervision to every detail of the business. The company's showrooms and office occupy an entire three-story and basement building, which is 27x210 feet in dimensions, and is supplied with every convenience, elevator, etc. The showrooms are elegantly fitted up having tiled floors and tiled ceilings, electric light, etc. Here is made the finest and most complete display in the United States of high-class artistic mantels in iron, wood and slate, and grates in the most elaborate handwrought patterns, and fireplace trimmings in brass, bronze and wrought iron, the output of marbleized iron mantels alone amounting to ten thousand in one year. Architects and the trade can here find exactly what they want in these lines to fit up the finest residences, offices, etc. Here also are shown full lines of the famous Arizona stoves and ranges, having many exclusive improvements, insuring economy of fuel, yet the utmost perfection as to cooking and baking. The company's trade covers the western, middle, and southern states, and extends into Mexico. Mr. Charles Pfeiffer has been identified with the business since 1866, and is a recognized authority therein. He is a public spirited citizen, an active member of the Board of Trade and in every way is fully qualified to extend and successfully guide this great industry. Mr. Phil. Brecker is widely known, and has been connected with the concern for many years, and is a business man of sound judgment. Mr. Ochsenbirt has been connected with the concern for a quarter of a century, and became the secretary and treasurer when the company was formed in 1885.

THE FISCHER LEAF COMPANY.
(See descriptive article on opposite page.)

WRIGHT & TAYLOR; Distillers and Wholesale Dealers in Fine Kentucky Whiskies; No. 319 West Main Street.—The production of a pure, mild and healthful whiskey, a true sample of the best stimulant, is a branch of industry requiring the utmost skill and soundest judgment, coupled with special facilities both for distilling and warehousing. In all these respects, the Wright & Taylor brands of whiskies are

justly celebrated and have come into general consumption with those who seek a superior article throughout the United States. The firm of Wright & Taylor was organized upwards of eleven years ago to engage in the distilling of high grade Kentucky whiskies. The retirement of Mr. Wright occurred four years ago, since when Mr. Marion E. Taylor has remained sole proprietor, retaining, however, the old familiar name and style. Mr. Taylor's distillery is located in Nelson County, Ky., in the Fifth District, a region famous for its superior whiskies, and it is one of the oldest and most complete in the state and dates its foundation back about one hundred years, and from time to time improvements and additions have been made until to-day it is one of the largest and most complete in the country, the premises covering an area of five acres. Here is a large three-story building for the distillery, malt house, boiler house, etc. The plant has a costly equipment of the latest type, and turns out some eight thousand barrels annually, five hundred bushels of grain being consumed daily. The greatest care is taken with every process, from the selecting of the grain to the barrelling of the finished product, and Mr. Taylor's brands are recognized everywhere as the highest grades of old fashioned hand-made sour-mash and pure rye whiskies. With such carefully selected grain, purest of spring water and approved methods of distilling, these whiskies are perfectly made. They are stored in three great warehouses of ten thousand barrels capacity each and left at an even temperature till thoroughly matured. Wright & Taylor's office and city storehouse are centrally located, a fine four story and basement building, 35x110 feet in dimensions. Here is carried an immense stock of fine Kentucky whiskies. The following famous brands are specialties; Fine Old Kentucky Taylor, eight years old, Fine Old Logan, a true fire copper handmade whiskey, eight years old, and the celebrated Pride of Louisville, a true sour-mash bourbon and pure rye whiskey, pronounced by experts to be the most palatable on the market. None is bottled until eight years old, and is a mild stimulant, positively free from all deleterious properties, and is strongly recommended for its health-giving, nourishing qualities, specially adapted for medicinal and family uses. All these goods are bottled and shipped direct by Wright & Taylor, and none are genuine without firm's signature on the labels. Another popular brand is their Cone Spring Whiskey. The house sells to the trade of the United States and Mexico and requires the services of a staff of fifteen travelers on the road. Wherever introduced these whiskies are much preferred thereafter. Mr. Marion E. Taylor is a native of Louisiana, and was formerly in the milling business at St. Louis. He is a pushing, energetic and successful business man, who has built up a flourishing trade within a few years, and permanently maintains the enviable reputation of his whiskies. He is a member of the Board of Trade and of the Pendennis Club, and is very popular socially, and has recently been elected secretary of the National Wine and Spirit Association.

J. C. KING UNDERTAKING COMPANY; No. 262 West Jefferson Street. It is only during the last thirty years, that any apparent progress has been made in the customs for the burial of the dead, and it is entirely due to the refinement of the present age, that the occupation of the undertaker has arisen from a trade to the dignity of a profession. In this connection special reference is made to the representative Louisville concern known as the J. C. King Undertaking Company, funeral directors and embalmers, whose establishment is located at Nos. 262 and 264 West Jefferson Street. This business was established March 1861 by Mr. J. C. King who was succeeded by Messrs. Pearson & King, Messrs. Owens & King and eventually Mr. J. C. King again became sole proprietor. On March 9th, 1892 he retired in favor of his son Mr. E. T. King who on May 13th, 1893 admitted Mr. W. T. Gregg into partnership, the firm being known as King & Gregg. Eventually on October 23rd 1894, the business was incorporated under the laws of Kentucky with ample capital, Mr. C. H. Boden being the president, Mr. J. H. Linn secretary and treasurer, and Mr. W. T. Boden, manager. Messrs. C. H. & W. T. Boden were formerly with Mr. King, the former of whom is a graduate of Sullivan's School of Embalming. W. T. Boden is also a graduate of the Boston School of Embalming. They cater to all classes of the population and furnish everything, requisite and necessary for the plainest and most imposing funerals, while they are prompt in meeting their engagements and can always be thoroughly depended on. In all matters relating to the last rites of burial. The premises occupied comprise a spacious three-story building, fitted up with every facility and convenience, and the stables are situated at Ninth and Madison Streets. They keep constantly on hand a carefully selected and choice stock of funeral requisites, including coffins, caskets, metallic cases, shrouds, plumes, etc., and also manufacture Patent Stone Burial Vaults, which are moulded to any size and can be used instead of wooden cases. Embalming when desired is performed according to the latest scientific methods and entire satisfaction is guaranteed patrons. Carriages and crapes are furnished at short notice for all occasions and the office is open at all hours day or night. Cemetery lots or graves are secured in any of the cemeteries of the city and its vicinity, and in a word they relieve bereaved relatives and friends of all care and trouble incidental to looking after these sorrowful details. Messrs. C. H. & W. T. Boden and J. H. Linn are natives of this city, the last named being a popular member of the Commercial Club. They are highly esteemed for their strict integrity and are active members of the Funeral Directors' Association of the Falls City, and have always made it a rule to charge only fair and equitable rates for their services.

A. BARTH; Tanner and Currier; New Albany, Ind.—This extensive business was established in 1864 by A. Barth & Company, the co-partners being Messrs. A. Barth and C. Grosecurth, who conducted it till 1885, when Mr. A. Barth became sole proprietor. Mr. Barth is a thoroughly practical and experienced tanner, who possesses an intimate knowledge of every detail of this useful industry, and the needs and requirements of a first-class trade. The premises occupied have an area of one and a half acres, and are connected by switches with the Belt Line Railroad and all lines entering New Albany. The plant includes six two and three story brick buildings, and here are in operation a one hundred and twenty horse power steam boiler, an engine of ninety horse power, three other steam engines, an electric motor, hydraulic pumps and all the latest improved machinery and appliances. Forty skilled workmen are employed during the busy season, and the capacity of the tannery is thirty thousand hides annually. Mr. Barth manufactures largely oak harness and oak collar leather, also fair leather and the lighter grades of harness leather suitable for bridles, saddles, etc., and the trade of the house now extends throughout the entire United States. The leather produced here is a recognized standard with the trade, and is unsurpassed for quality, finish and reliability, and has no superior in this or any other market. Orders are filled with care and dispatch at very moderate figures, and all leather is fully warranted to be exactly as represented. Mr. Barth is of German nationality, and learned his trade in his native land, and is highly regarded in trade circles for his strict integrity. He is ably assisted in the management of his business by his sons, Messrs. H. and A. Barth.

LOUISVILLE OF TO-DAY.

AMPHITHEATRE AUDITORIUM; City Ticket Office; No. 422 Fourth Avenue.—Our city has many distinctions, that place it far in advance as the great metropolis of the South, and chief among these is the possession in the vast Amphitheatre Auditorium. To the distinguished enterprise and energy of our popular fellow townsman, Mr. Daniel Quilp, is due the existence of this magnificent structure and its surrounding attractions. Mr. Quilp is the most enterprising theatrical manager south of Mason and Dixon's line, and in 1887-88 he arranged with Mr. Edwin Booth and Mr. Lawrence Barrett, to give a joint representation of Shakespearean dramas in this city, and a contract was entered into with them and the Southern Exposition, for the plays to be produced in his auditorium. To seat the immense audiences, Mr. Quilp purchased over three thousand folding chairs, and finally built a large music hall in which the chairs were utilized. In 1888 and 1889 the present magnificent theatre was erected, being first opened on September 23, 1889, by Messrs. Booth and Barrett, before a crowded house. Mr. Booth subsequently presenting Mr. Quilp with one of the only two busts in existence, showing Booth in his character of Brutus. The bust now stands in an enclosure near the entrance to the auditorium, and is an object of great interest. This theatre is adapted for the presentation of great attractions with large companies and much scenery. The stage is the largest in America, while the house readily seats over three thousand people. The auditorium forms a perfect square, one hundred and twenty feet from the stage line to the rear wall. The space is perfectly arranged, so that there is a view of the stage from every seat in the house, while the acoustic properties are perfect. The seating arrangements are as follows: Fourteen private boxes, seating seventy-two; parquette seats four hundred and fifty; dress circle, two thousand one hundred and thirty, and balcony, four hundred and fifty. The house is the best provided with exits in the world, being in excess of the requirements of law, there being no less than seven twenty twelve foot exits, with doors sliding into the walls, and if necessary an audience could leave the theatre inside of three minutes. All the modern improvements have been introduced here, Mr. Quilp's liberal policy being everywhere known of. At a cost of $35,000 he has put in a double electric light plant, so that he is independent of any outside service, and the theatre is most brilliantly illuminated, there being a profusion of arc and incandescent lights in and outside the building, besides gas light. It is the finest theatre in America, and from Booth and Patti down, all the great foreign and domestic celebrities have appeared here. Madame Patti declared that she had sung in all the principal theatres of the world, but in none with such satisfaction as in the auditorium, and this is the universal verdict of the profession. Mr. Quilp allows only the highest class of attractions to appear here, and the present season's engagements are of the most desirable character, and will be sure to draw large and appreciative audiences. Mr. Quilp's grand dancing pavilion and beautiful garden in the south auditorium are also worthy of special mention. Here is landscape gardening and scenery to perfection, besides an artificial lake. Near it is a grand band stand, and seating capacity for eight thousand people, while there is

a perfect bicycle track of six laps to the mile that cost $2,000. Around the lake and through the grounds are lovely promenades, while there is a deer park, and on one side of the amphitheatre is a perfect arrangement for exhibiting fireworks upon a gigantic scale. Mr. Quilp as sole proprietor and manager, is entitled to the warm praise and practical recognition bestowed upon his enterprise, in providing the city with such an amusement centre, and has the satisfaction of having erected in our midst by far the finest theatre in America. He is a business man of the highest standing, universally respected, and his spirit of enterprise might well be emulated by theatrical managers in other **great cities**.

ALEX. HARTHILL; Tobacco Buyer; No. 1001 West Main Street.—The marvellous growth of the tobacco interest in this, the largest leaf tobacco market in the world, is elsewhere in this volume set forth with some statistical array, and it is our purpose to give detailed description of the chief causes contributing to this end. There can be but little question but that the buyers and rehandlers have proven themselves prime factors in achieving the satisfactory result referred to, and prominent among such ranks Mr. Alex. Harthill, tobacco buyer, of No. 1001 West Main Street. He has filled this position for many years, and his extensive purchases are made on various accounts, most of the goods being shipped to the seaboard for export; contracting for a great deal of tobacco in the stemming districts, his purchases of such being shipped direct from there to the seaboard for export and consequently do not appear in the Louisville market at all, and heard of only through drafts and bills of exchange through bankers in Louisville. Like many others in the tobacco trade, Mr. Harthill is a native of Scotland, has been located in Louisville for twenty-three years, and enjoys an excellent reputation in the trade. His weekly reports of the market, which are published in the leading tobacco trade journals, are considered standard authority. Mr. Harthill does probably the largest all-around tobacco brokerage business, buying all grades and descriptions of tobacco for consumption in the United States, as well as for sale in all the leading tobacco markets in the world. He is a member of the Louisville Leaf Tobacco Exchange, as well as affiliated with the order of the Free and Accepted Masons. In buying, both at the auction sales in Louisville and privately in the country, he has had the able assistance of Mr. W. C. Herr for the past eight years, a gentleman well and favorably known both at home and abroad. Mr. Harthill does business entirely on commission, buying to the best advantage wherever he can for his customers.

JOHN E. AND FRANK WALTER; Proprietors of Clay Street Brewery; Nos. 812 and 814 Clay Street.—There may be breweries in Louisville employing more labor and having a larger output than the Clay Street Brewery, but there are none that enjoy a more enviable reputation or turn out a higher quality of beer. In 1856 Mr. C. Conrad Walter founded this industry and successfully conducted it until his lamented death which occurred in 1873. It was carried on after that by the estate until 1889, when Messrs. John E. and Frank Walter, sons of the founder, succeeded and under their able management the business is going ahead at a far brisker pace than ever before. The premises cover a large area and here are erected the brewery proper, the storehouses, the stables, etc. The equipment of the brewery is modern and complete. Everything in the line of machinery and appliances of the most approved pattern is supplied and motive power is furnished by steam. They manufacture cream beer, a specialty being made of brewing on order, and the output amounts to upwards of five thousand barrels a year. Several assistants and teams are employed and the output finds ready sale in all parts of the city. This is the oldest cream brewery in Louisville and its career from the outset has been characterized by the most liberal methods. Only the purest ingredients are used and the beer for purity, flavor and sparkling appearance is unrivaled. Hundreds of beer consumers will have nothing else and claim, rightly too, that it is equal to the best in the market. This is in sentiment the statement of the majority of the saloon keepers of Louisville. Messrs. Walter are natives of Louisville and are widely known and held in the highest esteem on account of their strict probity. They have been identified with this business since boyhood and understand its every detail, and we bespeak for the brewery, under their management, a future much brighter than its prosperous past.

C. C. MENGEL, JR. & BRO. CO; Logs and Lumber; No. 1609 West Kentucky Street.—One of the most important concerns is the South engaged in the manufacture of lumber is that of the "C. C. Mengel, Jr. and Bro. Company," which besides running two saw mills is proprietor of one of the largest planing mills and box factories in this city. The company makes a specialty of oak, poplar and cottonwood, and besides its heavy local trade, and throughout the United States, is a heavy exporter of logs and lumber to Great Britain. The business was established in 1877 by Messrs. C. C. Mengel, Jr. and Co., who early developed a flourishing trade. In 1888, their important interests were incorporated under the laws of this state, with a paid-up capital of $250,000, the old familiar name being retained. They are large owners of valuable tracts of timber lands in Tennessee, Arkansas, etc., covered with growths of the choicest old oaks, walnut, ash, cherry, hickory, sycamore, black birch, poplar, etc., which cut clear stuff to the largest dimensions, making this high grade of lumber specially desirable to the furniture manufacturer, cabinet maker, etc. The company's saw mills are located at Trimble and Tipton, Tenn., and have an immense annual capacity. The company yearly handles 30,000,000 to 35,000,000 feet of hardwood logs, and of this total, the mills in this city consume fully 15,000,000 feet. The plant is desirably located and has an area of two city blocks. The works comprise a large and splendidly equipped planing mill, an extensive box factory, etc. Connected with the mill are improved dry kilns, and large yards. The premises have switch connection with the railroads, entering the city and thus lowest freight rates are insured. The mills here are fully provided with saws and planers, run (with the box factory) by two engines of three hundred and fifty horse power. Poplar, cottonwood and quartered oak are largely cut here, made up into siding, ceiling, weatherboards and flooring, while the box factory turns out all kinds of boxes. The company employs one hundred and eighty hands here, and upwards of one hundred at the mills, and ships its product to every section of the Union, besides heavy exports of logs and lumber to Europe. Mr. C. C. Mengel, Jr., is a native of Mass., and is a valued and public spirited resident of this city. He is an active member of the Lumber Exchange, as also of the Builders' and Traders' Exchange, while he is the vice-president of the Board of Trade. Mr. C. R. Mengel, the secretary and treasurer, is a native of Brooklyn, N. Y., and is secretary and treasurer of the Columbia Veneer and Box Company. He also is a member of the Lumber Exchange and Builders' and Trades' Exchange, and is likewise connected with prominent social bodies.

NEW ALBANY MANUFACTURING COMPANY; Manufacturers of Quarry Machinery; Water Street, New Albany, Ind. Prominent among these leading industrial enterprises, which have exerted an important influence in the material growth and progress of the city of New Albany, will be found that which constitutes the immediate subject of the present sketch. What is now so widely and favorably known as the New Albany Manufacturing Company which originated in 1874 by Messrs. W. C. DePauw and Chas. Hegewald, who continued the enterprise till 1880, when Mr. N. T. DePauw bought his father's interest and in 1883, Mr. Chas. Hegewald retired from the firm. Eventually, January 1st, 1890, the business was incorporated under the laws of Indiana with ample capital, Mr. N. T. DePauw being the president, Mr. W. H. Coen, vice-president, Mr. T. H. O'Donnel, superintendent, and Mr. R. H. Bailey, secretary and manager. The premises occupied comprise a spacious brick building 50x130 feet in area, fully equipped with modern tools, machinery and appliances, operated by a superior one hundred horse power steam engine, and seventy-five skilled workmen are constantly employed. The company manufactures all kinds of quarry machinery, channellers, travellers, hoists, derricks, saw gangs, mill and steamboat machinery, and the trade of the concern, which is steadily increasing, extends throughout the central, western and southern states. Mr. DePauw is a native of Indiana and was educated in the DePauw University, while Mr. O'Donnel was born in St. Louis, where he learnt the moulder's trade and has had charge of various foundries in the Falls City for the last thirty years. Mr. R. H. Bailey is a native of Louisville, and has been engaged with this company since 1886.

AMERICAN RESTAURANT; J. Mivelaz, Proprietor; Nos. 425 and 427 Market Street.—It will be unanimously conceded, that a first-class restaurant is an important acquisition to any city. In this connection, prominent reference is made to the popular American Restaurant, of which Mr. J. Mivelaz is the enterprising proprietor. He opened this Louisville Restaurant in 1889 and at once by the excellence of its service and superior quality of its various dishes and meals, it secured a firm hold on public favor. The establishment is spacious, elegantly equipped and has lately been entirely redecorated and newly fitted up while fifty waiters, etc., are employed. Everything is selected with the utmost care and the bills of fare offer numerous courses of delicacies and staple dishes. A specialty is made of fine orders, the cuisine is unexcelled, and the coffee and lunch counter is unsurpassed in the Falls City. Superior meals can be obtained here at all hours of the day or night, while the prices charged in all cases are extremely moderate. Mr. Mivelaz, who is a thoroughly experienced caterer was born in this city in 1864, and is highly regarded by the community for sterling probity. For eleven years previous to starting on his own account, he was engaged at the English Kitchen, and at that time there were only four restaurants in the city, which supplied about 800 people daily. Mr. Mivelaz at the present day feeds about 1200 persons daily, and has on Sundays 2200, and having ample accommodations for providing meals for 3000 to 3500 people. A specialty is made of oysters in season, and to those requiring a first-class meal at a reasonable rate, we know of no establishment in this city more worthy of liberal patronage, than the American Restaurant, and a visit to Louisville is incomplete without a call at this popular resort.

H. H. WOLF'S RESIDENCE.

LOUISVILLE OF TO-DAY.

HENRY H. WOLF & CO.: Wholesale Manufacturing Clothiers; No. 644 West Main Street.—The leading wholesale clothing house of our city, is that of Messrs. Henry H. Wolf & Co., whose immense modern establishment is located so centrally at the above address. The importance of such a large and ably conducted concern to Louisville cannot be overestimated. It is such houses as these, employing hundreds of hands, and controlling a vast trade extending over more than a dozen states, that tend to the upbuilding and prosperity of a community, and the public spirited policy of Messrs. Henry H. Wolf & Co., in making our city a great manufacturing centre for the wholesale clothing trade is generally recognized and appreciated by the community. This business was established away back in 1848 by Messrs. Kahn, Wolf & Sons, afterwards succeeded by the firm of Levi Wolf and Newberger. In 1880, Mr. Henry H. Wolf formed the present firm in copartnership with Mr. I. G. Sternberger, who have greatly enlarged and extended the business. They were formerly located at Nos. 715 and 717 West Main Street, remaining there until 1889, when the present fine building was erected and occupied. It was planned to embrace every modern improvement, and is one of the handsomest structures in town devoted to mercantile purposes. It is six lofty stories and basement in height, and has dimensions of 25x210 feet. The premises are well arranged for the purposes of the trade, finished stock being shown and carried on the lower floors, while the upper ones are devoted to cloth cutting and manufacturing. A fast running elevator connects every floor. Men's and boys' fine and medium clothing is the specialty here, while both as to prices, workmanship and quality of material, the firm challenges competition with any house in the South. Messrs. Wolf and Sternberger select their woolens and other materials with the utmost care, while every bolt of cloth is most carefully inspected for defects, and every yard is shrunk and sponged, thus insuring perfect fitting and wearing garments. They employ the most expert cutters and impart to their clothing, the same grace and elegance of style as the most fashionable of tailor made. The work is largely given out, several hundred being thus employed, while seventy-five clerks, salesmen, cutters and workmen are kept busy in the house. The trade of the house is very extensive, their customers being found in every section of the South and Southwest, requiring the services of twelve travelers on the road. The firm have a well earned reputation for the superiority of their clothing, and they offer the most substantial inducements to retailers of any house in the United States to-day. Mr. Henry H. Wolf was born in Hopkinsville, Ky., and is a son of the original founder of the business, to which he was brought up, and has thus had vast practical experience, while he is a business man of the highest standing, universally respected and noted for sound judgment and conservative methods. He is a member of the Commercial Club and popular socially. Mr. I. G. Sternberger was born in New York city, and has been a permanent resident of this city since becoming a member of the firm in 1880. He is a business man of marked ability and very popular. He is also a member of the Commercial Club, while both partners have memberships in the Board of Trade, and their house is the great leading representative in its line in the South, with a record and a reputation of priceless value as regards their prompt, honorable dealings with everyone.

P. G. COKER: Importer of Millinery; No. 615 West Main Street.—In every branch of commercial activity in a large community, there is invariably one house that is justly and popularly spoken of as the representative of its class. In Louisville's millinery circles, the position of supremacy is held by the establishment of P. G. Coker, which is the leading exponent of the importation of and wholesale trade in fashionable millinery. This enterprise was established in 1879 by Mr. Coker, and by his energy and thorough knowledge of the requirements of the trade, it soon became widely known. Mr. Coker enjoys a very large and high class patronage, necessitating the services of seven traveling salesmen upon the road. The premises consist of a three-story brick structure, 25x80 feet in dimensions, giving ample accommodation for the manipulation and display of the exceptionally fine lines of goods carried. Mr. Coker is a direct importer of the latest modes in Parisian and London millinery, including flowers, feathers and ornaments in the greatest variety, and such are his foreign connections, that the newest correct styles appear here simultaneously with their display in the leading centres of fashion. The stock is one of the heaviest and most complete that is to be found between New York and St. Louis, comprising trimmed and untrimmed hats and bonnets, shapes, toques, ribbons, laces, feathers, silks, satins, flowers, ornaments, and all millinery novelties, steady employment being given to ninety skilled assistants, and the annual volume of trade being very large. Mr. Coker is a native of Georgia, and since coming here in 1862, has won universal respect and esteem for his ability, enterprise and honorable methods.

J. F. HILLERICH & SON; Wood Turners, Band and Scroll Sawing, Etc.; No. 216 First Street.—In reviewing the industries of this enterprising city, we find several houses which, owing to their many years of existence and the superiority of their productions deserve especially prominent mention. Such a concern is that of Messrs. J. F. Hillerich & Son, wood turners and woodworkers. This business was established in 1865 by Mr. J. F. Hillerich and conducted by him alone until the year 1888, when he took his son Mr. J. A. Hillerich in partnership, since which time the affairs of the company have passed more and more into the hands of the son, who now practically manages the business. The premises occupied comprise a two-storied brick building 26x135 feet in dimensions, fully equipped with the latest improved appliances and machinery for woodworking, in addition to band and scroll sawing of all kinds. They manufacture every description of bored porch columns, newel posts, brackets and poles, also manufacture fancy woodwork for interior and exterior decoration of buildings. They are also the manufacturers of the dairy swing churn, which is unquestionably the best, cheapest and most durable churn that has  yet been put in the market, and they also manufacture baseball bats, which have secured a national reputation for efficiency, strength and finish. From fifteen to twenty skilled hands are employed, and nothing but the very best work is ever turned out, perfect satisfaction as regards quality of materials and workmanship being fully guaranteed. Mr. Hillerich, senior, was born in Germany, but has made his home in Louisville for many years. Mr. J. A. Hellerich, the son, has long been known for business capacity and skilled ability. He was born in this city, and has gained the confidence of the firm's numerous customers.

FALLS CITY MANUFACTURING COMPANY; Manufacturers of Pants; No. 229 Seventh Street.—Among the noteworthy of the industrial enterprises located in Louisville, which have been founded within recent years, and which have developed into prominence and representative position in the business world, is that of the **Falls City Manufacturing Company** conducted under the able proprietorship of Messrs. George W. Roney, N. L. Fitschen and Frank J. Healine. This well and favorably known house was established in 1882, and the positive and permanent success that has attended the enterprise from the outset, amply attests the  general excellence of the goods produced, to say nothing of the energy and ability displayed in the management of the business. The premises occupied comprise the entire four-storied building at the address indicated, having frontage and depth of 24x105 feet, equipped with seventy-five sewing machines, operated by electric motor power, every provision being made for the cutting, packing, shipping and general business office departments. These departments are systematically divided so that the best results may be attained, and employment is provided for an average force of from one hundred to one hundred and twenty-five efficient hands. Here with the most complete facilities at their command, the company are carrying on general operations as manufacturers of the leather breeches brand of jean pants, also cassimere, corduroy, kersey and moleskin pants and suits; they also handle overalls and jackets. The goods are made of the best materials of their type, in the most substantial manner, and to quote from the facetiously worded business card of the firm, are full of stitches, warranted not to rip, plenty of room in leg and hip. That these statements are not by any means overdrawn, is amply evinced, firstly by the signal success the company marked from the start, and a consideration of the fact that their trade is rapidly increasing in volume and value. Mr. Roney was born in Lagrange, Ky., and prior to engaging in this enterprise, conducted a general mercantile establishment as Belmont, Bullitt County, this state. Mr. Fitschen hails from Hanover, Germany, and has resided in Louisville since 1869, being formerly engaged in the merchant tailoring line. Mr. Healine was born here, and was formerly employed as cutter with leading firms in this same branch of business, with which this company is so favorably identified.

LOUISVILLE OF TO-DAY.

M. T. LEWMAN & CO.; Contractors and Builders; No. 815 Columbia Building.—Among the enterprising and trustworthy firms engaged in the contracting and building line in Louisville, who have become well known throughout the southern states by reason of the length of time they have been engaged in the business, and the many large buildings of prominence throughout the country they have constructed, are Messrs. M. T. Lewman & Co. The business of this concern was founded thirty-five years ago by the late Mr. M. T. Lewman, at Greencastle, Indiana. Subsequent removal was made to Louisville owing to the many facilities this city offered and its splendid location by which a business of this kind could be extended throughout the South and so easily managed from this point. In 1888 the founder of the house died and the business has since been carried on by his sons, Messrs. J. B., H. L. and L. D. Lewman, under the present firm style; and under their enterprising management, the business of the house has been materially augmented, the concern ranking among the most prominent of its type in the South and Southwest, branch offices of the firm being maintained at Savannah and Atlanta, Georgia. Messrs. Lewman devote their energies to the contracting and erection of public buildings, hotels, churches and kindred edifices throughout the southern states, evidences of their skill abounding all over this section of the country. In fact the largest and most prominent buildings in a majority of the southern cities were built by them. Notable among contracts more recently completed by them may be mentioned the De Soto Hotel, Savannah, Ga.; the Insane Asylum, Marion, Va.; the Blind Asylum, Macon, Ga.; Natchez Hotel, Natchez, Miss., etc., and many others too numerous to mention. The firm employs often from one to three hundred hands. Messrs. Lewman are members of the Builders' and Traders' Exchange at Louisville and Atlanta.

THE SOUTHERN OIL TANK LINE; Manufacturers of Petroleum and its Products; Brook and Lee Streets.—The Southern Oil Tank Line, manufacturers and refiners of petroleum and its products, has a large plant established in Louisville. The premises occupied are spacious and well equipped, and several large storage tanks of many thousands of gallons capacity, are utilized. The headquarters of the Southern Oil Tank Line, as well as the main refinery, is situated at Oil City, Penna. Agencies are established at both Dayton, Ohio, and Louisville, the local branch having been in operation since 1890. It is situated on the main line of the L. & N. R. R., and employs twelve men. Being an independent refinery, the company had to contend against strong efforts which larger rivals made to crush it, but it held its ground and gradually established a fine trade in both illuminating and lubricating oils, owing to the superior quality and reliability of its goods. Its oils are always exactly what they are represented to be, and inferior goods are never put on the market. The Louisville agency has for its territory the entire South, and operates seventy-five tank cars continually out of Louisville, selling heavily to the large manufacturers and dealers. The Southern Oil Tank Line has the reputation of handling the best illuminating oils on the market, its finest brands being Electric and Calcite oil; these goods are absolutely odorless, clear, and never produce any smoke when burning. "Mutual" gasoline has also become the favorite both with the trade and the consumer, and the company's engine and machine oils always give complete satisfaction, while their lubricating qualities are unexcelled. Mr. S. W. Bennett has been the manager of the Louisville branch since June, 1894. Mr. Bennett has a complete knowledge of the oil business, having formerly been the agent at this point for the Cleveland Refining Company. He is one of the most widely-known business men in the city and is also an active Freemason.

THE LOUISVILLE BRYANT & STRATTON BUSINESS COLLEGE; Third and Jefferson Streets.—The importance of giving the youth a sound business education need not be enlarged upon. It grows more and more in evidence daily. The benefits to be derived therefrom can scarcely be overestimated. A young man or woman who has had a training in a first-class modern commercial institute certainly starts with a decided advantage over those not so favored, and in respect to such advantage we direct attention to the Louisville Bryant & Stratton Business College, which stands first in public esteem. It has a splendid record, and its popularity increases with each year. It takes rank among the foremost institutions of its kind in the United States, and is widely and favorably known. The history of the Louisville Bryant & Stratton College covers a period of thirty-one years, and its career has been marked by steady progress. It was organized in 1864, and has ever since been conducted with uninterrupted success. About sixteen years ago, Mr. James Ferrier assumed control, and the institution was duly incorporated under the laws of the state of Kentucky in 1894. It is officered as follows: James Ferrier, president and treasurer; Edwin J. Wright, vice-president and superintendent of instruction. The course of instruction here is the result of many years of experience, and is eminently practical and systematic. The Louisville Bryant & Stratton Business College is conveniently and pleasantly located, and occupies very spacious and commodious premises. The classrooms are neatly and excellently appointed, airy and thoroughly ventilated. The institution is well lighted and heated, and the sanitary arrangements and general accommodations are of a superior character. The average attendance is upwards of two hundred scholars.

LOUISVILLE OF TO-DAY.

THE JOSEPH DENUNZIO FRUIT COMPANY; Importers and Jobbers of Foreign and Domestic Fruits and Nuts; Nos. 316 to 322 Jefferson Street. This is one of the oldest and largest houses of the kind in the South, and was originally established by Mr. Joseph Denunzio, twenty-five years ago, who, after successfully conducting it for fifteen years alone,

admitted Mr. Chas. Scholtz, Jr., into partnership, and in 1893 the present company was organized. It is incorporated under Connecticut laws with ample capital paid in, and the present officers are: President, Charles Scholtz, Jr.; secretary and treasurer, Fred Scholtz, the lamented death of Mr. Denunzio having occurred September 18th, 1894. The salesrooms and storehouses consist of a three-story and basement building, 60x130 feet in dimensions, with a large sub-cellar, located at 316-322 West Jefferson Street, and a large storehouse at Fifteenth Street and High Avenue. Large ripening rooms, kept at a temperature of sixty degrees; cold storage apartments with a capacity of seven thousand barrels are included in the equipment, and in all respects there is no house of the kind in this part of the country, equipped in a more complete or modern manner. Fruits and nuts of all kinds are handled in immense quantities and specialties are made of tropical productions. Shipments are received direct from Italy, Spain, West Indies, as well as California, Florida and other sources, and with producers the house enjoys exceptionally advantageous trade relations, owing to its long and unblemished career. The extent upon which they operate enables them to offer advantages to the trade, which few, if any houses in the country can duplicate. Thirty-five assistants and twelve teams are employed and the trade, though extremely heavy in this city and locality, is by no means confined here, but extends to all parts of the United States. Under its present able management the house is advancing with greater strides than ever and a future, much brighter than its enviable past, awaits it. The active management of the house devolves upon the president and secretary and treasurer, Messrs. Charles Scholtz, Jr., and Fred Scholtz. These gentlemen are brothers and have been identified with the house seventeen years and fifteen years respectively. They are members of the Produce Exchange, and of the National League of Commission Merchants of the United States, and in business life they rank among the most prominent of Louisville's merchants.

FRANK P. BARON, Jr.; Harness, Saddles, Bridles, Collars, Whips, Etc.; No. 1314 Preston Street, Near College.—Mr. Baron commenced business on his own account in a small way in 1885, and is a self-made man, who has risen by his own industry, frugality and honesty to his present leading position in the saddlery trade of Louisville. Harness is made promptly to order in the very best style from the best quality of leather and mounted in nickel, brass, etc, being noted for its superior workmanship and lasting durability, while it is warranted to give the best of service. Mr. Baron has lately added to his business a feed department and deals largely in hay, oats, grain and feed. He was born in Louisville in 1869. He is highly esteemed for his mechanical skill and strict probity, and has gained the entire confidence of his numerous customers in all sections of the country.

— — LOUISVILLE OF TO-DAY. — —

CARTER DRY GOODS COMPANY; Nos. 729, 731 and 733 West Main Street. Our city permanently maintains her supremacy as the great mercantile centre of the South. The enterprise and the ability of her merchants is proverbial, and notably so in the wholesale dry goods trade, in which line the leading representative is the famous Carter Dry Goods Company. This is a very old concern, the business having been founded away back in 1859 by Messrs. John A. and J. G. Carter. They were succeeded by the firm of Carter Bros. & Co., thus continuing until July 1st, 1892, when the concern was reorganized and incorporated under the present title of the Carter Dry Goods Company, with a paid-up capital of $250,000. It has continued to steadily enlarge the flourishing and extensive trade of the old house, and the highest credit is due to the officers, who are as follows: Mr. J. C. Bethel, president; Mr. Edward Rowland, first vice-president; Mr. E. D. Clark, second vice-president; Mr. W. H. Bradbury, secretary, and Mr. H. Dumesnil, treasurer. They are direct importers and jobbers of staple and fancy dry goods, and carry an immense and freshly assorted stock in their spacious store, so centrally located at Nos. 729, 731 and 733 West Main Street. The business has been carried on at this stand for nineteen years past, and was prior to that in premises on the opposite side of the street. The present building is a modern five-story and basement structure, 63x210 feet in dimensions, and is equipped with elevators and all improvements. The salesrooms are handsomely fitted up, and here are displayed the latest novelties in English, German, French and domestic dry goods, notions, fancy goods, gents' furnishing goods, etc. A specialty is made of silks and dress goods in all the latest patterns, shades and textures; while the most complete stock of cottons, sheetings, calicoes, cambrics and muslins in the South is to be found here. In notions, fancy goods, laces, embroideries, ribbons, hosiery and furnishing goods generally, the house has always maintained a similar enviable reputation. A New York office is maintained at No. 115 Worth Street, where the company's resident buyer is constantly on the market, securing bargains in new goods from importers, commission merchants and eastern mills direct, and shipments of new goods are daily being opened in the store here, so that the southern and western trade can fully rely upon the fullness and freshness of this stock, while buying with such good judgment and for cash, the Carter Dry Goods Company offers substantial inducements in prices which cannot be duplicated elsewhere. Upwards of sixty clerks, packers and porters are required in the store, while the company requires a staff of twenty travelers on the road, covering every section of the South and Southwest to the Gulf, with customers all through Indiana and Southern Illinois. To merchants in the south, the company has long been known as headquarters in the trade, dealing in the same class of goods as could be found in New York, at quite as low—often lower prices than are quoted there, with a certainty of liberal and honorable treatment from this responsible old concern. Mr. J. C. Bethel, the president, is a native of Kentucky, and has been permanently identified with the house since 1866. His sound judgment and intimate knowledge of the trade are too well known of, to require special comment here, and the enterprising policy of the company, with its resultant success, reflects the highest credit upon his guidance. Mr. Edward Rowland, the first vice-president, is a native of Alabama, and became identified with the company in July, 1892, when the business was reorganized. He was formerly auditor of the Louisville and Nashville Railroad, and is universally respected. Mr. E. B. Clark, second vice-president, is a native of Virginia, and has been connected with the house since 1885, and in this line for twenty-five years. Mr. W. H. Bradbury, the secretary, is a native of Steuben County, N. Y., and was connected with the old firm for twelve years. Mr. H. Dumesnil, the treasurer, joined the company in 1894, and was formerly of Dumesnil Brothers brick manufactures. All the officers give close attention to business, and the company is one of the oldest conducted, most progressive and popular in the wholesale dry goods trade of America.

BAKER & SMITH COMPANY; Heating and Ventilating Apparatus, and Power Plants; No. 298 Third Street. This is undoubtedly an age of progress, and each year witnesses fresh triumphs in the field of invention. Perfection is rapidly approaching in every article of manufacture, and nowhere is this more clearly to be seen than in the production of low steam and hot water heating apparatus, for warming and ventilating public buildings and institutions, private residences, stores, etc. It is in such connection we make due reference in the pages of this industrial review to the noted Baker and Smith Company of Chicago, whose Louisville branch, under the able management of Mr. Fred. A. Clegg, is located at No. 298 Third Street. This flourishing concern was duly incorporated under the laws of the state of Illinois some fifteen years ago. The company has a cash capitalization of $200,000 and is ably officered as follows: J. J. Smith, president; P. S. Hudson, vice-president and general manager; C. C. Turner, secretary and treasurer. The superiority of the steam and water heating and ventilating apparatus manufactured by the Baker and Smith Company bids fair eventually to supersede all other modes of heating. It is at once the most effective, manageable and economical of all inventions and contrivances for distributing and producing artificial warmth. The company manufacture single joint direct steam radiators, sectional cast and wrought iron boilers, culinary and laundry apparatus, revolving and stationary ventilators,

as also equipment for power plants. The premises here occupied consist of a substantial three-storied building, 18x60 feet in dimensions, admirably subdivided for the purposes of the business as follows: first floor, general business office and fitting rooms; second and third floors, storage of stock. An examination of the goods here exhibited readily reveals the fact that the greatest care and scientific experimentation have been expended to bring these specialties for warming, heating and ventilating to their present point of perfection. They are adapted for all kinds of service and are particularly suited for schoolhouses, public and private buildings, churches, stores, railroad depots, etc. Through this agency apparatus has been more recently supplied for the Louisville Trust Co., Bamberger, Bloom & Co., Kenyon Building, Calvary Church, Kentucky School of Medicine, etc. The trade may be said to be broadly distributed all over the United States, Mr. Clegg controlling and considerably enhancing the same which radiates from this point south of the Ohio River. He is a native of Chicago, and a thoroughly practical steamfitter. Prior to being appointed to this superintendency, he was for twelve years favorably associated with the company at their Chicago headquarters, No. 193 to 197 East Van Buren Street. He is an active member of the A. O. U. W.

CHAS. W. SPRINGER; Manufacturer of Mineral Spring Waters; No. 1534 Preston Street.—Among all the manufacturers and bottlers of mineral waters in the city, no one is more widely known as a merchant of the highest probity and reliability, whose goods are always of the highest class sold at the lowest prices, than Mr. Chas. W. Springer. Mr. Springer has been constantly engaged in the business for thirty-five years, and there is nothing pertaining to its conduct which he is not perfectly familiar with. He has occupied his present plant for fifteen years, a commodious two-story brick structure. The building was erected especially for this purpose, and is fitted with every appliance necessary, including generators of the finest pattern. The factory is manned by six employees, and a team is used for making deliveries. Mr. Springer handles both foreign and domestic mineral spring waters, and enjoys a tremendous patronage, which receives substantial additions every year. The leading brands sold by this house are Selters, Kissinger, and Karisbad, all of which are famous beverages. Also Vichy, carbonic and Lythia waters. He also manufactures ginger ale and soda waters of the highest standard, which can be found in all first-class hotels and restaurants in the city. He is a native of Germany, but has resided in Louisville since 1862. He is a prominent member of both the Liederkranz and the A. O. U. W. societies.

LOUISVILLE OF TO-DAY.

EITEL & CASSEBOHM; Manufacturers of High Grade Cigars; No. 547 East Madison Street.—Among the various interests that diversify the industries of Louisville, none deserve more prominent mention than that of cigar making. In this connection special reference is made to the newly established and reliable house of Messrs. Eitel and Cassebohm, which was established in 1894 by Messrs. Bopke, Eitel & Co., who conducted it till 1895, when Mr. Bopke retired and Messrs. Otto F. Eitel and H. D. Cassebohm continued the enterprise under the firm name of Eitel and Cassebohm. From the start they determined to manufacture an honest cigar, well worthy of the good opinion of critical smokers and have already secured a liberal and influential patronage, not only in Kentucky, but also in the adjacent states. The factory is well equipped and only really competent cigar makers are employed. All cigars are made from choice selected stock, no poor tobacco being used, and none but really superior and first-class goods are turned out. These splendid cigars are confidently recommended to retail tobacconists, hotel men, restaurant keepers and the smoking public generally. In being absolutely unsurpassed for quality and uniform excellence, and are offered at prices that cannot be discounted by any other reliable house in the trade. Messrs. Eitel and Cassebohm are expert cigar makers, who possess an intimate knowledge of the needs of a first-class trade, and are highly regarded in business circles for their strict integrity. They have gained the entire confidence of their numerous customers, owing to the superiority and intrinsic merits of their cigars, and their future prospects in this important industry seem well assured.

BOSQUET, SILBERG & CO.; Wholesale Grocers; No. 825 West Main Street.—One of the most enterprising and pluckiest firms in the city is the young grocery firm of Bosquet, Silberg & Co., which shows what can be accomplished by young men if they have the necessary energy, ambition, and courage coupled with a thorough knowledge of business. Thirteen years ago last July, Henry Bosquet and John Silberg commenced business in a very small way as their means were very limited in the retail grocery business. After three years, during which time they were very successful owing to their close attention to business and courteous treatment of their customers, realizing that the field in the retail business was too limited for their energy and ambition, they branched out into the wholesale business realizing full well that they would meet with many obstacles, with no practical knowledge of the wholesale business, no customers and no reputation, in competition with old and established houses, but they had pluck and it finally carried them to victory until to-day they are one of the most prosperous firms in Louisville. Their salesmen are welcomed wherever they go, as they are a jolly set and can always be relied upon having something new to offer, the firm making a specialty of introducing new ideas and new goods and they carry the most complete grocery stock in the city. It is a pleasure to see in what neat manner their stock is arranged and the systematic manner in which they conduct their business. The firm is one of the youngest in the city, Mr. Bosquet being forty years of age, Mr. Silberg thirty-six, and Mr. Gottbrath twenty-five, and they may well be proud of the phenomenal and unprecedented success they have achieved by their unlimited stock of energy and courage.

H. W. WERST PLUMBING COMPANY; No. 553 Third Avenue.—Marked progress has been made in recent years in gas and steam fitting also in plumbing and electric lighting, etc., which are now conducted upon exact principles, and a representative concern engaged in this important trade, in Louisville is that of the H. W. Werst Plumbing Company. This house dates its existence back twenty-two years, it having been founded by Messrs. C. O'Connor and H. W. Werst, under the firm style of O'Connor and Werst. The business was thus conducted till the year 1891, when a dissolution of partnership took place, and in 1892 state corporate charter was secured under the existent trading title. The original president of the corporation, which is capitalized at $25,000, was the late Mr. H. W. Werst, who died in 1894, the personnel of the present executive being as follows: Wm. H. Werst, son of the recently deceased founder of the house, president; William Griffin, vice-president, and B. C. Graft, secretary and treasurer. The premises occupied comprise a commodious salesroom, 25x45 feet in dimensions, giving ample accommodation for the storage and display of the exceptionally fine line of plumbers' specialties carried, the assortment of ornate gas and electric light chandeliers being an eminently well selected one. An average force of from twenty to thirty skilled hands is employed, and the company are at all times prepared to execute plumbing, gas and electric lighting commissions, charges being invariably based upon a uniform scale of strict moderation. Evidences of their skill abound all over the city and vicinity, among more recent contracts satisfactorily completed being the work in their line on the several residences of Dr. Curran Pope, Jno. C. Lewis, J. M. Atherton, Sam. Ouerbacker, and many others. The officers of this progressive corporation are all natives of the city, and members of the Master Plumbers' Association.

GRAN. W. SMITH & SON; Funeral Directors and Embalmers; Corner Eighth and Jefferson Streets.—The vocation of an undertaker is essentially a very delicate one involving for its successful prosecution peculiarly important qualifications, which comparatively few individuals possess, and it is only by experience as well as natural aptitude that a man is enabled to discharge his duty to the entire satisfaction of bereaved friends and relations. An old established and widely-known firm in this section of Louisville actively engaged in this line, is that of Messrs. Gran. W. Smith & Son, funeral directors and embalmers. In 1834 the business was founded by J. V. W. Smith, father of Gran. W. Smith and 1868 Messrs. Gran. W. Smith & Bro. succeeded to the control and conducted it till 1878, when Mr. Al. S. Smith retired and Mr. Gran. W. Smith continued alone. In 1882 he admitted his son Mr. John V. W. S. Smith into partnership, which was continued until his death in 1892, when Mr. Al. S. Smith was admitted. Mr. Gran. W. Smith has had long experience and is a graduate of Professor Clark's school of embalming. They are prompt in meeting their engagements, perform their duties with accuracy and propriety, and can always be depended on in all matters relating to the last rites of burial. The warerooms are elegantly fitted up, and are fully stocked with coffins, caskets, metallic burial cases, trimmings, shrouds and other funeral goods, and the house has ever made it a rule to charge only moderate prices. A specialty is made of embalming, which is performed in a superior and scientific manner at short notice. Burial plots are secured in any cemetery in the city or its vicinity, while hearses and carriages to any required number are supplied and all calls are immediately attended to day or night. Miss Kate Smith is the lady assistant and embalmer, preparing ladies and children a specialty, and everything requisite is furnished for the plainest or most imposing funerals. Messrs. Gran. W. and Al. S. Smith are honorable and energetic business men, who have secured a liberal patronage by honestly deserving it. Mr. Gran. W. Smith is an active member of the Catholic Knights of America and also Catholic Knights of Ladies, and was the first organizer of both in this city.

GRAN. W. SMITH.

ALS. S. SMITH.

LOUISVILLE COLD STORAGE COMPANY; Nos. 228 to 234 West Jefferson Street.—The steady development of Louisville has been manifested in numerous ways, but in few more so that in the facilities afforded our merchants for the cold storage and warehousing of perishable products. We are led to make these remarks after having paid a visit to the admirably appointed establishment of the Louisville Cold Storage Company. This representative concern has been in successful operation since 1891, and its plant is recognized as the leading headquarters for cold storage in the Falls City. The building is a substantial brick structure, four stories in height with frontage on Jefferson Street and ice manufactory in rear, equipped with the latest improved refrigerating machinery, having a capacity of forty-five tons of pure distilled water ice per diem. The main building has one hundred thousand cubic feet of storage, and the finest products of the dairy and farm, such as butter, eggs, cheese, poultry, fish, fresh and pickled meats, etc., are perfectly kept while awaiting consumption and the most delicate domestic and foreign fruits are here preserved for our tables for months. The company's rates for storage are as low as those of any other first-class company. The management of the business is vested in the hands of S. M. Lemont, president, and Chas. A. Cox, secretary and manager.

JOHN H. KUHN; Manufacturer of Riding Saddles; Fourteenth and Walnut Streets.—As the business of this country has grown to such stupendous proportions, and mammoth enterprises and combinations are formed every day, the tendency of all manufacturers is to specialize. The day when one factory turned out all the articles used in a community is passed, and the producer now as a rule devotes his entire time and attention to one line of goods or even to one article. Mr. John H. Kuhn, the manufacturer of riding saddles, is a prominent and successful example, being the largest manufacturer of riding saddles in the world. He established his business fourteen years ago at No. 739 Market Street, but the tremendous trade which he rapidly acquired, compelled him to seek larger quarters, and he removed four years ago to his present plant. The factory consists of a solid three-story brick structure, with dimensions 90x200 feet, and a rear extension of 130 feet. The establishment is located on the Pennsylvania Railroad tracks, and has switch connections with every road entering the city. He employs a force of eighty-five men, the superior quality and fine workmanship of his saddles necessitates their being made entirely by hand. The capacity of the factory is eight hundred saddles weekly, and is the only manufactory of riding saddles exclusively in the country. His custom is not confined to any particular locality or district, but is spread over the entire United States. Mr. Kuhn is a native of Louisville and has had long experience in his present business. He is thoroughly practical himself, and personally supervises the manufacture of his goods.

J. H. KUHN.

P. G. BERLE; Dealer in Boots, Shoes and Rubbers; No. 439 East Market Street.—An old established footwear emporium in this section of Louisville where one is always assured of obtaining perfectly fitting and first-class goods at popular prices, is the house of Mr. P. G. Berle, which ranks as one of the most reliable boot and shoe establishments in the city. The business was founded in 1857 by Mr. G. Berle, who conducted it till 1883, when he was succeeded by his son, Mr. P. G. Berle, the present proprietor. He is a thoroughly practical shoemaker, who deals in all kinds of footwear, and also furnishes promptly custom goods to order. The store is commodious, and is fully stocked with a superior assortment of fine and medium boots and shoes for both sexes in all styles, also slippers, sandals and rubbers, while a specialty is made of first-class custom goods and of repairing. Every pair sold in this establishment is warranted to be exactly as represented, and all work to order is guaranteed to render entire satisfaction as to fit, finish and material. Mr. Berle was born in Louisville in 1858, and is highly regarded for his business skill and strict rectitude. He is a prominent Freemason and an active member of the Order of Elks, and is very popular in social circles.

P. C. BERLE.

W. L. WELLER & SONS; Wholesale Liquor Dealers; Nos. 240 and 242 East Main Street.—One of the oldest established firms of wholesale liquor merchants in this city and the South, is that of Messrs. W. L. Weller & Sons. This house enjoys an international reputation for the superiority of its old Kentucky rye and bourbon whiskies, and is a favorite concern with which to place orders for assorted lines of the most famous brands. The business was established in 1849 by Mr. W. L. Weller, whose long and active identification with the trade, renders him a recognized leading authority therein. The firm of Weller & Gonterman was subsequently formed, succeeded by that of Messrs. W. L. Weller & Bro. Mr. W. L. Weller afterward became sole proprietor, thus continuing until in January, 1879, he admitted into co-partnership his son, Mr. George P. Weller, under the style of W. L. Weller & Son. In 1886 his second son, Mr. John C. Weller, was admitted under the present firm name of W. L. Weller & Sons. Messrs. George P. and John C. Weller have both been brought up to the business, and have a thorough practical knowledge of every detail. The firm's warehouse is located conveniently, and is a three-story and basement building, 50x200 feet in dimensions. Here is carried the finest stock of old Kentucky whiskies to be found in town, or in fact anywhere. The firm handles only straight goods, the selected distillings of leading concerns, all of which have become thoroughly mellowed and aged before being put on the market. Absolute purity and finest quality are the guarantees accompanying all goods sold by this honorable old house, which sells exclusively to the trade, and covers every section of Kentucky, Indiana, West Virginia, Virginia, North Carolina, Alabama, Georgia, Florida, Mississippi, Louisiana, Texas, Arkansas, Indian Territory, etc., etc. Seven travelers are employed, and the sales of the house are annually enlarging. Mr. W. L. Weller was born in Kentucky, and is universally respected, and throughout his lengthy career has ever retained the confidence of leading financial and commercial circles. Messrs. George P. and John C. Weller are natives of this city, and are members of the Board of Trade, and are public spirited in support of those measures calculated to benefit our city, and to which their house has for so long been such a prominent and valued factor.

HOFFMAN, AHLERS & CO.; Distillery and Brewery Coppersmiths; No. 629 East Main Street.—The oldest and best known concern in this section of the country engaged in the production of distillery and other specialties, is that of Messrs. Hoffman, Ahlers & Co., distillery and brewery coppersmiths. This house dates its existence back to 1831, when it was founded by Messrs. Wardell and Kierstead at Cincinnati, which is still the headquarters of the concern. The changes of proprietorship have since been many from that date, and the firm consists of Mr. Isaac A. Hoffman, Louis H. Hoffman and George L. Ahlers. The Louisville branch was established in 1889, the premises occupied being as follows: Three-storied brick office and store house, two-storied brick copper and brass foundry and two-storied brick pipe bending works. The machinery is of the latest pattern, operated by gas engine. The firm manufacture a general line of copper and brass work for distilleries, breweries, candy factories, soap and glycerine works, and are patentees of the Horn and McGroen continuous beer stills and the Bevis spirit and vapor condensers. The trade extends over the entire United States and the Canadian provinces. Among contracts completed by this firm may be mentioned $10,000 worth of work for the Hiram Walker Distilling Company, at Walkerville, Ont., Canada, $78,000 worth of work for the Great White Spirit Distilling Company, of Cambridge, Mass. The firms are likewise proprietors of the Cincinnati Copper works. Mr. Hoffman is a native of Cincinnati, a member of the Commercial Club, this city, and the orders of Foresters, Elks, Knights Templar, and Freemasons. Mr. Louis H. Hoffman was also born in Cincinnati, while Mr. Ahlers is of German nationality, but has lived in Cincinnati since 1857, and manages the business controlled from that point.

TAPP, LEATHERS & CO.; Manufacturers of Kentucky Jeans; Nos. 823 and 825 West Main Street.—The houses engaged in the manufacture of clothing are important factors in the commercial prosperity of the Falls City, and prominent among the number ranks the corporation of Tapp, Leathers & Co. The business was originally established by Messrs. Tapp, Leathers & Co., thirty-five years ago, Mr. Leathers retiring from the partnership in 1891, and state corporate charter under the existing trading title being secured in 1893. The company has a cash capital of $100,000, the executive officers being: P. H. Tapp, president, a native of Florence, Ala., and a director of the Mutual Life Insurance Company, of Kentucky; H. C. Turner, vice-president, born in Tennessee, and now identified with the house for the past twenty years; J. S. Carr, secretary and treasurer, a native of Indianapolis, Ind., and resident in Louisville since 1878. The premises occupied comprise a substantial five-storied and basement building, 50x70 feet in area, with elevator and all the latest appliances known to the clothing manufacturing industry, operated by thirty-five horse-power engine. Here five hundred skilled hands are employed, the range of production embracing Kentucky jeans, and men's, youths' and boys' fancy and staple clothing in all the latest and most fashionable styles. They give close attention to the selection of their fabrics, and as they employ none but first-class cutters, the trade and the public have permanently retained their confidence in the clothing of the Tapp, Leathers & Co. corporation. The house controls a trade extending all over the United States, Canada and Mexico.

F. R. TOE WATER; Representing Liggett & Myers Tobacco Company; No. 1007 West Main Street.—Special attention is directed in this volume to the Liggett & Myers Tobacco Company, of St. Louis, for whom Mr. F. R. Toe Water is the able representative and buyer in Louisville, because of their recent arrangements for the erection in St. Louis of what will be beyond all question the largest plant for the manufacture of tobacco in the world. It is to cover three city blocks and to cost $1,000,000, and a unique feature is to be the licorice factory, which will be the only one in America. This business was begun in 1832 by Messrs. Liggett and Danemann, and in 1873 Mr. Geo. S. Myers bought out the interest of Mr. Danemann, the firm becoming Liggett & Myers. In 1878, the Liggett & Myers Tobacco Company was incorporated, Mr. John E. Liggett, president, and Mr. George S. Myers, vice-president; both gentlemen have retired from active management, the chief officers, at present, being M. C. Wetmore, president; Chas. Halliwell, vice-president. The business of the company is of mammoth dimensions, requiring the services of two thousand hands, and in addition to an immense trade with all sections of this country, a heavy export business has been built up, requiring the manufacture of nearly thirty million pounds of plug tobacco each year. The best known brand is the Star, which enjoys a greater sale than any other in the world, and has received the widest recognition for purity, flavor and adaptation to the requirements of the trade. Mr. Toe Water has represented this great house here for eighteen years, and is known as one of the best judges of tobacco and shrewdest buyers on this market. He is a native of St. Louis, and has won the entire confidence and esteem of all with whom he has had dealings.

BEN. S. WELLER; Cash Jobber of Boots, Shoes and Rubber; No. 527 West Main Street.—Prominent among the reliable houses in Louisville actively engaged in the wholesale boot and shoe trade, is that of Mr. Ben. S. Weller, who established this business May 1st, 1893, which has proved extremely successful. The premises occupied consist of a four-story brick structure, 25x200 feet in area, utilized for offices, salesrooms and stock, and is expressly adapted for the rapid transaction of the business. The stock is immense, including everything in the line of footwear for both sexes and all ages, and representing the best product of the most noted eastern and western manufacturers. A specialty is made of eastern goods, and also of filling special orders in any desired style, the trade extending throughout Kentucky, Indiana and the adjacent states. A thorough knowledge of the business followed and exceptional trade relations with the best sources of supply, enables Mr. Weller to buy to the very best advantage, and consequently to offer inducements to the trade that few houses in the line can approach. Mr. Weller is a native of Nashville, Tenn. In 1865 he began life as a bookkeeper for the shoe house of Lisby, White & Cochrane, and was identified with this establishment in various capacities, until 1880 when he became a member of the firm of Weller & Payne. In January, 1891, this firm consolidated with Satcliffe & Owen and the Woolfolk-Payne Company was organized. In 1893, Mr. Weller sold out his interest to embark upon his present venture. In the city he is highly esteemed for his honorable characteristics, and takes rank among our most influential citizens.

EAGLE BRASS WORKS; No. 225 Eighth Street.—A prominent establishment in its line in Louisville, is that of Messrs. Fowler & Co., Eagle Brass Works. This industry was founded in 1868 by Mr. John Fowler, who is sole proprietor. He is a thoroughly practical brass founder and finisher, and the liberal patronage bestowed on his works furnishes abundant proof, that his brass goods meet with the approval of a first-class trade. The premises occupied, which were designed and built especially for the purpose by Mr. Fowler, comprise a spacious four-story brick building, 30x100 feet in area, the first floor being devoted to the foundry and offices, while the other floors are utilized for finishing shops and storage. The foundry and workshops are fully equipped with modern appliances, etc., and one hundred and twenty-six skilled workmen are constantly employed. Mr. Fowler manufactures to order, all kinds of copper and brass castings, distillery and water company's ferrules and cocks, metallic letters for pattern makers, phosphor bronze castings, etc., and makes a specialty of Fowler's patent steam shifter, Fowler's patent vacuum valves and Fowler's patent pumps, which are unrivalled for efficiency and reliability. His trade is chiefly local and throughout the adjacent states, and the prices quoted for all work are extremely moderate. During the civil war, he enlisted in 1861 in the Home Guards, Twenty-ninth Kentucky Infantry, and on August 6th, 1862 was transferred to the Sixth Kentucky Cavalry. He rose from the rank of private to first lieutenant before he was twenty-one years old. Mr. Fowler is a native of this city, a Thirty-second degree Freemason, a member of the Board of Trade, I. O. O. F., Commercial Club, Knights of Honor, and is also treasurer of the Kentucky Fish and Gun Club.

W. B. TRUMBO COMPANY (Incorporated); Dealers in Furniture, Carpets and Oil Cloths; No. 228 West Market, and Ninth and Market Streets.—Prominent among the leading houses of enterprise and refinement in Louisville, actively engaged in handling furniture, carpets, etc., is that known as W. B. Trumbo Company, whose warerooms are filled to repletion with original and exclusive styles of medium and fine furniture sets for the parlor, bedroom, kitchen, dining-room, library and hall. Here also can be found single pieces in antique and other styles such as desks, cabinets, easy chairs, lounges and screens, and the same remark applies to the complete stock carried in their carpet and oil cloth departments. Limit of space prevents an attempt at describing the many beautiful and exclusive designs displayed, the assortment being unsurpassed by any similar house in Louisville. The W. B. Trumbo Company is prepared to furnish a home throughout, and estimates are cheerfully furnished at any time. Only the best goods are handled in all departments, and the sales amount to over one hundred and fifty thousand dollars annually, which will be increased considerably this year. Employment is given to twenty-five experienced salesmen and assistants, and the trade extends over this state and Indiana. This incorporated concern was founded by the present co-partners, Messrs. W. B. Trumbo and W. T. Armstrong in May, 1889, and from its inception has been a most marked success. The basis on which the business is transacted is characterized by liberality and equity, so that transactions once begun with their house may not only be pleasant for the time being, but of such nature that it will be pleasant and permanent.

FALLS CITY PLANING MILL; Nos. 1967 Portland Avenue and 1900-06 High Avenue.—Among the woodworking industries of this city, the Falls City Planing Mill, of which the J. P. Will Company, are proprietors, has for a period of twenty years maintained a most enviable reputation for the superiority of its products. The business was established in 1875, by the late Mr. J. P. Will, who subsequently associated with him in the management of the works, his sons, Messrs. Philip Will, Jr., and Geo. Will. The lamented decease of Mr. J. P. Will occurred in August, 1893, since which date the industry has been actively continued by his sons; Mrs. Philippina Will, his widow, still retaining her interest in the concern. The mill and yards are located at Portland and High Avenues, and the premises covered is an area of 160x500 feet in dimensions. The mill is a substantial three-story brick structure, specially erected for the purpose. It is equipped with all the latest improved woodworking machinery, planers, saws, etc., run by heavy steam power. The company makes a specialty of the manufacture of doors, sash, blinds, mouldings, etc., also newel posts and stair work of all kinds. They also dress lumber for flooring, ceiling and siding, and for all building purposes, and fine interior work and hard wood finish can be contracted for here on advantageous terms. Builders' hardware, pumps, etc., can also be secured here at moderate prices. Mr. Philip Will, Jr., is the manager of the business, and is noted for his enterprise and sound judgment, both partners having been brought up to the business, and thoroughly understanding all details. Both partners are active members of the Builders' and Traders' Exchanges.

JOHN MITCHELL & CO.; Manufacturers of Boilers, Tanks and Sheet Iron Workers; Nos. 312, 314, 315 and 317 Eleventh Street.—In few branches of industry in the United States has such notable progress been made in recent years as in the construction of steam boilers, tanks and kindred work. In this connection special reference is made to the reliable Louisville firm of Messrs. John Mitchell & Co., manufacturers of boilers, tanks and sheet iron work. This business was founded in 1872 by Mr. John Mitchell, who eventually admitted his sons, Messrs. John H. and Edgar Mitchell into partnership. Mr. John Mitchell, the founder, was born in England in 1833, and came to Louisville in 1854, where he worked several years with his uncle, Mr. Joseph Mitchell, and is recognized as one of the ablest boiler makers in the country. Mr. Mitchell's father was likewise one of the best boiler makers in England, and he intends soon to retire from active business and spend the remainder of his life looking after the interests of his family. Messrs. John H. and Edgar Mitchell have been brought up and thoroughly trained in the boiler making trade, and are highly esteemed for their mechanical skill and just methods, and their future prospects in this useful and important industry are of the most favorable character. The premises occupied comprise two spacious buildings, respectively 52x105 and 44x95 feet in area, full supplied with the latest improved machinery, tools and appliances operated by steam power, and a full force of skilled mechanics is employed. They manufacture promptly to order all kinds of boilers, tanks, chimneys, sheet iron work, fire fronts, grate bars, etc., and make a specialty of repairing and of steamboat work. Only the choicest grades of iron and steel plate are utilized, and their work is unrivalled for strength, durability and workmanship, while their prices in all cases are noted for the moderation, and their trade extends throughout Kentucky and the adjacent states. They promptly furnish estimates for all kinds of boiler and plate work, and no more reliable boiler makers can be found in the ranks of the trade in the city.

D. **H. EWING & SONS**; Creamery; No. 312 West Breckinridge Street. The question of milk and cream concerns the entire community, and our mission would be but poorly fulfilled, were we not to call special attention to a Louisville establishment, the purity of whose products have gained for it widespread recognition. We refer in this connection to the reliable house of Messrs. D. H. Ewing & Sons, proprietors of Ewing's creamery. This is the largest concern of the kind in the city, and was established in 1885, the present co-partners being Mr. D. H. Ewing and his three sons, J. M., T. R. and C. O. Ewing, who were previously engaged in the dairy business in the country. They are constantly receiving the purest and best milk and cream from selected dairies in Kentucky and Indiana, and have two large skimming stations at Bloomfield, Ky., and at Waddy, Ky., where they skim by centrifugal force. When they first began business here, only one can of cream was shipped to the city daily and it is now received in car load lots, and as regards butter, at the start they made from twenty-five to fifty pounds daily, and now turn out fifteen hundred in the same time. The premises are spacious, fitted up with all modern conveniences, refrigerators, etc., but owing to a steadily increasing patronage, they contemplate the erection of a much larger building, fully equipped with modern appliances. A heavy stock of milk, cream, buttermilk and butter is always on hand, and customers have always the satisfaction of knowing that none but the purest dairy products will be sold to them. Twenty men and ten wagons are employed, and customers are promptly supplied in any part of the city or suburbs at lowest rates. Mr. D. H. Ewing was born in Virginia, while his sons are Kentuckians. They are highly esteemed for their business ability and strict probity, and have built up in spite of strong competition, the finest business of the kind in the city.

H. **ADOLPH PFINGST**; Apothecary; Southwest corner, Hancock and Chestnut Streets.—In every community a well-managed pharmacy fills an important position, and in this connection prominent reference is made to the popular establishment of Mr. H. Adolph Pfingst the widely-known Louisville druggist and apothecary.

Mr. Pfingst, who is a duly qualified pharmacist, commenced business in 1859, corner Eleventh and Market Streets and remained there till 1890 when his store was totally destroyed by the great cyclone; he then removed to his present location and now numbers among his permanent customers many of the leading families of this section of the city. The store is provided with every convenience and having a good prescription trade ample provision is made for this important part of the business, which is conducted under Mr. Pfingst's immediate supervision. The stock embraces a full assortment of fine drugs and chemicals, proprietary medicines, toilet and fancy articles, perfumery, mineral waters, etc. Physicians and the public have long recognized the fact that what they obtain at Pfingst's pharmacy is not only good but of the best quality. Mr. Pfingst was born in Germany fifty-four years ago and came to Louisville in 1855. He is an honorable gentleman, prompt and reliable in all matters pertaining to his business and enjoys the entire confidence of his numerous customers.

RUFER'S HOTEL; Fifth Street, between Market and Main.—Rufer's hotel is one of the most popular houses in this city, and is under the able management of Mr. John C. Rufer, and is a model in every respect, while it has been recently remodeled and refurnished throughout, making it to-day the most comfortable hotel in the South. The name of Rufer is a familiar one to the public, for as far back as 1856, the late Mr. C. C. Rufer opened the present hotel. He early developed a flourishing trade, resulting in the repeated enlargement of the premises. For upwards of twenty-seven years, Mr. Rufer continued to manage the hotel, until his lamented decease in 1883, since which date the proprietorship has remained vested in his estate, with the management devolving upon Mr. John C. Rufer, his brothers Messrs. Charles and Rudolph Rufer being his assistants. The hotel is a handsome brick structure, three and four stories in height and 80x120 feet in dimensions. It has all modern improvements, including electric call bells, annunciators, electric light, steam heat, etc. The arrangement of the premises is as follows: On the first floor are the handsomely decorated office reading and writing rooms, first class bar and barber shop, and a large and well appointed public restaurant, comfortably seating eighty persons. On the second floor are the main dining-rooms, seating one hundred and twenty-five, the richly furnished parlors, and a number of fine sleeping rooms. The two upper floors are devoted to sleeping rooms. The hotel is conducted upon the European plan, at a most moderate tariff of prices for rooms, while the restaurant service is perfect, all the delicacies of the season being on the bills of fare. The house is a great favorite with commercial men, being so central to the principal business sections, the depots, steamboat landing and places of amusement. Mr. John C. Rufer is a native of Louisville. He is a member of the Hotel Men's Association, of the Knights Ancient Essenic Order of America and is worthily sustaining the enviable reputation Rufer's hotel had during his father's lifetime. Messrs. Charles and Rudolph Rufer, were also born here, and assist in the management of the house, and are deservedly popular young men.

WILLIAM KLEIN & SON; Confectioners; Nos. 516 and 518 Fourth Avenue.—One of the best known houses engaged in the confectionery business of the Falls City, is that of Messrs. William Klein & Son, which was established by Mr. William Klein in 1863. He conducted it with great success, the patronage being derived principally from among the most refined people of our city. In 1890 he admitted his son Mr. John W. Klein to an interest in the business and the present firm style was adopted. Messrs. Klein are thoroughly conversant with every detail of the business and the fame of this establishment is annually increasing.

The main business premises consist of a substantial and three-storied basement brick building 25x210 feet in dimensions, with thoroughly equipped bakery and kitchen in rear. The store, which includes retail counters, ice cream parlors and restaurant, with seating capacity for one hundred and twenty-four guests, is one of the finest in Louisville, being equipped with electric lights and fans, steam heat, elaborate soda fountain, etc. The productions of the house embrace the purest and finest qualities of ice cream, water ices, cakes of every description, candies and bon-bons, pastries, such as meringues, charlotte russe, jellies, delicious confections, etc. They also promptly cater to and supply balls, receptions, weddings, etc., and control the first-class patronage of the surrounding country. They do twice as much in this line as all their competitors put together, and give complete service in every particular. You give them the order, kitchen and dining-room, and they will attend to the balance, relieving you of all bother and worry. The service in all departments is unsurpassed and competent assistants are employed. Mr. Klein is a native of Germany and has been a highly respected resident of Louisville, where his son was born and brought up in the business for the past thirty-five years.

MARTIN NILEST & CO.; Clothing, Shoes and Furnishing Goods; Nos. 116, 118 and 120 Third Street.—Prominent among the old established houses of Louisville is that known as "Martins," dealers in clothing, etc., which was established many years ago on a small scale compared with its present extensive proportions and there is no house in the city more widely or favorably known. The business premises are ample and convenient, consisting of the ground floor and basement of two stores, one of which is 80x120 feet in area and the other 20x60 feet. The basement is devoted to the manufacture of shoes and for the wholesale trade in shoe uppers, this department being supplied with every modern appliance. On the main floor is the retail department and here we find advantageously arranged an extensive stock of clothing, shoes and furnishing goods of all kinds, representing the productions of the best factories in the country and all grades to suit all classes of trade. Twenty-five assistants are employed and the trade is by no means confined here but is also derived from all parts of the surrounding country. Shoes and shoe uppers are made to order and these goods have a reputation for durability and excellence, second to none on the market and are strictly handmade. The firm's influential connections enable it to offer special inducements to the trade and to quote prices which smaller houses cannot duplicate. The members of the firm are Messrs. M. Nilest and L. M. Frazer, both of whom give personal attention to the business. Mr. Nilest was born in Louisville and succeeded John Graff, his stepfather as proprietor, over twenty years ago. Mr. Frazer was born in Portland, Oregon, but was raised and educated in Mount Vernon, Ky. He has been identified with the house for four years, having formerly been a salesman for the Louisville Tin and Stove Company. Both are honorable merchants and their enterprise is a credit to the city.

THE WESTERN INSURANCE COMPANY OF LOUISVILLE, KY.; No. 309 West Market Street.—Without the organizations now engaged in affording protection against loss by fire, Louisville would not present the splendid appearance she does to-day, with lofty and expensive buildings, equal to any in the country. In this connection prominent mention should be made of the well-known Western Insurance Co., of Louisville. This concern dates its incorporation back to 1865, when it was known as the Western Insurance and Banking Co. In 1872, however, the Kentucky Legislature passed an act that made it imperative that banking and insurance companies should be distinct enterprises under corporate charter. Conforming to such legislation, the Western Bank and the Western Insurance Co., have since conducted business in the same building, though their interests are wholly disconnected, while the executive management of both is commercially associated. The progress of this company has been marked by a guidance of judicious ability, resulting in presenting before the public at the end of each year a statement that speaks for itself in the strongest terms, and forms a most convincing proof to insurers, that the Western Insurance Co. of Louisville is built upon a solid financial basis. The cash capitalization of the company, as authorized is $250,000, $100,000 of which is paid in, irrespective of a handsome surplus fund, amounting to nearly $100,000 more, the management of the affairs being vested in the hands of the following well-known honorable business men, viz: A. F. Coldewey, president; B. Frese, secretary, and Henry Miller, solicitor.

L. MOSES & CO. Manufacturers of Clothing at Wholesale; Nos. 640 and 642 West Main Street.—Among the old established and representative clothing houses in Louisville, is that of Messrs. L. Moses & Co., manufacturers of fine and medium grade men's, boys', youths' and children's clothing. This prosperous concern was established by Mr. L. Moses forty years ago, the present firm style being adopted on the admission of his sons, Messrs. Joseph E. and Simon Moses, to an interest in the business in 1876. Operations were primarily commenced at No. 713 West Main Street, premises of which were destroyed by the cyclone which swept the city March 27th, 1890, removal being made to the present commodious quarters subsequent to that mishap. They consist of a substantial six-storied and basement building, 25x150 feet in dimensions, equipped with all modern conveniences, cutting machinery, etc. In the home premises thirty skilled hand are employed, the finishing of the garments being attended to by a force of five hundred out-door operatives. They manifest excellent judgment in the selection of all cloths and suitings, while at the same time they are always among the first to secure and make up all the new styles and textures. A large stock of the firm's clothing is constantly on hand, and the trade of the house extends throughout all sections of Kentucky, Indiana, Tennessee, Illinois, Mississippi, Alabama and Louisiana. Twelve traveling salesmen are employed, and the operations of the house are exclusively of a wholesale character. Mr. Moses, Sr., is a stockholder in the German Bank and member of the Board of Trade. His son, Mr. Joseph E. Moses, is a Knight Templar, a thirty-second degree Royal Arch Mason and a member of the Standard and Commercial Clubs. His brother, Mr. Simon Moses, is likewise a member of the Standard and Commercial Clubs and Board of Trade.

EISENMAN, SHALLCROSS & CO.; Produce Commission Merchants; Nos. 105 & 107 Third Street; Warehouse, Nos. 218 to 228 Water Street. —The quantities of hay, corn, oats, fruits and produce disposed of annually through the medium of the commission merchants in Louisville, reach extensive proportions, and one of the most noted firms in this line is that of Messrs. Eisenman, Shallcross & Co. This flourishing business was established by Mr. Landelin Eisenman, the business being subsequently conducted under the firm style of Messrs. Eisenman and Brothers, the present co-partnership consisting of Messrs. L. F. Eisenman and M. B. and J. W. Shallcross, being formed several years ago. This is by common consent one of the leading and most reliable concerns of the kind here—none maintaining a higher reputation for integrity, and few enjoy a larger measure of merited recognition. They handle everything comprehended in produce, making leading specialties of hay, corn, oats, mill feeds, wheat, straw, apples, onions, potatoes, fruits, etc., etc., and their connections are of a most substantial character, extending to all parts of the South and Southwest. Special attention is given to car and boat load lots, consignments are solicited, liberal advances made thereon when desired, and prompt sales, quick returns and highest ruling market prices are guaranteed in every instance. Here also can be obtained at all times timothy, clover and prairie hay, corn, oats and straw, mixed horse, cow and sheep feed, dried distillers feed, pearl, bolted and feed meal, cracked corn and crushed oats, sheaf oats and hay chop, oil meal and rock salt, wheat and mixed chicken feed. The members of the firm are natives of the city, who devoting unfiring attention to the interests of those entrusting consignments to their care, well meriting the extensive patronage they are now enjoying.

ERNST H. KOCH; Boots and Shoes; No. 254 East Market Street.—A leading footwear emporium in this section of Louisville, where can always be found a comprehensive assortment of everything in this line from the dainty lady's kid shoe, to the most durable brogan, is that of Mr. Ernst H. Koch. This business, which is one of the oldest of the kind in the city, was established in 1842 by Mr. John F. Koch, who was succeeded in 1875 by the firm of Mullenschinger & Koch. Eventually in 1882, Mr. Ernst H. Koch became sole proprietor, and is noted for his business capacity and strict probity. He has built up a large and fashionable trade in the city and adjoining counties, and there are few houses whose goods are held in such esteem by a critical public. The store is attractively fitted up and provided with every convenience for the comfort of patrons. The stock includes ladies', misses', gentlemen's, youths' and children's boots and shoes in all sizes, widths, shapes and designs, both in fine and medium grades, also a full assortment of slippers, sandals and rubbers. Only the choicest goods are handled and the prices quoted defy competition. Fine custom work is a specialty with this house, and in this department, Mr. Koch makes boots and shoes to order, which are unsurpassed for style, quality, fit and appearance at very moderate figures and every pair of shoes sold in this establishment is warranted to be exactly as represented. Mr. Koch was born in Louisville in 1850, and is an honorary and has been an active member of the Liederkranz for over twenty years, and is extremely popular with all classes of the community.

BRINKE & PAUST; Groceries, Meats, Etc.; Nineteenth and Madison Streets.—The trade in groceries and meats is the most important in any community and is well represented in the Falls City by several first-class houses and prominent among these is that of Messrs. Brinke & Paust. This business was established twenty-six years ago by Brinke & Co., who conducted it till 1874, when Mr. George Paust became a partner, the firm being known as Brinke & Paust, and both are able business men, who possess an intimate knowledge of the requirements of a first-class trade. They occupy a spacious three-story and basement brick building 50x100 feet in area, equipped with every convenience, refrigerators, etc., and they deal largely in staple groceries, feed, fresh meats, vegetables, oysters, canned fruits, butter, eggs and all kinds of country produce and are always prepared to offer substantial advantages to patrons. Only the best and freshest goods, in all lines, are handled and customers have always the satisfaction of knowing that nothing inferior will be sold to them and lowest market prices prevail and they include among their permanent customers many leading hotels, restaurants and families of this section of the city. Messrs. Brinke & Paust were both born in Germany, the former having resided in Louisville thirty-five years and the latter twenty-seven years, and are highly esteemed for their strict integrity. Mr. Brinke is a popular member of the Liederkranz and Garfield Club, while Mr. Paust is an active member of the Legion of Honor.

MANSFELD & SON; Manufacturers of Bank Fixtures; No. 319 East Main Street.—A representative firm in its line in Louisville, is that of Messrs. Mansfeld & Son, manufacturers of bank and store fixtures, etc. This business was established in 1865, by Mr. Robert Mansfeld, who eventually admitted his son, Mr. Fred Mansfeld, into partnership. They are expert cabinetmakers and designers, who possess an accurate knowledge of the requirements of the most critical patrons, and their trade extends throughout the principal cities and towns of Kentucky and the adjacent states. The factory is spacious and is fully supplied with the latest improved woodworking machinery, tools and appliances, operated by steam power, and forty skilled workmen are constantly employed. They manufacture largely to order bar and store fixtures, druggists', confectioners', hatters', and milliners' wall cases, counters, shelving, show cases, etc., all of the latest modern designs, also fancy grille work for arches. Messrs. Mansfeld & Son have fitted up some of the finest bars in the city to the entire satisfaction of patrons,

ROBERT MANSFELD.

and are sole agents for the liquid carbonic beer pumps. They use all kinds of rare woods and turn out all work in a first-class manner at extremely moderate prices. Messrs. Robert and Fred Mansfeld are widely known in trade circles for their ability and strict probity.

NICK. WIEST; Baker and Confectioner; Corner Main and Clay Streets. —In August 1883 Mr. Nick. Wiest established his present flourishing enterprise, and from the first it has proven an unqualified success. Patronage began to flow in from all sides, casual customers became permanent patrons, and before a year had rolled by the success of the venture was assured and time only served to render the hold upon popular favor stronger. The premises occupied consist of a three-story brick building of large proportions, thoroughly modern in its appointments, while the salesrooms are splendidly and tastefully finished and furnished. The bakery is located in the rear and is supplied with all modern appliances. The stock carried consists of bread and cake of all kinds, choice confectionery, ice cream, sodas, etc., etc., all of the highest order, the house catering specially to high-class trade. The supplying of parties, weddings, etc., with cake and pastry is a special feature of the house, and in this Mr. Wiest has a heavy patronage. Several assistants are employed and the patronage though large in the eastern section of the city is by no means confined there, but comes from all parts of Louisville and its vicinity. By maintaining his product at the highest standard of excellence and offering the most liberal inducements, the trade of the house has been built up, and time can only further develop it, so firm a footing has it already established. Mr. Wiest was born in Germany, coming here in 1872, and having always followed this line, is a master of its every detail. He is highly esteemed in business and social circles, and it is a pleasure to eulogize an establishment so largely patronized as this, which is unrivalled in the city.

NICK. WIEST.

BYRNE & SPEED; Wholesale and Retail Coal Dealers; No. 415 Jefferson Street.—The firm of Byrne and Speed, wholesale and retail dealers in coal, was established twenty-five years ago under its present style, and from the very outset has been characterized by constantly increasing prosperity. Each year has seen the trade limits expand, the volume of the sales increase, until from a modest beginning and a scarcely local reputation, it has become one of the most powerful concerns of its kind in the state, and derives its patronage from all parts of Indiana, Kentucky and Tennessee. The yards are at Fourteenth and Canal, while branches are maintained at Thirteenth and Kentucky Streets, Sixth and River Streets and Floyd and River Streets. The yards are spacious and are thoroughly appointed and equipped, while the best receiving and shipping facilities by rail and water are provided. The yards also contain an elevator with a capacity of four hundred tons a day. Anthracite and bituminous coal, representing the finest products of the leading mines of the country are dealt in, and a heavy stock is always carried in the yards. Orders are filled of all sizes from cargo lots down to the smaller wants of the household, and the same liberal and reliable methods characterize all operations. The members of the firm are J. B. Speed, J. P. Byrne and A. P. Speed, all of whom take rank among the most progressive and influential citizens, and they are identified with many of the leading industrial and commercial enterprises of the city.

E. A. BURFORD & CO.; Manufacturers' Agent and Commission Merchant; No. 441 West Main Street.—One of the most reliable of manufacturers' agents in Louisville, actively engaged in handling sheetings, ducks, etc., is that of Mr. E. A. Burford, under the firm style of E. A. Burford & Co. This concern dates back some fifty-three years, it having been founded by Messrs. John P. Howard & Co., in 1842, such firm consisting of Messrs. Jno. F. Howard and George C. Hunter. In 1868 the business was conducted under the style of George C. Hunter & Co., in 1880 as Hunter, Deering & Co., later as E. A. Burford & Co., the present proprietor assuming control in 1883. Mr. Burford acts as special agent for the sale of Trion, Pinewood and Georgia sheetings, ducks, cotton yarns, grain bags, twines, batting and also largely in field seeds in the capacity of general commission merchant. The premises occupied comprise a commodious five-storied and basement building 25x175 feet in dimensions, with L shaped annex, extending to Nos. 153 and 155 Fifth Street, equipped with elevator, etc. He sells at wholesale to the trade only acting as selling agent for the Mount Vernon and Guyers Mills, ducks and sheetings, Baltimore, Md.; Pinewood Mills, Rome, Ga.; Trion Mills, Trion, Ga.; Eagle Mills, Madison, Ind., and many other representative concerns of this type. All orders are promptly filled, and complete satisfaction is guaranteed patrons. Mr. Burford was born in Kentucky, and has made Louisville his home and the centre of his business operations for the past twenty-seven years. He is highly esteemed for his integrity, and is a popular member of the Board of Trade.

J. HENRY DOERR; Photographer; Twelfth and Market Streets.—In no department of the arts are the improvements of the past quarter of a century so conspicuous as in photography. In this connection prominent reference is made to Mr. J. Henry Doerr, the popular Louisville photographer. Mr. Doerr opened this gallery in 1865, and during his long business career, has gained the esteem and confidence of the entire community. The parlors and gallery are spacious and elegantly furnished, while the light, accessories and all appliances are perfect. Photography in all its branches is here executed, and the best and finest class of work is produced. Pictures are taken by the instantaneous process, and thus patrons are enabled to obtain accurate and perfect photographs of themselves and children—a specialty is made of life size portraits in crayon, oil, pastelle and india ink. Mr. Doerr's work is of the highest artistic merit, and at such reasonable prices as cannot fail to satisfy the most critical customers. His imperial cabinets are general favorites with the refined and educated classes of society. He was born in Bavaria, Germany, but has resided in Louisville for the last forty-three years, and is highly esteemed for his artistic ability and strict probity. He is a popular member and one of the committee on membership of the Board of Trade, while he is also an active member of the Photo Association of America.

SENG BROS.; Diamonds, Watches, Jewelry, Silverware, Etc.; No. 430 East Market Street.—In the jewelry trade of this section of Louisville, one of the most reliable firms is that of Messrs. Seng Bros. This business was established in 1891 by Chris. J. and Chas. E. Seng, who have since secured a liberal patronage. Both partners are expert jewelers and watchmakers, who are noted for handling only genuine and first-class goods in all departments, and the store is elegantly equipped with plate glass windows, cases, etc., and is fully stocked with a carefully selected assortment of diamonds, watches, solid gold jewelry, silverware, marble clocks, eyeglasses, spectacles, gold pens, gold headed canes and umbrellas, and they possess many matched diamonds of rare beauty, which cannot readily be duplicated elsewhere. Repairing of watches and jewelry is a specialty and in solid gold jewelry, the stock includes a superior line of rings, earrings, pins, brooches, necklaces, chains and lace pins, and we also recommend this firm for its reliability in dealing in the finest mounted diamond jewelry and precious stones set in all the popular styles, and the prices in all cases are extremely reasonable. They are also prepared to test eyes and furnish proper glasses. Messrs. Chas. E. and Chris. J. Seng, are natives of this city and are highly esteemed by the community for their ability and integrity, and their future prospects in the jewelry trade of Louisville are of the most favorable character.

SCHOENING & MATTMILLER; Merchant Tailors; No. 637 Market Street.—Louisville has long been the centre in the South for fine tailoring, and a thoroughly representative house in this line in this section of the city is that of Messrs. Schoening & Mattmiller, the popular merchant tailors. The co-partners, Messrs. E. H. Schoening and Jacob Mattmiller, who are thoroughly practical and expert cutters and custom tailors, established this business in 1890, and already have secured a liberal patronage. The store is spacious and is fully stocked with a superior assortment of broad cloths, tweeds, worsteds, cassimeres, overcoatings, suitings, etc., including all the newest shades and patterns. Fashionable tailoring in all its branches is executed by the firm on correct principles, and all the niceties of attire are given strict attention, and the garments turned out are recognized by a critical public, as perfect in style, fit and artistic workmanship, while the prices quoted for all goods are noted for their moderation. Mr. Mattmiller was born in Germany, in 1849, and came to Louisville in 1867. Mr. Schoening, however, is a native of this city, having been born in 1862. They are highly esteemed for strict probity, and are very popular with the community.

AMERICAN CORPORATE AGENCY; Sole Agents for the Sale of the American Improved Anti-Friction Metal; No. 139 Third Street.— Those who have traveled much either on railroads or steamships, are more or less acquainted with the hot-box, which really means a hot journal-bearing. Various ingenious contrivances have been constructed to overcome this difficulty, but no real practical advance was made until the discovery of what is now termed the American Improved Anti-Friction Metal. This company are the sole agents for this wonderful product for the states of Michigan, Wisconsin, Illinois, Missouri, Kansas, Iowa, Minnesota and Nebraska. It absolutely prevents hot bearings, nearly all friction being destroyed, and it increases motive power and saves sixty per cent. In oil, while its lubricant does not precipitate. This company was incorporated in 1888, the officers being Mr. E. Barbaroux, president, and Mr. Lewis Barbaroux, secretary. Already two million pounds are in use, and its sale is increasing rapidly. Messrs. Lewis and E. Barbaroux were born in this city, and are highly regarded for their strict probity. Mr. E. Barbaroux has been engaged forty years in the machinery business, and since 1872 has occupied the same building. He deals largely in all kinds of iron and wood working machinery, and retired from manufacturing in 1890.

ST. NICHOLAS HOTEL AND RESTAURANT ; Henry Seekamp, Proprietor; Corner Sixth Street and Court Place.—For home-like surroundings and superior table at moderate prices, the popular and old established St. Nicholas hotel and restaurant, is one of the best stopping places in Louisville. This is one of the oldest hotels, saloons and restaurants in the Falls City, and was opened about fifty years ago. In 1859 Mr. Henry Seekamp became the proprietor, and has continued to manage the St. Nicholas up to the present day. He makes every guest comfortable, and is one of those genial men, whose friendship is prized and his hospitality sought again and again, whenever the traveler or guest returns to the city. The hotel is a spacious four-story brick building, elegantly equipped and furnished throughout, and is supplied with all modern improvements, while the sanitary arrangements are perfect. The table is always amply supplied with the best in the market, and the attendance upon guests is all that can be desired. It is conducted on the American and European plan, the rates for the former being only $1.50 per day. The bar is supplied with the choicest wines, liquors, ales, beers, cigars, etc., and first-class meals can be obtained in the restaurant at all hours. Mr. Seekamp was born in Hanover, Germany, in 1836, and came to Louisville in 1854. He is highly regarded for his strict integrity, and we heartily recommend those who appreciate the comforts of a home to make their stay when in the city at the St. Nicholas.

D. M. OSBORNE & CO.; Manufacturers of Harvesting Machinery; No. 311 Main Street.—One of the most noted and successful agricultural machinery houses in America, is that known as D. M. Osborne & Co., manufacturers of harvesting machinery and farm implements. The headquarters and works of the company are in Auburn, N. Y., which are the largest and best equipped in the United States, and give constant employment to fifteen hundred skilled workmen. This business was founded in 1855, and has since been incorporated with large capital, the present executive officers being Mr. T. M. Osborne, president; Mr. E. D. Metcalf, treasurer; Mr. J. H. Osborne, secretary, and Mr. F. W. Terpening, manager. The company has been represented in Louisville since 1880, and its present branch was opened in 1891, Mr. C. L. Elliott being the general agent and manager. The premises occupied in the Falls City comprise a spacious foundry and basement building, which has an area of 25,000 square feet, fully equipped with every convenience. D. M. Osborne & Co., manufacture extensively, mowers, reapers, binders, hay rakes, corn harvesters, hay tedders, steel disc harrows, cultivators, etc., and also keep in stock at their branches, surreys, phaetons, wagons, harness, etc., without entering into a technical description of the company's various machines and farm implements, which have completely revolutionized the farmers' business, it may be justly stated that for lightness of draught, ease of management, simplicity of construction, strength, durability and working qualities, the Osborne machines lead the world. Mr. Elliott, the manager of the Louisville Depot, is a native of London, Ontario, and previously represented the Milwaukee Harvester Company, at Columbus, O., and is an active Freemason and a member of the A. O. U. W.

FRANK METTLER; Practical Watchmaker and Jeweler; No. 1036 West Market Street.—Among the popular and reliable jewelry establishments in this section of Louisville, actively engaged in the sale of watches, diamond goods, etc., is that of Mr. Frank Mettler, where as to price, quality and general superiority of stock, we know of no place in town, where such substantial inducements are offered to the public. Mr. Mettler established this business in 1871, and has since built up a liberal and influential patronage with the best classes in the city and its vicinity. The store is well appointed, and the stock embraces a full line of American and foreign gold and silver jewelery, diamond goods, rings, earrings, pins, bracelets, lace pins, sterling silver and plated ware, marble clocks, optical goods, etc. Only really genuine and first-class goods are handled and customers have always the satisfaction of knowing that nothing inferior will be sold to them. Mr. Mettler makes a specialty of the finest Waltham, Elgin and other noted American watches at prices that cannot be discounted in the city, and carefully repairs fine watches and jewelry, the work being entrusted only to first-class workmen. He was born in Switzerland in 1853, and came to Louisville in 1865. He is an honorable, energetic and liberal business man, who is very popular with all classes and has built up in spite of strong competition, one of the finest jewelry businesses in this section of the city.

JOHN KIEFER; Dealer in Meats, Groceries, Produce, Etc.; Corner Third and Breckinridge Streets.—There is probably no house in the city, devoted to the retailing of groceries and provisions, that enjoys a better reputation than that of John Kiefer, who established it twenty years ago, and from the outset prosperity has characterized it. The premises have a ground area of 45x120 feet, and are equipped in a superior style, being in all respects a model of the up-to-date business house. The stock consists of the choicest staple and fancy groceries, butter, eggs, cheese, game, poultry and fresh meats of all kinds and the utmost care is exercised in the selection of these, for the trade is strictly first-class that the house caters to. An idea of the extent of operations may be gained from the fact that nine skilled assistants are employed in the salesrooms, while three wagons are constantly delivering orders. The secret of the success of this business may be traced to the liberal and reliable methods rigidly adhered to from the outset, and to advance the interests of patrons has been the constant aim of the management. Mr. Kiefer was born in Germany, and came to Louisville twenty-five years ago. Possessed of the characteristics of his race, perseverance, enterprise and integrity, he cast his lot in Louisville, with the firm determination to succeed, and to-day he takes a leading position among the progressive business men of the city. We bespeak for this house a future, far better than its successful past.

BERNHEIM BROS.; Whiskies; Nos. 135-137 West Main Street.—This concern was established in 1872 on a very small scale in Paducah, Ky., and has developed along with the development of the Kentucky whiskey interest, only in a far greater ratio. Besides the distilling properties owned and controlled by them, they occupy in this city a building at Nos. 135 and 137 West Main Street, which is thirty feet front by two hundred feet in depth, extending through from West Main to Washington Street, and consisting of five floors. The rule with Bernheim Bros. is to give the trade exactly what the trade want, and in consequence, they carry an enormous stock of both straight and blended goods. They can always furnish sweet or sour-mash, young or old, floor stock or stock in bond. They control a number of prominent brands, but the whisky that they recommend most highly, and the one that their enterprise has pushed to the front as a staple in all parts of the country, is the celebrated "I. W. Harper." This brand is known in every state in the Union, and it may truthfully be said, that with a very large proportion of our population, it stands as a synonym for fine whiskey. They also carry in stock a large quantity of tax paid and bonded rye whiskies of Kentucky, Maryland and Pennsylvania. In conclusion we might state, that Messrs. I. W. and Bernard Bernheim, stand socially, as business men, and in all movements of a public nature, among the first citizens of Louisville. In the Board of Trade, and the Commercial Club, they are influential workers, and in every subscription for charities of a broad and non-sectarian character their names can always be found among the first.

Interior view of T. P. Taylor & Co.'s Drug Store.

T. P. TAYLOR & CO.; Druggists and Pharmacists; Corner of Third Avenue and Jefferson Street.—No branch of business is of more importance than that of the pharmacist, and in these days, when so many mishaps are occurring through incompetency, it is a matter of importance to the public to know where they can obtain accurate and careful service. Such a drug store in this section of Louisville is that of Messrs. T. P. Taylor & Co., which was opened in 1875 by Mr. A. C. Williams, who conducted it till 1881, when Mr. T. P. Taylor purchased the business. Mr. Taylor is a thoroughly qualified pharmacist, a graduate of the Louisville College of Pharmacy, and an active member of the Botanical

Club. The store is spacious, elegantly equipped and fitted up with every modern convenience, handsome plate glass front, electric lights, superior soda fountain, etc., while the laboratory is in the rear. The stock is one of the choicest in the city, embracing all kinds of pure fresh drugs and chemicals, mineral waters, proprietary medicines, physicians' supplies, druggists' sundries, toilet and fancy articles, perfumery, etc., also the best brands of imported and domestic cigars. Physicians' prescriptions and family recipes are compounded accurately at all hours of the day or night, and only thoroughly competent assistants are employed. Patrons receive always prompt and intelligent service, and prices in all cases are extremely moderate. Mr. Taylor compounds several preparations of his own, which are highly recommended by leading members of the faculty for their general efficiency and excellence, and employs in his pharmacy five assistants. He is a native of this city, and previous to succeeding to this business, conducted several drug stores in Louisville. He is highly esteemed by the community for his professional skill and integrity, and his success as a pharmacist, is as substantial as it is well merited.

FALLS CITY STABLES; Livery, Sale and Boarding Stables; Nos. 315, 317 and 319 Second Street.—A well managed livery and boarding stable is a positive convenience to any community, and a valuable acquisition to this section of Louisville is that of the Falls City Stables, of which Mr. D. W. Holmes is the popular proprietor. Mr. Holmes first commenced business in this line in 1889 at Floyd Street, and eventually in 1892 removed here having purchased the business of the Falls City Stables. The stables are spacious, and have excellent accommodations for sixty horses. Mr. Holmes has had long experience and is recognized as an authority and judge of horses, and handles and sells more first-class saddle and buggy horses, than any dealer in the city. For livery purposes he has a superior outfit, comprising new stylish carriages, buggies, etc., and a fine stock of driving and saddle horses. Orders receive immediate attention and carriages are promptly furnished for funerals, weddings, parties, balls, etc., at very reasonable rates, and Mr. Holmes already numbers among his permanent customers, many of the leading families of the city and its vicinity. He was born in Louisville in 1844, and has always resided within two squares of his present stables. He is highly regarded for his strict integrity, and we predict for him a steadily increasing patronage.

PRESTON STREET POTTERY; John Bauer, Proprietor; Nos. 2122 to 2128 Preston Street. Seventeen years ago Mr. John Bauer established the Preston Street Pottery, and has strenuously endeavored to meet the demands of the public in every particular. The pottery is a three-story structure, 60x35 feet in area. Its appointments and equipments render it a model of up-to-date completeness, and the various modern machines and appliances are operated by a fifty horse power steam engine. There are three large kilns operated, and the output amounts to fourteen thousand gallons capacity, and six thousand flower pots, of all sizes and

designs weekly. Twenty-five expert workmen are employed, and the trade is derived from all parts of Indiana, Kentucky, Tennessee, North Carolina and Virginia, sales being mostly made to jobbing houses and large retailers. Adjoining the pottery are large storage yards, and a switch of the Louisville and Nashville Railroad passing through these, furnishes excellent shipping facilities. For design, workmanship and material, these goods are unsurpassed, and have always commanded patronage solely upon their merits. Mr. Bauer is of German descent, but has resided in Louisville for many years. He is a man of liberality, energy and public spirit.

A. **A. CHICKERING**; Coal, Groceries, Chop and Crushed Feed; Nos. 400 and 404, corner Main and Preston Streets.—A representative and the oldest established house in this section of Louisville, actively engaged in handling groceries, is that of Mr. A. A. Chickering, who founded the business in 1860, and has since secured a liberal patronage. The premises occupied are well adapted for the business, and eight assistants are constantly employed. Mr. Chickering carries at all times a choice stock of teas, coffees, spices, canned goods, table delicacies, dried fruits, provisions, sugars, syrups, etc., and also deals largely in chop and crushed feed, and the finest grades of anthracite and bituminous coal. Only the purest and best groceries are handled, and customers have always the satisfaction of knowing that nothing inferior will be sold to them, while the prices quoted for all goods are extremely moderate. Patrons buying coal here, can always depend on getting full weight and coal free from slate and other impurities, and at the same time the best burning fuel in the market. He makes all kinds of mixed feed, and his leading specialty is Chickering's celebrated chop and crushed feed, the great blood purifier and bowel regulator for horses and cattle, and he is likewise proprietor of Chickering's famous hoof oil, which is unrivalled for cracked hoofs. Mr. Chickering was born in Westmoreland, N. H., and came to Louisville in 1849, and was engaged in the bottling business up to 1860. When a young man in Baltimore, he became a member of Lodge 1. I. O. O. F., the first lodge of the kind in the United States. Mr. A. A. Chickering, Jr., the son of the founder, has now the entire control of the business. He is highly esteemed for his integrity, and has already served eight years in the Common Council, being an earnest supporter of all measures, conducive to the permanent welfare of the Falls City.

JACOB H. MAYER & SON; Collar Manufactory; Nos. 308 & 310 East Green Street.—One of the most reliable firms in this section of Louisville is that of Messrs. Jacob H. Mayer & Son, manufacturers of horse collars. This business was established in 1862 by Messrs. Mayer & Christian, who conducted it till 1886, when on the death of Mr. Christian, Mr. Jacob H. Mayer became the proprietor. Eventually in 1894 he admitted his son Mr. Fred. J. Mayer into partnership. Mr. F. J. Mayer is a thoroughly practical collar maker, who possesses an intimate knowledge of the needs and requirements of the trade. The factory is well equipped with modern appliances, and a full staff of skilled workmen is employed. The firm has introduced several useful improvements and makes a specialty of the finer grades of patent leather work, its goods being standards with the trade, and have no superiors in this country. Orders are carefully filled at lowest figures, and the trade of the firm now extends throughout all sections of Kentucky, the southern and southwestern states. Mr. Jacob H. Mayer, who was born in Germany in 1836, came to Louisville in 1854, while Mr. Fred. J. Mayer is a native of the Falls City. Mr. J. H. Mayer is highly regarded for his strict probity, and has been for many years president of the German Protestant Orphans Home. Both partners are active members of the A. O. U. W., of which order Mr. J. H. Mayer has been for many years a charter member and recorder.

FOWLER AND CONSTANTINE; Druggists; Corner Seventh and Market Streets.—Among the various learned professions, there are none that require so much skilled accuracy as that which is devoted to the preparation of drugs and medicines. In this connection we make due reference to the noted pharmacy conducted by Messrs. Fowler & Constantine, which dates its existence back some fifteen years, it having been founded by Messrs. Newhouse & Co., in 1880, the present proprietors, namely, Dr. J. W. Fowler and E. R. Constantine purchasing the good will and interest in 1892. This is one of the finest stores of the kind in the Falls City, the fixtures and show cases being the acme of good taste. Electric lighting and every possible convenience are at hand, inclusive of a superior fountain. The stock is complete, embracing a full line of drugs and medicines, together with a complete assortment of proprietary medicines. Special attention is given to the accurate compounding of physicians' prescriptions, while in toilet articles and perfumery, we have scarcely seen a stock equal to this. Dr. Fowler is a native of Fredericksburg, Ky., and a graduate of the Louisville College of Medicine. He is likewise a member of the American Pharmaceutical Association, the Kentucky Pharmaceutical Association, president of the State Board of Pharmacy and editor of the pharmaceutical columns of the Medical Herald. Mr. Constantine is a native of Fairfield, Ky., and was formerly chief clerk in the pharmacy still conducted by Dr. Fowler at the junction of Second and Green Streets. He is a graduate of the Louisville College of Pharmacy, also a member of the American Pharmaceutical Association and the Louisville College of Pharmacy. Mr. Constantine was also assistant professor of chemistry in the Louisville College of Pharmacy for a number of years but resigned in 1894 in order to devote his entire attention to his business located at Seventh and Market Streets.

BOSSE BROS. & SON; Funeral Directors and Embalmers; No. 522 Green Street.—An old established and representative Louisville house in its line, is that of Messrs. Bosse Bros. & Son, the popular funeral directors and embalmers. This business was established in 1857 by Mr. Joseph Haarmann, who was succeeded in 1866 by Messrs. Henry and

Joseph Bosse. They continued it under the firm name of Bosse Bros., till 1889, when Mr. Henry Bosse, Jr., the son of Mr. Henry Bosse, Sr., became a partner, and the present title of Bosse Bros. & Son was adopted. The premises occupied comprise a spacious ground floor, 45x210 feet in area, fully equipped with every convenience. Here they keep a large and choice stock of coffins, caskets, burial cases, trimmings, shrouds and all kinds of funeral goods. They cater to all classes of the population, furnishing hearses, carriages, etc., and supplying everything necessary for the plainest or most imposing funerals, while they have always made it a rule to charge only moderate prices. Interments are procured in any of the city or suburban cemeteries, while a specialty is made of embalming according to the latest scientific methods. Mr. Henry Bosse, Sr., and Mr. Joseph Bosse were born in Germany, the former in 1838, and the latter in 1840, and came to Louisville in 1853 and 1857 respectively, while Mr. Henry Bosse, Jr., is a native of this city. They are prominent members of the Undertakers' Association, and the Catholic Knights of America, and are highly esteemed by the community for their strict integrity.

J. C. PARKER; Wholesale Paper and Twine; No. 439 West Main Street. —Louisville as the metropolis of Kentucky thoroughly maintains her supremacy in every line, having establishments that compare favorably with anything of the kind elsewhere in the United States; and the paper line is not an exception to the rule, for example, the wholesale paper and twine house of Mr. J. C. Parker, located at No. 439 West Main Street, who has developed a large and growing business with the best and largest firms in the country. He has developed and maintains his business by the uniform excellence of the stock he carries and the promptness and dispatch in filling orders. This business was established many years ago by Dupont & Co., who were manufacturers and large paper dealers, handling everything that is carried by a first-class paper house. They conducted this business until 1887, when Mr. J. C. Parker succeeded them in the jobbing business. Mr. Parker brings great practical experience to bear in his business, while his facilities are the best and his connections with the largest manufacturers enable him to fill special orders with unusual promptness, and enable him at all times to offer substantial advantages to large buyers. The premises occupied by him comprise five floors and basement, fitted up with modern conveniences for the storage and handling of his large and extensive stock, which consists of a full line of paper supplies, including card board, book paper, newspaper, flat and writing papers, besides a large stock of wrapping papers and twines, that are offered to the trade at prices to meet the very closest competition. Only the best grades of paper are handled and this house is one that does not make specialties of job lots, but makes it a policy to carry all standard grades of papers, at bottom prices, which has been fully appreciated by the large and extensive trade which extends throughout Kentucky, Indiana, Tennessee and the southern states. Orders are filled with the greatest care, whether they are sent in through the mail or through his traveling salesmen. Mr. Parker is a native of Fayette County, Kentucky, and is highly esteemed in business circles and his establishment is an important factor of mercantile activity in the Falls City. His extensive stock enables him to reach and sell the printers, stationers, dry goods, hardware, boots and shoes, grocers and every branch of trade.

KENTUCKY JEANS CLOTHING COMPANY; No. 631 West Main Street. —No industrial interest of the city of Louisville is of more importance than the manufacture of clothing. Among the thoroughly reliable and representative houses engaged in this branch of industry in its special line, is that of the Kentucky Jeans Clothing Company. This prosperous concern was established as an individual enterprise by Mr. A. V. Thomson in 1888, the policy of forming a joint-stock company being decided upon in 1889 and state corporate charter being secured under the existent trading title during that year. The company has an ample cash capital, and is ably officered as follows: A. V. Thomson, president; Chas. Mendel, vice-president, and Hardin Wilson, secretary and treasurer,—all Kentuckians and favorably known in the financial and commercial circles of this section. They have great practical experience, give close personal attention to all the details of the manufacture of their goods, and provide constant employment for a force of two hundred skilled operators. The premises occupied comprise a substantial four-storied and basement building, 25x210 feet in area, fully equipped with every facility for the systematic conduct of this extensive business, including elevator, and one hundred and twenty-five sewing machines, operated by electric power. The range of production embraces jeans clothing, cottonades, cassimeres, kerseys, corduroys, etc., the firm being proprietors of the famous Lion brand of goods and turning out one hundred dozen of men's, youths' and boys' pants per day, supplying the demands of an extensive trade, which radiates broadly throughout Kentucky, Indiana, Tennessee, Georgia, Mississippi, Illinois, Ohio, West Virginia, Arkansas, Iowa, Missouri, Alabama, Texas and Wisconsin. Two traveling salesmen are employed, and the nature of the firm's operations are exclusively wholesale to the trade. The officers are highly regarded for their integrity, and those who enter into business relations with them, can always rely upon securing advantages and inducements in goods and prices very difficult to be obtained elsewhere in this section of the Southwest.

GOFF & CO.; Makers of Fine Cigars; Nos. 121-128 West Jefferson Street.—Among the various industries of Louisville, few deserve more prominent mention in this volume, than that of cigar making, and considering the vast quantities produced in the United States, it might be reasonably supposed, that an excellent smoking article could easily be produced anywhere at a very moderate price. Such is not the case, and often it is very difficult to obtain a first-class cigar. Some of our manufacturers, however, have always adhered to honorable methods, handling only the choicest leaf, and turning out nothing but superior goods. Prominent among this number is the firm of Messrs. Goff & Co. This business was established in 1894 by Mr. Thos. L. Goff, who is sole proprietor. He now occupies the premises, which were previously for seventeen years in the occupation of Mr. J. C. Bamburger, cigar dealer. Mr. Goff is a thoroughly practical and expert cigar manufacturer, who possesses an intimate knowledge of the needs and requirements of a first-class trade. The factory is spacious and well equipped, and fifty skilled hands are constantly employed. All the cigars produced by Goff & Co., are made from choice selected stock, no door tobacco being used, while none but really first-class goods are turned out. A specialty is made of the widely known and favorite ten cent "El Tropico" cigar, which is manufactured from the choicest growths of Havana and Sumatra tobacco, and for delicacy of flavor, true fragrance, perfect workmanship and select leaf, is rapidly distancing all competition wherever introduced. We cannot too strongly recommend hotel men, restaurant keepers, druggists and the trade generally, to sample these splendid cigars, as they always give entire satisfaction, and will be found to sell quickly, hold custom, and give a good profit to the retailer. Orders are filled with care and dispatch, and the trade of the house now extends not only throughout Louisville and Kentucky, but also to Indiana, Ohio, Illinois and Tennessee. The store is elegantly equipped and a heavy stock of cigars, etc., is constantly on hand, while a specialty is made of box trade. Mr. Goff was born in Mason County, Ky., and from there moved to Shelby, where his father was for many years engaged in the leaf tobacco trade, and they sold at the prize sale at Richmond, Va., in 1888, the highest priced hogshead of burley tobacco ever sold in the world. He is an honorable, progressive and liberal business man, who is very popular in trade circles, and we predict for him a very successful career in this important industry.

AMERICAN GROCERY COMPANY, (Incorporated); Wholesale Grocers and Provisions Dealers; No. 741 West Main Street.—This staunch old house was founded twenty-five years ago by Messrs. H. C. Armstrong & Company. The senior partner died in 1892, and for some time the business was conducted, prior to his decease under the firm style of H. C. Armstrong, and eventually it was incorporated under the laws of Kentucky, July, 1893, as the American Grocery Company, the officers being J. W. McGee, president, a native of Kentucky and a prominent member of the Masonic Order; Morton Armstrong, secretary; son of the late H. C. Armstrong, attorney-at-law. The house has ever maintained a first-class reputation for just dealing, and its trade extends throughout Kentucky, Indiana and Tennessee. The premises occupied comprise a substantial four-storied and basement building, 25x200 feet in dimensions, and the stock comprises full lines of staple and fancy groceries, sugars, coffees, teas, provisions, etc., of the best quality, pure and wholesome. Eight assistants are employed, while seven traveling salesmen represent the house on the road.

C. G. BECKER & SON; Grocer; No. 2882 Portland Avenue. One of the most reliable grocery establishments in this section of Louisville is that of C. G. Becker & Son, which has been in operation since 1869. In 1885 Mr. C. G. Becker assumed control and eventually admitted his son, Mr. Joshua Becker into partnership. The premises occupied comprise a spacious floor fully equipped with every convenience.

Here they keep a heavy and choice stock of select teas and coffees, pure and fresh spices, condiments and table delicacies in great variety, standard grades of sugar, syrups and molasses and everything usually found in a first-class grocery store, also a large stock of feed. They have a large general trade throughout the city and neighboring sections, and deal also in the choicest of fruits and vegetables in their season. Mr. C. G. Becker was born in Germany in 1844 and came to Louisville in 1852. Joshua Becker, his son, is a young man of ability and promise in his business. He is an active, energetic, enterprising citizen, has inherited the energy and integrity of his father. They are both exceedingly popular with all who know them, and always ready to further any project intended to promote the welfare of the city.

EDWARD J. O'BRIEN & CO.; Leaf Tobacco Brokers; No. 1032 West Main Street. This business was established nine years ago by Mr. Edward J. O'Brien, who eventually admitted Mr. J. F. Nash into partnership. Mr. Nash died March, 1895, and the business is still conducted under the old firm name of Edward J. O'Brien & Co. Mr. O'Brien brings great practical experience to bear on the business, and is considered one of the best judges of leaf tobacco in the country, and a test by him is always sufficient to finally fix the quality and value of any particular lot. He conducts a strictly brokerage business in leaf tobacco, and buys largely for export to European and other foreign countries. Orders are filled with care and dispatch, and complete satisfaction is guaranteed the most critical patrons. Mr. O'Brien is a native of the Falls City, and is an honorable, energetic and able broker, who is very popular in trade circles, and is a prominent member of the Louisville Leaf Tobacco Exchange.

WM. G. MEIER & CO.; Leaf Tobacco; Seventh Street near Main Street.—Louisville is the largest leaf tobacco market in the world, and it is but fitting that those agencies chiefly contributing to this commercial pre-eminence should be duly recognized in a volume such as this purports to be. The brokers and buyers have unquestionably largely aided in the consummation of this satisfactory result, and as prominent participants in such direction may be mentioned the old established house of Messrs. Wm. G. Meier & Co. This time honored concern was established in 1861 by the late William G. Meier, who fourteen years later formed the firm of Wm. G. Meier & Co., consisting of Wm. G. Meier, his brother, R. Meier, and F. H. Wulkop. In 1886 the founder of the house died, and the business has since been successfully conducted by the surviving partners, who have still retained the well-known firm style. These gentlemen enjoy the reputation of owning the largest tobacco warehouse of a private character in the Falls City. Their purchases and dealings are for both home and foreign account, their trading connections covering the entire United States and the leading European ports, using their extensive city warehouse for the sorting of leaf tobacco only. Mr. R. Meier is of German nationality, but has now been on this side of the Atlantic for many years. He resides at Cincinnati, O., where a branch office of the firm is conducted at the northwest corner of Second and Vine Streets. He is a member of the Leaf Tobacco Exchange and Board of Trade. Mr. Wulkop, who is also associated with the above named organizations, was born in this city, and has been identified with the house for the past twenty-five years, becoming an interested partner in the firm in 1875.

116   — — LOUISVILLE OF TO-DAY. — —

NANZ & NEUNER; Florists; No. 504 Fourth Avenue.—Louisville has acquired quite a national reputation as one of the leading centres of the flower and seed trade, and a prominent house engaged in this business is that of Messrs. Nanz and Neuner, the widely known florists. The business was established in 1850 by Mr. H. Nanz, who eventually admitted his son Mr. H. Nanz, Jr. into partnership, and in 1870 Mr. C. Neuner became a partner, and in 1872 for want of space, the plant was removed to St. Mathews, where they have thirty acres under cultivation, five acres of which are covered with greenhouses. Eventually in 1877, Mr. A. Neuner who was then located in New York City, became a member of the firm, and Mr. H. Nanz the founder died in 1882 aged seventy-two years, after an honorable career, being the oldest florist in the Falls City. The present store was opened eighteen years ago, and they now supply a large demand for all kinds of flowers, foreign and native flowering plants, shrubs, palms, etc., and their trade extends throughout the entire United States. They also furnish bouquets, wreaths and various emblematic designs for weddings, parties, balls and funerals in new and original conceptions of artistic forms. All orders by mail, telegraph, telephone or in person, receive prompt attention, the firm being fully prepared to fill all commissions not only promptly, but with that intelligent apprehension of design, that make their efforts so highly appreciated by patrons. Choice cut flowers of all kinds can always be had here at reasonable prices in profusion in winter or summer. Mr. C. Neuner has personal charge of the greenhouses and cultivation, while Mr. H. Nanz manages the city and local trade. Mr. A. Neuner has charge of the correspondence and foreign affairs of the firm. They are highly esteemed for their strict integrity, and are very popular in trade circles. The firm issues annually thirty-five thousand illustrated catalogues, relating to seeds and flowers, which are promptly mailed free to any address.

SLOAN & DAWERS; Tailors; No. 231 Fifth Street.—Among the leading houses actively engaged in artistic tailoring in this section of Louisville is that of Messrs. Sloan & Dawers, whose reputation for first-class work is unsurpassed in the city. The co-partners Messrs. Ed. B. Sloan and C. H. Dawers established this business in 1890, and have since built up an influential and permanent patronage, not only in the city but also in the Southern states. Both partners are thoroughly expert custom tailors, whose ability to cater to a fashionable trade is shown by the number of our leading professional and business men, who are among their regular customers. Their store is spacious and is attractively fitted up, and only really first-class cutters and journeymen are employed. The stock embraces a fine assortment of imported fabrics from the best European looms, as well as all kinds of domestic goods, suitings, cassimeres, broadcloths, vestings, etc., in all the latest styles, shades and qualities, so that even the most fastidious customer can readily be suited here. Every suit and garment that leave this establishment are made of the best quality of materials, are beautifully finished and of the most stylish and fashionable patterns. The partners give close personal attention to all details of the business, and their prices for all garments are noted for their moderation. Mr. Sloan was born in Nashville, Tenn., in 1861, and came with his parents to Louisville in 1869; Mr. Dawers, however, is of German nationality, and has resided in the Falls City since 1876. Both partners are connected with several societies, Mr. Sloan being a member of the Order of the Elks and Knights of Pythias, while Mr. Dawers is also a member of the Knights of Pythias and treasurer of the Louisville Division, No. 1. They are highly regarded for their skill and probity, and their future success as merchant tailors seems well assured, and we predict for them a steadily increasing patronage.

S. ROBERTS & CO.; Wholesale and Retail Dealers in Coal; No. 508 First Street.—The consumption of coal has naturally assumed proportions which eclipse that of any other material in Louisville, and as a result, many large establishments are here located to supply the ever augmenting demand for that staple fuel. Not only is the best quality of coal in demand for use by manufacturers, but also in private dwellings, public institutions and all industrial establishments and an important factor in supplying this city with all kinds of hard and soft coal is the firm of Messrs. S. Roberts & Co. This business was established in 1862, under the present firm style, but from 1888 to 1893 was conducted by Mr. Ed. Roberts alone, the present co-partners Messrs. S. Roberts and L. P. Rammers, assuming the control April 1st of the latter named year. This firm make a specialty of Pittsburg and Youghiogheny coal and coke, as also the best grades of Kentucky mined fuel, while they carry several thousand tons of different varieties in stock at all times. The yards of the firm, (which are connected by telephone with the main office call No. 198, rings 2 and 4) are situated on Shelby and Franklin Streets, cover a lineal ground area of 150x450 feet, and are amply supplied with shedding, coal cars, trestles, etc., and employment is given twenty hands, and the firm operate ten delivery wagons, and are doing a business of a wholesale and retail character, amounting to $100,000 per annum. Their connections enable them to offer purchasers every possible advantage in prices, while they have every facility for filling all orders with dispatch. The operations of the house in the past have been commendable, and have given ample evidence of a strong adherence to business principles, which constitute the foundation of a career eminently successful and prosperous.

N. U. WALKER SEWER PIPE CO.; Warehouses, No. 142 Third Street.—This concern dates its existence back to 1864, and became a corporate organization under the existent trading title some twenty years later. The company has a capitalization of $275,000, the management of its affairs controlled from this point, being in the able hands of Mr. Frank B. Burrell, who has efficiently filled that appointment since 1881. The works of the concern are located at Walkers on the Ohio River, some two miles from Wellsville, and not only enjoy the distinction of being the oldest of their type in the United States, but in point of machinery equipment, rail and river transportation facilities, etc., stand without a peer on the American continent. The premises here occupied at No. 142 Third Street, consist of a substantial five-storied main building, 25x110 feet in dimensions, supplemented by extensive yardage, as also rear warehouse two stories in height, and having a lineal frontage and depth of 80x220 feet. The stock carried is an immense one, and embraces vitrified salt glazed sewer pipe, culvert pipe, hot air and flue linings, patent chimneys, Walker's patent plain and fancy chimney tops, vitrified lawn and parlor vases, flower pots, terra cotta work, paving brick, fire brick, fire and grate tile, fire clay, Michigan & Newark brands, land drain tile, plastering hair, cements (Black Diamond, also imported and domestic Portland), stove thimbles, etc. The trade from this point radiates broadly throughout the entire South and West, and some criterion of Mr. Burrell's management may be gleaned from the statement that the sales here effected average $175,000 per annum. He is a native of Memphis, Tenn., but has been settled here since early youth.

A LB. C. TAFEL; Surgical Instruments; No. 117 Third Street.—The name of "Tafel" will ever be honorably identified with the progress and development of the manufacture of surgical instruments in the city of Louisville. This business was established in 1855 by Mr. Fred Siegal, who conducted it till 1880, when Mr. Albert C. Tafel became the proprietor. He is thoroughly conversant with every detail of this important industry, and his patronage now extends not only throughout the southern and western states, but also to Mexico and Central and South America. The premises occupied consist of a commodious four story brick building 20x50 feet in area, with factory on upper floors 20x40 feet in size. The factory is fully equipped with modern tools and appliances, operated by electric motor power, and a force of skilled workmen is employed. Mr. Tafel manufactures and keeps in stock, all kinds of surgical instruments, etc., and also deals in rubber goods, crutches, trusses, supporters, glass eyes, and sells largely to graduates of medical colleges here. He is also known all through the South for fitting trusses and making most approved appliances for cripples. The firm's surgical instruments are unsurpassed as to purity of metal, improved designs, perfect temper, general high quality and superior finish, and is a great favorite with the profession, while they are offered at extremely moderate prices. Mr. A. C. Tafel is a native of Cincinnati, O., and is an honorable and able business man, whose success in this useful industry is as substantial as it is well deserved.

EMPIRE DRILL COMPANY; No. 134 Second Street.—The head office of this enterprising concern is at Shortsville, New York, and in presenting this enterprise to our many readers, in order to do full justice to the Empire drills, it would be necessary to explain somewhat more in detail than space in this work would permit, what advantages it possesses over all other manufacture. Therefore only a few of the chief features of these interesting and highly useful contrivances can be touched upon. Their grain drill has a positive force feed, and sows with the same gear, the same quantity of wheat or oats. It plants corn perfectly without requiring any special device for this purpose. The quantity sown being regulated by gear makes it eminently reliable and satisfactory. It is the lightest draft drill made, and is so evenly balanced, that it rests very lightly on the horses' necks, and for the quality of material used, workmanship and finish, it is simply unsurpassed. There are many other practical and useful points which as previously indicated, space here does not permit of having reproduced. These drills have no equal and no farmer should be without one, nor would he be were he once practically acquainted with its merits. The premises in this city comprise a three-storied and basement building, the office and salesroom being situated on the first floor, the rest of the building being used for storage of drills and interchangeable parts. Six traveling salesmen are kept constantly on the road, the territory covered from this point being the entire Southwest. Mr. C. H. Brackett, the manager of this branch, is a native of York state, and represented the concern on the road, previously to taking charge here, some ten years ago. Under his energetic and able management, the business of the company has increased to a remarkable extent, and exceeds in volume that of any of the other branches. Personally Mr. Brackett is a genial, courteous gentleman, honorable, liberal and fair in all transactions, possessing a sterling integrity and force of character, which invariably achieve substantial success in any undertaking.

LOUISVILLE OF TO-DAY.

HEATH-MORRIS COMPANY; Manufacturers of Berry Boxes and Baskets.—This business was established about 1871 and conducted since 1880 by Smith, Young & Co., who eventually were succeeded by Messrs. Heath, Morris & Co. On December 6th, 1893 the enterprise was incorporated under the laws of Indiana with a paid-up capital of $10,000, executive officers being Mr. W. B. Heath, president; Mr. W. F. Morris, vice-president, and Mr. John F. Miller, secretary and treasurer. They manufacture largely all kinds of berry boxes and baskets, also fruit packages of all kinds and sizes, while a specialty is made of stave and splint baskets in

car lots. One hundred and thirty skilled hands are employed, and last year the company turned out two million quart baskets alone, also vast numbers of baskets and other packages. The trade of the company extends throughout the entire United States. The factory is connected by a switch with all the railroads entering the city, and they likewise have a large three-story warehouse 60x120 feet in area located on Thomas and East Streets. The company also has a branch in Cincinnati, O. Mr. Heath is a native of Benton Harbor, Mich., where he was previously engaged in the same business twelve years, while Mr. Morris was born in New Albany and is superintendent of the factory. They are highly regarded for their strict integrity and are very popular in trade circles, justly meriting the substantial success secured in this useful industry. Mr. Miller is a young man of marked ability, a native of this city and has been with the company since 1891.

E. B. NUGENT; Dry Goods; No. 501 Fourth Avenue.—This house was established by Mr. E. B. Nugent, in 1858, on West Market Street, and was there continued by him with great success till 1893, when, the exegencies of a rapidly increasing trade, necessitated removal to his present eligible quarters. They consist of a commodious three-storied and basement structure, 30x200 feet in dimensions, with L-shaped extension to Green Street, having lineal frontage and depth of 25x100 feet. The trade is chiefly of an urban and suburban character, and so far as the character and extent of the stock is concerned, it may be confidently stated that it has no superior in this section of the country. It embraces a diversity of departments, the following being the principal ones, viz: dress goods of all descriptions and fabrics, shades and colors, gloves, millinery, hosiery, ladies' underwear, corsets, laces, children's outfits, fancy goods, and that vast array of articles summed up under the comprehensive term of "notions." The store is steam heated, electric lighted, and in every respect thoroughly equipped with a view to the advantageous prosecution of the business in all its branches. Mr. Nugent's liberality and promptness have always characterized the operations of this house, and the success which has attended it is but the just reward of a commercial policy, without which no permanent prosperity is possible.

THE H. A. THIERMAN COMPANY; Distillers and Wholesale Whiskey Dealers; Nos. 227 and 229 West Main Street.—Louisville has long been the leading centre in the United States for the distillation and wholesale trade in whiskies, and among the prominent concerns engaged in this important industry, a position of leadership is held by The H. A. Thierman Company. This business dates back to 1864, when it was founded by H. Thierman & Co., the firm name becoming two years later, Thierman, Pratt & Co., while the present style was adopted in 1872. The large interests involved were incorporated in 1882, under the laws of Kentucky, with a capital of $50,000, which is now supplemented by a handsome surplus. The company utilizes a substantial four-story building, 35x94 feet in dimensions, and is able to store in this place no less than five thousand barrels of whiskey. The president of the company, Mr. H. A. Thierman, is a prominent member of the Board of Trade and the Commercial Club, as is also the secretary, Mr. William Buedeman, whose connection with the house dates from 1873. The company are proprietors of the Rugby Distillery Company, whose plant located at Thirty-sixth Street and Missouri Avenue, has a daily capacity of one thousand bushels of grain and a storage capacity of thirty-five thousand barrels of whiskey. Mr. Thierman is president, Mr. Buedeman, vice-president, and C. M. Babbett is secretary of this concern, which has a capital of $50,000. They are also the owners of the Mayflower Distillery Company, having a cash capitalization of $25,000, and a plant situated in Jefferson County, Ky., whose storage capacity is twenty thousand barrels, and daily consumption four hundred bushels. Mr. Buedeman is president and Mr. Thierman, vice-president of this corporation, and E. M. Babbett, secretary. With these exceptionally fine facilities for the production of high grade whiskies, the company transacts an immense business, broadly distributed over the whole of the United States, the total of which average $750,000 each year. Their special brands, Belle of Louisville and Mayflower, sour-mash bourbon, rye and Indian Hill bourbon rye whiskies and Belle of Jefferson, are prime favorites wherever introduced, especially with good judges and connoisseurs. The success of the company is due alike to the merits of their products, and to the enterprise of those charged with the management of its affairs.

S. C. SHEPPARD; Steam Forge and Machine Works; No. 317 Ninth Street.—One of the most reliable industrial establishments in this section of Louisville is that of Mr. S. C. Sheppard the widely known machinist which, from a modest beginning, has attained to its present important dimensions. The works were established fifteen years ago by Mr. Sheppard, who by strict attention to business and an honorable course of dealing has built up a liberal patronage extending all over Kentucky, and the South. The steam forge and machine works are 22x125 feet in dimensions provided with the most improved machinery and appliances including five forges, and a thirty horse power engine. From twenty to twenty-five skilled hands are employed and the range of production embraces all kinds of castings and forgings of every description, special machine forging and crank axles made to order, while a large trade is done in manufacturing iron derricks, railings, window guards, door chains, bolts, turnbuckles and everything in the line of blacksmithing and wrought iron work. Mr. Sheppard has executed several contracts for iron and steel work for jails in the South and the work done here has given entire satisfaction. Mr. Sheppard is a Pennsylvanian. He is a man of great practical experience and is highly esteemed by all classes for his personal worth.

PRICE & LUCAS CIDER AND VINEGAR CO: Fifteenth Street and Portland Avenue.—The use of prepared condiments, vinegar, cider, etc., is almost universal among civilized people the world over. In this connection special reference is made in these pages to the noted Price & Lucas Cider and Vinegar Company, which dates its existence back some twenty-five years, it having been founded by Messrs. Price and Lucas in 1870, state corporate charter being secured June, 1893. The company has a cash capital of $250,000 and is ably officered as follows: Vernon D. Price, president, a native of Ohio, and member of the University Club and Board

of Trade; Jno. W. Lucas, vice-president, a Virginian by birth and resident here since 1869; W. B. Lucas, son of John W. Lucas, secretary and treasurer, member of the Commercial Club and Elks Society. The premises occupied comprise a substantial three-storied and basement building, connected with commodious warehouse on the southern branch of the K. and I. Bridge railroad. The equipment embraces the latest improved appliances, employment being provided for a force of thirty skilled hands. Here is turned out one hundred and thirty barrels of pure malt vinegar, also a large quantity of cider pressed from sound selected fruit at the proper season, the company being likewise extensive jobbers of superior Worstershire sauce, pepper sauce, catsup and mustard, for which they find a ready demand at good prices. The trade of the house extends throughout the entire South and West, and under able management is rapidly increasing in volume, the products of this company having but to be tried to be permanently appreciated.

J. H. PAYNE & CO.; Builders and Contractors; Mill and Office, Twenty-eighth and Cane Run Road.—The extensive building operations in Louisville of late years, have given rise to a number of prominent firms devoted to that important line of industry, and among these none stand higher in popular form or entail a more extensive patronage, than that of J. H. Payne & Co., builders and contractors. The business was founded in 1886 by E. A. Grant, Jr., and two years later Reese and McKenzie, succeeded. In 1892 the style changed to the Parkland Lumber Company, and in September, 1894, J. H. Payne & Co. became proprietors. Though the firm name has changed so often, there has been no variation in the success which has characterized the venture from the outset, and to-day no firm in the city in this line, has a reputation more to be envied. The premises occupied, cover in all an area of one acre of ground, the best receiving and shipping facilities are provided, and the yards contain unexcelled conveniences for handling and storage of lumber. The planing mill has a ground area of 100x130 feet, and is in its appointment thoroughly modern and complete. The most approved steam machinery and appliances are provided, an engine of thirty horse power furnishing the motive force, and a large number of expert operatives are employed in the various departments. Planing mill work is done in all its branches, a specialty being made of interior woodwork. As contractors and builders, the firm has executed some very large contracts, many of the best buildings of the city furnishing excellent examples of their handiwork. The members of the firm are J. H. Payne and W. W. Riggs. Mr. Payne was born in Glasgow, Ky., and has always followed this line of business. Mr. Riggs has been identified with the house since 1894. He is secretary of the Commercial Building and Trust Company of Louisville. Both gentlemen possess business qualifications of a high order, and must be classed with the progressive, reliable and influential citizens.

THE KENTUCKY PUBLIC ELEVATOR COMPANY; Fourteenth Street, between Kentucky and Oak Streets.—The prominent position which the Falls City now occupies in the grain trade, has been reached by the unsurpassed shipping facilities afforded by the different railroad lines, tapping the best producing regions of the West which converge to this point, while a good idea can be obtained of the magnitude of this trade, from a personal inspection of the numerous grain elevators here. In this connection we make due reference in the pages of this review to the establishment of the Kentucky Public Elevator Company, handlers of and storers of grain. This concern was duly organized and incorporated under the state laws in 1881, and under able and efficient guidance, has continuously prospered to date. The company has a cash capital of $150,000, the executive officers being as follows: Oscar Fenley, president, also cashier of the Citizens' National Bank, director of the East End Improvement Company, the Columbia Finance and Trust Company, and a trustee of the Orphans' Home, F. C. Dickson, manager, now identified with the company for the past six years and Chas. A. Villier, secretary and treasurer, member of the Board of Trade, and now connected with this company for the past nine years. This elevator was erected at a cost of $250,000 and has a storage capacity for five hundred thousand bushels of grain, constituting the largest and best appointed establishment of its class south of the Ohio River. The transportation facilities could not be improved upon, direct connections being maintained with the lines of the L. and N. R. R., the Louisville Southern R. R., Louisville, St. Louis and Texas R. R., B. and O. S. W. R. R. and Louisville, New Albany and Chicago R. R., the C. O. and S. W. R. R. and the P. C. C. and St. Louis Railway. The elevator has an area of 85x92 feet, the building rising one hundred and fifty feet in height, the smoke stack one hundred and fifty-two feet, the plant including wagon, blacksmiths' and carpentering shop, capacious storage accommodation being provided for sacks,—no less than twenty million bushels of grain being handled and stored here per annum. This company are owners of one and one-half miles of tracks, furnishing room for two hundred cars, something that no other elevator in the country can claim for itself.

D. SHANAHAN SONS & COMPANY; General Railroad Contractors and Bridge Builders; No. 610 Columbia Building.—The firm of D. Shanahan Sons & Company, of Louisville has become too widely known to require explanation as being prominently identified with bridge building and railroad contracting throughout the United States. The business was established in 1862, by Mr. D. Shanahan and Mr. C. R. Mason, under the style of Mason, Shanahan & Company. In 1869 they dissolved and Mr. D. Shanahan formed the present firm, taking his sons, Messrs. C. M. and D. A. Shanahan into co-partnership, both of whom are experienced contractors and accomplished engineers. While the firm's headquarters have been permanently located in this city, they have extended their operations over a vast area of territory, accumulating their working plant, where the contract calls, and they are now engaged upon one of the most extensive undertakings of the age, namely the contract for the excavation of the famous Chicago drainage canal. They have a vast plant employing fully twelve hundred men upon the various sections. Among the great contracts for railroad construction executed by them are those for the National, Florence & Sheffield Railroad; the R. N. I. and B. Railroad from Versailles to Irving, Ky., at a cost of $290,000. The Chesapeake & Ohio Railroad from

Ashland to Cincinnati, O., including the famous Hunting bridge across the Ohio River from Covington to Cincinnati. They also constructed one-third of the entire road of the Kentucky Central extension from Paris, Ky., to Livingston, Ky. Mr. D. Shanahan was born in Ireland, and has spent fully two-thirds of his life in Allegheny County, Va. He is president of the famous Rich Patch Iron Company of Virginia, and has large interests in this city. The firm is to-day one of the most representative in its line in the United States, and Louisville is to be congratulated upon the permanent headquarters for its widely extended operations.

CHESS, WYMOND & CO.; Cooperage; No. 17 Board of Trade Building.—The leading cooperage house in the South is that of Messrs. Chess, Wymond & Co. of this city. They are the largest manufacturers of high-class tight barrels for liquors, oils and other liquids in the United States, and have long maintained the representative position in their line. Such an extensive industry, employing so many men, is one of great value to our city. The concern was established about seventeen years ago by Mr. W. E. Chess and Mr. W. S. Wymond, under the style of Chess & Wymond. In 1887 the interests were incorporated, thus continuing until 1893, when the present firm of Messrs. Chess, Wymond & Co. was formed as successors, the co-partners being Messrs. W. E. Chess, W. S. Wymond, C. S. Wymond, L. H. Wymond, A. Cunningham and C. M. Pate. These gentlemen are all practical cooperage manufacturers, and give the business their close personal attention. Their plant is extensive, covering an area of twelve acres. It is advantageously situated, having direct railroad connections, and the equipment of machinery is of the most elaborate character, run by four steam engines, of five hundred, one hundred and fifty, fifty, and thirty-five horse power respectively. The firm employs two hundred and fifty hands, and turns out twenty-five hundred barrels daily—largely, the best class of tight cooperage, specially designed for the storage of fine whiskies, brandies, wines, etc., also for oil manufacturers. The firm has developed a large patronage and its trade extends into every state in the Union from New England south to the gulf. They own large tracts of choice oak timber lands, whence they secure an abundant supply of standard staves. All their fine cooperage is strictly the best grade of work, made by the best machinery in the world. This extensive industry has been developed strictly on the basis of quality, no inferior materials or unskillful workmanship being allowed, and this is the place to have work done promptly at moderate prices. Mr. W. E. Chess is a native of Indiana. During the Civil War he was a lieutenant in the Twenty-first Indiana Artillery, and is a member of the Board of Trade. Mr. W. S. Wymond is also a native of Indiana, and is a member of the Board of Trade and of the Commercial Club. Mr. W. S. Wymond is chairman of the finance committee of the G. A. R., and was the principal means of bringing the Grand Army to Louisville. Mr. C. S. Wymond, his brother, is likewise a native of Indiana, and has been connected with the house for eight years. Mr. L. H. Wymond is a son of Mr. W. S. Wymond and joined the house some years ago. Mr. A. Cunningham is a native of Pennsylvania, identified with the house for eight years. Mr. C. M. Pate is a native of Kentucky, also identified with the house eight years ago. This house is a solid source of prosperity to the Falls City.

COOPER & CLARK; Electrical Specialties; Nos. 313 and 315 West Main Street.—This business was established three years ago by Messrs. L. H. Cooper and James Clark, Jr., both of whom are thoroughly practical and expert electricians and graduates in electricity at the Technological School, Boston, Mass., and occupy a spacious new four-story building situated at Nos. 313 and 315, West Main Street, which has an area of 17,000 square feet, the whole being utilized for stock, the workshops being in the rear. The workshops are fully equipped with modern tools and appliances and are in charge of Mr. C. F. Willey, a practical and able electrical engineer and machinist, who carefully supervises repairs and the fitting up of new plants before they are sent out. Messrs. Cooper & Clark keep in stock all kinds of electrical supplies and specialties, and are agents in Western Kentucky and Southern Indiana for the General Electric Company, of New York, manufacturers of motors, dynamos and all kinds of electrical goods. They are likewise agents for Messrs. Holmes, Booth & Hayden, Waterbury, Ct., manufacturers of copper wire, etc., Bryant Electrical Company, Bridgeport, Ct., general electric supplies, and are also sole agents for the Okonite wires and cables. They furnish complete plants for power or lighting either incandescent or arc, and have supplied plants for street lighting to Shelbyville, Ky.; Morganfield, Ky.; Corydon, Ind., and others to the entire satisfaction of patrons, also to the Galt House, Fifth Avenue Hotel, Enterprise Hotel, Crescent Bath House, etc., this city and power plants for street railways in Owensboro and Henderson, Ky.; Estimates are promptly furnished by the firm for electric plants, dynamos, etc., and they carefully superintend the construction and fitting up of all work entrusted to them according to the latest scientific and improved methods. From fifteen to twenty skilled workmen are constantly employed, and their work is highly endorsed by leading electrical engineers as being unrivalled for reliability, efficiency and perfect workmanship. Both partners are natives of this city. Their honorable business methods have secured for them the respect and esteem of a wide circle of business acquaintances, and no more reliable and skilful electrical engineers can be found in the ranks of the profession.

SULZER-VOGT MACHINE COMPANY; Manufacturers of Ice and Refrigerating Machinery, Etc.; East Main Street.—This great industry was established in 1872, by the firm of Tilley & Co., of which Mr. Henry Vogt was a member. The original firm was subsequently succeeded by that of Messrs. Sulzer & Vogt. In 1885 the business had grown to such proportions that Mr. Henry Vogt and his associates wisely decided to incorporate, which was done under the laws of this state, with an authorized capital of half a million dollars, of which $250,000 was paid in, and under the presidency of Mr. Henry Vogt, and Mr. Adam Vogt secretary and treasurer, the corporation has been remarkably prosperous. The buildings are all of a substantial character, specially designed for the purpose. The machine shop fronts on East Main Street, and is a very large three-story brick building, with boiler house adjoining. The office building and forging shop also front on East Main Street. The foundry, erecting and blacksmith shops are in rear, while there is also a fully equipped wood-working shop. The pipe fitting and tank shops are located on north side of Washington Street, and west of Preston Street, while the extensive boiler works are on the east side of Preston Street north of Washington Street, where they do sheet iron work and pipe bending. The works throughout are specially fitted up with the latest improved machinery and appliances, and about two hundred hands are here employed in the manufacture of the most improved type of ice machines for breweries, cold storage plants, ice making plants, etc. Besides ice machinery, refrigerating plants, etc., the company manufactures boilers for stationary and marine uses, hangers, pulleys, etc., and they make a specialty of elevators, and have placed on the market, the latest improved and most efficient electric elevator for passenger and freight services ever invented, and they have them in operation at Cincinnati, Indiana, Nashville, Chattanooga, and a large number in Louisville, and have just issued a pamphlet giving a full description of the same, which they will mail on application, and they also furnish catalogues of their ice and refrigerating machinery. Either for brewing, cold storage or artificial ice making purposes, their machines are the most practical, and embody every improvement, are all of best materials and perfect workmanship, while with such splendid facilities at command, the company can quote prices not possible to duplicate elsewhere.

HEINIG & CO.; Metal Novelties; Nos. 222-228 Eighth Street.—The manufacture of novelties in sheet metal is well represented in Louisville by a number of enterprising concerns which are known far and wide by the extent and quality of their output. Among them the house of Heinig & Co. fills a niche. They manufacture a line of metal goods, making specialties of combination lard pail covers, Overland and Locomotive oil cans being the best inventions of their kind on the market.

The land paid covers reduce the cost of packing, the Overhead oil can saves time and oil and the Locomotive, the great railroad oiler, saves at least thirty-three and one-third per cent. of oil. Mr. Heinig established his business on a nominal scale in 1882, his entire capital aggregating some $10 as opposed to a cash capital lying to his credit to-day of upwards of $35,000. Some idea of his success may be learned from the statement that he owns and occupies his present commodious plant consisting of a three-story and two two-story buildings, equipped with a twenty-five horse power steam engine and all modern machinery calculated to expedite the processes of manufact-

ure, including every description of lithographing on metal. Mr. Heinig gives steady employment to sixty-five skilled operatives. Many of the various appliances utilized are the outcome of Mr. Heinig's own inventive genius, and are duly covered by letters patent. Mr. Heinig is a native of St. Louis, where he learned every detail of this trade, and prior to locating at Louisville, was for some time favorably identified with this industry in New York city. He is the type of the self-made man who has risen to prominence by his own exertions, and enjoys the respect and esteem of both social and business circles. He is an active member of the Commercial Club and Order of the Knights of Pythias.

SOUTHERN CHAIR MANUFACTORY: Fred. Weikel, Proprietor; Nos. 1236 to 1241 Ninth Street.—Among the various business enterprises of Louisville none is more widely and favorably known than the Southern Chair Manufactory, owing both to its long and prosperous commercial existence and its reputation for supplying the trade with chairs of unequaled make at the lowest prices. The business was established in 1873 by Mr. John Glock, who united with him, two years later, Mr. Fred. Weikel. The concern under the firm name of Glock & Weikel, by their energy and enterprise succeeded in securing a trade, of the very best class, never losing any customer once made and adding largely to their number every year. In 1884 Mr. Glock retired leaving Mr. Fred. Weikel sole proprietor and manager. The concern occupies one of the largest factories owned by a single company in the city, an extensive three-story and a half brick structure, 90x130 feet in dimensions, surrounded by large yards. Steam power is utilized entirely in the plant which is equipped with a great variety of tools and machinery, and its superior equipment enables the factory to turn out two hundred dozen chairs weekly. The cane, rattan, and split seat chairs manufactured here are greatly preferred by the trade on account of their strength, durability, and general superior workmanship. A specialty is also made of upholstered and cobbler seat chairs and rockers of various sizes and styles. Their customers are found in all parts of Kentucky, Indiana, and Ohio, as well as throughout the entire South, and a large stock is always carried, which insures the prompt shipment of all orders. Mr. Weikel, the proprietor of the business is a native of Kentucky, and during his twenty-two years' experience in the chair business has mastered its smallest details, in addition to possessing the broad commercial knowledge necessary for the successful conduct of so large an enterprise, and is highly regarded in trade circles for his promptness in meeting his engagements and strict rectitude. He is fully alive to the necessity of keeping fully abreast of the times and the demands of the trade and is among the first to introduce the latest designs in chairs, that always command a ready sale.

THE MUTUAL LIFE INSURANCE COMPANY OF KENTUCKY; Corner of Fifth and Market Streets.—That talented, but somewhat eccentric American divine, the Rev. T. DeWitt Talmage is responsible for the utterance when speaking of the matter of life insurance, that "if a man could pay the premium on a policy, and neglect to do so it would be a mean thing for him to go up to heaven, while his family went to the poorhouse." And, as a matter of fact, the necessity of insuring one's life in this intelligent age is no longer a debatable question, the whole problem resolving itself into a decision of with which responsible company to place your risk. An organization, justly worthy of popular confidence in this section of the country, is the noted Mutual Life Insurance Company of Kentucky. This concern was organized under the usual state laws as the Southern Mutual Life Insurance Company in 1866, conforming to the requirements of insurance legislation four years later, the present corporate title being assumed in 1886. The company issues all the best forms of life and endowment policies, on the most equitable terms, and dividends may be reserved and the surplus and cash surrender value paid at any period of five years, or dividends may be applied on the second and subsequent payments to reduce the premiums or increase the insurance. This company enjoys an honored record, and has promptly paid every just claim. It has the reputation of being the oldest, staunchest and most reliable life insurance company in this state. The latest available statement of its affairs issued December 31st, 1894, go a long way towards verifying our remarks in this direction. The figures, in fact, speak for themselves, and furnish the best possible proofs of the continued integrity and solidity of The Mutual Life of Kentucky. The roster of the executive management embraces the subjoined list of prominent and successful men: Hon. Charles D. Jacob, president; George W. Morris, vice-president; Wm. W. Morris, secretary; David Meriwether, treasurer, and James B. Steedman, M. D., medical director.

LOUISVILLE STEAM FORGE COMPANY; Manufacturers of Car Axles, and other Forgings; Shipp Avenue, corner Sixth Street.—Among the great industries permanently located in Louisville is that of the "Louisville Steam Forge Company," manufacturers of the highest grade of car axles and other forgings including the best quality of shafting. The company was incorporated under the laws of Kentucky with an original paid-up capital of $50,000, since increased to $75,000. The late Dr. Norvin Green, with his sons, Messrs. Warren and John E. Green were the prime movers in the establishment of this industry. Upon the decease of Dr. Green, three years ago, (who at that time, and for many years previously, had been the president of the Western Union Telegraph Company, with headquarters in New York), Mr. Warren Green became president and treasurer; while Mr. John E. Green, retained the offices of vice-president and secretary, with Mr. Jacob Losey as superintendent. The plant covers about six acres, on the main line of the Louisville & Nashville Railroad. The equipment of machinery and appliances in the works is of the latest improved description, including four steam hammers, etc., and power is supplied by a fifty horse engine. From sixty to seventy-five hands are employed, turning out about five hundred axles a week besides shafting, etc. Mr. Losey was formerly the president of the "New Albany Steam Forge Company," and his skilled supervision insures a uniformity of quality in the products.

DR. J. A. KRACK; Druggist; Eighteenth and Chestnut Streets.—If there is one drug store in Louisville that is worthy of, and receives the confidence of the public it is that conducted by Dr. J. A. Krack. This is one of the oldest drug houses in the city, having been favorably known to the public for almost a half century. In 1851, at the corner of Shelby and Market Streets, Dr. Krack first opened business and after successfully conducting it for some years, gave up the drug business and established a glass factory. This also proved a success and was carried on until 1872, when it was given up and the drug business reinstated. The premises occupied are 25x100 feet in area and are artistic in their equipment. Nothing has been neglected to render the store at once attractive and convenient, while the laboratory, equipped with everything in the line of apparatus of modern style, is a model of up-to-date completeness. The stock carried embraces the purest drugs and chemicals, standard patent medicines, perfumery, toilet articles, etc., etc. All goods are purchased direct from the leading sources of supply while the various preparations put up by the house meet with especial favor. The compounding of physicians prescriptions and family recipes are made a specialty of. Dr. Krack was born in Carroll County, Md., but has resided in Louisville for the last forty-eight years. After graduating, with credit, from the Kentucky school of medicine in 1851, he began the practice of his profession at the same time conducting his pharmacy. He still practices medicine to some extent, his long medical experience and thorough knowledge rendering his services especially valuable in special cases. In public and business life in Louisville none of her citizens stand in higher esteem. Dr. Krack has filled successfully a great number of public positions. He was a member of the school board from 1852 to 1857; a member of the common council for the first ward from 1857 to 1858; from 1866 to 1871, was a member of the board of aldermen; from 1875 to 1886, one of the city assessors.

ARMSTRONG LUMBER COMPANY; Corner Twenty-seventh Street and Broadway.—Of the many industries belonging to a great city none occupies a wider sphere of usefulness than that of lumber and timber. Prominent among the leading concerns engaged in this business in Louisville well worthy of notice in the pages of this review ranks that of the Armstrong Lumber Company. This enterprise was incorporated under the laws of the state of Kentucky, in 1890, and has since enjoyed a prosperous career. The company has a cash capital stock of $20,000, and is ably officered as follows: Thomas Armstrong, president and treasurer, a native of New Albany, Indiana, now resident in Louisville for the past twenty-eight years. He is also a director of the Home and Savings Fund Company, the Builders' and Traders' Exchange, proprietor of the Pond River Saw Mills (the plant of which covers some eight hundred acres) and a prominent member of the Louisville Lumber Dealers' Association. Mr. C. F. Thomas has been manager since 1892, and is greatly respected for his ability and strict probity. The premises have an area of 208,670 feet, and are connected as regards transportation facilities with the Twenty-ninth Street switch of the Louisville and Southern Railroad, storage capacity being here provided for four million feet of lumber. The company are extensive manufacturers of and dealers in oak, poplar, ash, gum, elm, walnut, and pine lumber, likewise joists, scantling, flooring, siding, fencing, posts, shingles, sheeting, doors, blinds, etc. The trade of the house extends throughout the entire state, Indiana, and also Chicago. Estimates are furnished promptly on application, and orders are not only filled with promptness and dispatch, but the facilities of supply controlled by the company are such as to enable it to quote figures to builders, contractors, carpenters and large consumers that few of its competitors in the lumber trade in this section of the country can profitably afford to duplicate.

JOHN F. SEEBOLD; Wholesale and Retail Dealer in Pittsburg Coal; No. 227 Third Street.—No business interest is more important to Louisville than that of the coal trade. In this connection we desire to make mention of the reliable establishment of John F. Seebold, dealer in Pittsburg coal. Twenty-two years ago, under the style of Rogers & Seebold this house was established and conducted until six years ago when Mr. Seebold became sole proprietor. The yards are spacious, 60x210 feet in area, with extensive dock frontage, and are equipped with every facility. Large storage sheds are provided and four barges are owned by the house. The amount handled annually, is about sixty-five thousand tons, requiring the employment of thirty workmen and twelve teams. The trade is wholesale and retail, extending throughout Louisville and vicinity. Both hard and soft coal is handled, the specialty however, being the celebrated "Pittsburg bituminous coal," which is admitted to be unrivaled for steam and manufacturing purposes. Orders for a ton or car lot are filled, and great care characterizes all operations. Mr. John F. Seebold was born in Jefferson County, Ky., but has resided most of his life in Louisville. He is a prominent member of the Board of Trade and the Masonic Order, and is secretary of the Louisville Coal Exchange. Progressive, and honorable, Mr. Seebold is classed among Louisville's influential citizens, whose efforts have made her what she is to-day.

ACME BRICK COMPANY Manufacturers of Vitrified Street Paving and Hard Building Brick; Office, Room 905 Columbia Building.—In 1892 under the style of the Acme Vitrified Brick Company, this enterprise was established to manufacture vitrified street paving brick, and was thus conducted for two years, when, in April, 1894, in order to enlarge the scope of operations, it was reorganized and the present style "Acme Brick Company," was adopted. The company is incorporated under the laws of Kentucky, with ample capital, and the officers being, president, Charles R. Long; vice-president, Fred. Hoertz, and general manager, G. K. Bikes. They manufacture vitrified street paving and hard building brick, and the works are located at Cloverport, Kentucky. These cover an area of forty acres and the various departments contain all the latest appliances for rapid and perfect production. Six kilns are in operation and the output amounts to fifty thousand brick daily, thirty-five workmen being employed in the different departments. The trade extends to all parts of the South and West, no similar products enjoying greater popularity than these. These unrivaled brick have been used in the following buildings, etc., to the entire satisfaction of patrons, viz: Ahrens & Ott Manufacturing Company's building, Louisville Jockey Club House, Paul C. Bath Engine House, residence of Wm. McCauley, of the McCauley Opera House, etc., while in street paving, Third, Twenty-sixth, Twenty-fourth, Twenty-eighth, Main, etc., in Louisville and numerous streets in St. Louis, Memphis, Nashville, New Orleans and many other cities have been paved by them. The officers of the company are too well known to require extended introduction from us, Charles R. Long being also president of the Louisville Water Works Company, and the Car Roofing Company, while Mr. Hoertz is a director of the Union National Bank and the National Building and Loan Association. Mr. G. K. Bikes, the general manager, has been identified with the enterprise since 1894. He was formerly deputy sheriff for Jefferson County for twelve years, and is a director of the Louisville Turnpike Company.

LOUISVILLE OF TO-DAY.

J. S. MINOR & SONS: Contractors; No. 1815 Garland Ave.—Twenty years ago Mr. J. S. Minor commenced business as a millwright and machinist, and after successfully operating in that line for ten years, turned his attention to contracting and building. In December, 1884, Mr. Minor admitted into partnership his sons, E. T. and O. R. Minor, and the present style of "J. S. Minor & Sons" was adopted. They make a specialty of

Bonded Warehouse, near Lawrenceburg, Ky., built by J. S. Minor and Sons.

building warehouses and distilleries, and in this line are unsurpassed, and have erected every new bonded warehouse in Louisville during the last three years. The yards are 250x200 feet in area, while the lumber yards cover an acre of ground. Four portable steam plants of twenty horse power each are used by the firm, these being transferred to whatever place they are working. From one hundred to two hundred skilled workmen are employed and the trade comes from all parts of the South and West. Among some of the large contracts executed by the house may be mentioned a distillery for J. T. S. Brown & Sons, of Louisville, cost $40,000; distillery for John T. Barbier, at Woodford, Ky.; High Wine distillery plant, capacity six thousand five hundred bushels of grain a day, cost $150,000; fire proof bonded warehouse for Rosenfeld Bros., of Chicago, located at Twenty-eighth Street, Louisville; grain elevator for the Cleveland Grain Elevator Company of Cleveland, Ohio; dryer plant for the Chicago Grain Elevator Company at Clybourne Avenue, Chicago; dryer plant for S. G. Greenbaum, of Midland, Ky.; Columbia Laundry of Louisville, Ky.; bonded warehouse for J. S. Roach & Co., distillers, etc., etc. This firm has invented a machine for preparing lumber, brick and stone for building purposes and erecting same, all being done by machinery. This device was exhibited at the World's Fair and received the highest commendation. From the list of buildings we have given, the extent of the firm's operations will be rendered more apparent to our readers than by any words we could employ. Mr. J. S. Minor is one of the most influential and public-spirited citizens of Louisville and is too well known to require further comments at our hands. His sons, Messrs. E. T. and O. R. Minor, are young men of wide experience and ability and have signally aided in bringing the business to its present prosperous condition.

WM. KELLY: Groceries, Wines, Liquors, Cigars and Tobacco; Corner of Twenty-second and Duncan Streets.—A prominent establishment in this section of Louisville is that of Mr. Wm. Kelly, the popular dealer in fancy and staple groceries, etc. This business was established sixteen years ago by Mr. Kelly who has since secured a liberal patronage. He conducts not only a grocery but also a saloon, the entrance to the latter being on Twenty-second Street. The grocery is well appointed and the stock includes fresh crop teas, coffees, spices, dried fruits, canned goods, butter, eggs, provisions, etc. Only the purest and best goods are handled, and the prices quoted cannot be discounted in the city. In the saloon Mr. Kelly handles only the choicest wines, liquors, brandies, cigars, etc. He was born in Ireland and came to Louisville twenty-four years ago, and is highly esteemed by the community for his strict integrity, and is an active member of the Catholic Knights of America.

RUDOLPH & BAUER; Wholesale and Retail Candies; No. 234 West Market Street.—Americans are the largest consumers of confectionery in the world, and a representative house in Louisville actively engaged in the wholesale and retail trade, is that of Messrs. Rudolph and Bauer, whose premises are fitted up in the most tasteful and attractive manner, the heavy stock of caramels, creams, marsh mallows, etc., being displayed to the very best advantage. A complete line is also carried at

Interior view Rudolph & Bauer Candy Store.

their other retail establishment at No. 515 Fourth Avenue. This concern was established by the present co-partners, Messrs. Joseph Rudolph and Frederick A. Bauer in 1889, at No. 224 West Market Street, where they commenced manufacturing their own candies for their retail store on Market Street, where they soon won for themselves substantial patronage. A force of experienced hands is employed, and their goods are noted for their fine flavor and absolute purity. They are to-day the largest retail confectioners in the city. Mr. Rudolph superintends the factory, while Mr. Bauer attends to the wholesale department. Both partners have gained the confidence of the purchasing public, by their fair and liberal dealings which have ever characterized all their transactions.

HWEIRICH; Manufacturer of Boots and Shoes; No. 328 Fifth Avenue.—Who is there that has not experienced the misery caused by an ill-fitting and badly made boot or shoe, and on the contrary what ease and comfort are obtained by having these indispensable articles made by a first-class bootmaker. For the benefit of those of our readers, who are suffering from the effects of badly fitting shoes in Louisville, the house of Mr. H. Weirich is mentioned as being unexcelled in the manufacture of the finest grades of ladies' and gentlemen's footwear. This business was established twenty-three years ago by Mr. H. Weirich, who has since secured a liberal patronage, numbering among his permanent customers many of the leading families and citizens of the Falls City. The store is well equipped, and Mr. Weirich, who is one of the ablest shoe-makers in the country, combines comfort, elegance and durability. He employs only first-class workmen, while he uses only the best leather and findings, all work being handsewed, and the prices are extremely moderate for such excellent goods. Every pair of shoes made here is fully warranted, and the trade of the house extends throughout the city and state. Mr. Weirich was born in Germany, but has resided here since 1865. He is highly esteemed for his skill and integrity, and we cordially recommend him to our readers, as one justly meriting their patronage. Persons residing in the country can have an accurate fit by sending one of their shoes to Mr. Weirich, and a simple outline drawing of the foot, which is made by placing the foot on a piece of paper, and drawing a pencil around it.

FALLS CITY BUGGY TOP COMPANY; No. 116 West Main Street.—One of the most noted establishments in its line in Louisville, is the Falls City Buggy Top Company, conducted under the able proprietorship of Messrs. Robert O. and Thomas H. Rubel. This prosperous concern was established by its present proprietors four years ago, who by strict attention to business have since succeeded in rearing an extensive patronage, which is broadly distributed throughout the entire South and Southwest. Operations were first commenced at No. 372 East Main Street, removal being made to the present quarters during the current year. They consist of a substantial three-storied and basement building, 25x210 feet in area, thoroughly equipped with all the latest tools and appliances for the reproduction of strictly handmade goods. Fifteen skilled hands are employed, the range of manufacture embracing tops, cushions and buggy trimmings of every description, a large and comprehensive stock of which is invariably kept on hand for the accommodation of the trade, and the steady demand for these goods testifies to their high quality, character, usefulness and superiority, and only the best materials are used and the highest skilled labor is employed. Both members of the concern are natives of Louisville, Mr. E. O. Rubel being engaged with Messrs. I. F. Stone & Son, carriagemakers and dealers in wood work supplies, the active management of the enterprise devolving upon Mr. T. H. Rubel. The latter gentleman is likewise a member of the Order of Chosen Friends and an active Freemason.

KENTUCKY PLANING MILL; G. E. Moody, & Co.; Ninth Street, near Broadway.—Planing mills are to builders a most important factor and the number that are located in Louisville has created a great competition in this branch of industry. In this connection we make special reference in this volume, to the old established enterprise, known as the Kentucky Planing Mill now operated under the able proprietorship of Messrs. G. E. Moody & Co., which was founded thirty-eight years ago by Mr. John Christopher, several changes in proprietorship having since occurred, the present firm consisting of Messrs. G. E. Moody and John Mitchell succeeding to the control in 1878. The plant covers a ground area of forty thousand square feet, the mill being a substantial three-storied brick structure having a frontage and depth of 100x200 feet equipped with all the latest wood working machinery operated by steam power, the balance of the premises being devoted to yards, shedding, etc. Forty to fifty skilled hands are employed, the output consisting of sash, blinds, doors, mouldings, flooring, ceiling and all kinds of building lumber, rough and dressed, a specialty being made of the construction of stairways. The trade of the house is chiefly among our leading city and suburban contractors and builders. This firm supplied the interior woodwork for the Presbyterian Church, Second Street and Broadway ; the Broadway Baptist Church, the Theological Seminary, the Kenyon Building, Columbia Club, City Hall, etc., etc., L. & N. Depot and Custom House, Quincy Ill.; Custom House, and post-office at Lynchburg Va., Oxford Miss., and Frankfort, Ky. Mr. Moody is a native of Henry County, this state, and has resided in Louisville since 1857. Mr. Mitchell is of Scotch nationality but has made the Falls City his home for many years. Apart from this interest he is likewise one of our leading contractors and builders.

T. C. COLEMAN; Steam and Street Railway Supplies; No. 232 West Main Street.—Prominent among those in Louisville, who have built up an excellent reputation for handling first-class goods is Mr. T. C. Coleman, the widely-known manufacturers' agent in steam and street railway supplies. Mr. Coleman, who is an able mechanical engineer and machinist, established this business in 1876, and his patronage now extends throughout the entire United States. He has influential connections with some of our most celebrated manufacturers, and represents in Louisville, the following first-class companies, etc., viz: The Weir Frog Company, Cincinnati, O., street railway frogs, crossings, etc.; Anderson, Dupuy & Co., Pittsburg, Pa., spiral steel springs, bar steel; Cleveland City Forge and Iron Company, forgings, railroad axles, etc.; Latrobe Steel Works, Latrobe, Pa., locomotive tire, etc.; Chicago Tire and Spring Company; the Johnston Company, Johnston, Pa., steel street girder rails, etc.; the Hale & Kilburn Manufacturing Company, Philadelphia, Pa., railroad seats and chairs ; Missouri Car and Foundry Company, St. Louis, Mo., railroad cars, axles, etc., and several others. Mr. Coleman promptly fills orders at manufacturers' prices, the goods and supplies, which are unrivalled in America or Europe, are shipped direct from the works and factories. He was born in Cork, Ireland, but was brought up and educated in Louisville, and is highly esteemed for his ability and probity, and is a popular member of the American Society of Engineers, and was formerly president of the Louisville Rolling Mill Company, now out of existence, and also secretary and a stockholder in the Johnson Company.

WILLIAM KOPP; Manufacturer of Wardrobes, Safes, Tables, and Furniture Ornaments; Main, Twenty-first and Crop Streets.—In no line of industry has such marked advancement been made of late years, as in the manufacture of furniture. A leading establishment in this line is that of William Kopp, which he established thirteen years ago. Mr. Kopp commenced business, devoting himself at that time to the furniture trimming trade, and successfully conducting it until 1884, when he established his present industry. He manufactures a variety of articles, making a specialty of wardrobes, safes, tables, refrigerators, china closets, furniture ornaments, etc., which are unsurpassed in the market. The premises have an area of 140x250 feet, and here is erected a spacious modern factory, 80x140 feet in dimensions, two stories high. Wood-working machinery and other appliances are provided through all departments, and motive force is furnished by a fifty horse power engine. Sixty experienced workmen are employed, and two million feet of lumber are consumed annually. Only the best seasoned woods are used, and the workmanship is of the highest order. Beauty and originality of design characterizes all goods made here and these find ready sales through all parts of the South and West. Mr. Kopp was born in Germany, and came to Louisville thirty years ago. He is a member of the Liedekranz and other organizations, and takes rank with our most esteemed and successful citizens, and we bespeak for this house a bright future.

KENTUCKY TITLE COMPANY; No. 234 Fifth Street.—All owners of property are agreed on the desirability of having a policy of title insurance, the only question arising, is which corporation engaged in the issuance of these policies in Louisville is most judiciously organized. We unhesitatingly affirm that the Kentucky Title Company, of the Falls City, completely meets the wants of the public in this direction, and under its present efficient management, fully enjoys the confidence of conservative property owners. This company was incorporated as the Louisville Abstract Association in 1874, the title under reorganized management taking place later, when the company's affairs were conducted under the style of the Louisville Abstract and Loan Association, the present corporate title being assumed in 1887. This is the only organization in Louisville authorized by law to guarantee or insure titles, no other company having the requisite capital or such legal authority. The maintenance of a permanent guaranty fund is required by the state, not to be less than $80,000, which in the instance of this progressive corporation is now $100,000, the paid-up general capitalization being $250,000. The officers of the company are as follows: Embry L. Swearingen, president, succeeding his father to such office during the current year. He is a native of this city, and has now been associated with this company since 1891, a director of the Union National Bank and member of the Pendennis Club; R. T. Durrett, vice-president, attorney-at-law; Chas. M. Lindsay, attorney; W. C. Priest, appraiser, real estate operator.

WATKINS & COWLES; Coke, Coal, Scrap, Pig Iron, Etc.; No. 215 Sixth Street.—Prominent among the representatives in the coal, coke, and pig iron trade of Louisville, is that of Messrs. Watkins & Cowles. This business was established January 1st, 1892, by Messrs. Adams and Watkins, who conducted it till January 1st, 1894, when Mr. John H. Cowles became a partner. Mr. Adams retired March 1st, 1894, and the business is now the property of Messrs. W. J. Watkins and John H. Cowles, the former of whom was previously for twenty-five years bookkeeper for the firm of Geo. S. Moore & Co., of this city, in the same line of trade. They are honorable and able business men, whose connections are of a most influential character, thus enabling them to offer substantial advantages to patrons. Their yards which are supplied with every convenience, shedding, etc., are situated at Thirteenth and High Streets and Fulton and Brook Streets, and here they keep a heavy and carefully selected stock of foundry and furnace coke, blacksmithing coal, scrap and pig iron, also sewer pipe, chimney tops, fire brick, fire clay, terra cotta, etc. Orders are filled at lowest rates, and the trade of the house now extends throughout Kentucky and the southern states. The sales of the firm which are steadily increasing amount to about $60,000 annually. Both partners are natives of this city, Mr. Cowles being treasurer of the Globe Building and Loan Company, whose office is situated in that of this firm.

PABST BREWING COMPANY; Frank E. Gazzolo, Louisville, Manager; No. 1328 Jefferson Street.—It is an interesting fact that Louisville has within her limits a thoroughly equipped branch of one of the most noted breweries in the world, whose output carries with it the unqualified endorsement of the press, the public and the medical profession. This is the famous "Pabst Brewing Company" of Milwaukee, Wisconsin, whose interests in this great southern distributive centre are ably looked after by Mr. Frank L. Gazzolo. The success of this colossal concern has been so publicly portrayed in the elaborate printed matter issued by the company that we shall content ourselves in this place, with the simple recapitulation of the more salient points as they affect the admirably appointed branch of the "Pabst Brewing Company," located here in the Falls City. The present premises were erected for the purpose in November, 1894, the ground area, covering 60x210 feet; the main building rising two stories in height and equipped throughout with the latest improved machinery and appliances. Some criterion may be formed of the business done by this company from this point from the statement that the sales from this branch alone reaches four hundred thousand dollars per annum. To dilate upon the superlative qualities of the "Pabst" brand of draught or bottled lager beer would be superfluous on our part. Suffice it to say that it is simply one of the most palatable malt beverages on the market, of a beautiful clearness and bright color, delicious flavor and having all the tonic properties and strengthening elements found in this class of liquids—their "Select," "Bohemian and Hoffran" brands being specially recommended for table use and invalids by the medical profession. The company's Bohemian beer is sold in kegs and bottles, while "Standard" is sold in kegs only. The "Best" tonic is carried in stock for supplying the jobbing trade for the south.

130 — — LOUISVILLE OF TO-DAY. — —

HENRY DISSTON & SONS (Incorporated); Proprietors Keystone Saw, Tool, File and Steel Works; No. 923 West Main Street.—The development of Louisville as one of the great commercial distributing centres of the Southwest, for every class of manufactured goods combines to render it of the utmost importance to the leading establishments of the United States to be directly represented in the Falls City. In this connection we desire to refer to the famous house of Messrs. Henry Disston & Sons, proprietors of the Keystone Saw, Tool, Steel and File Works of Philadelphia, whose interests here are represented by Mr. Frank E. Gould. The record of this time-honored house is an unprecedented one, to-day the concern ranking as the largest of its kind in the world, while their primary capital in 1843 was represented by but three hundred and fifty dollars. The house has now had representation here for the past twelve years, the trade here controlled heavily radiating throughout Kentucky, West Virginia, Indiana, Tennessee, Missouri, Ohio, Alabama and a part of Illinois. The premises occupied in this city consist of a substantial three-storied and basement building, 25x100 feet in dimensions, the range of manufacture in Louisville being fully equipped for manufacturing circular saws. Twenty hands are employed, and a full line of the Disston Company's general output is at all times carried, including saws of every description for saw mills, planing mills, spoke and stave factories, files and rasps of every description, scroll saws and band saws and brazing outfits, emery wheel grinding machines, saw clamps, anvils, hammers and straight edges, board and log rules, mill and Peavey cant hooks, pike poles, cables, etc., a special feature being made of the repair of saws at short notice. Mr. Gould is a Philadelphian by birth, and for fifteen years prior to accepting the Louisville superintendency, was connected with the home office of the house. He is a member of the Commercial Club, and has a wide business and social acquaintance throughout the southern states.

S. ZORN & CO.; Receivers and Shippers of Grain; Nos. 60, 61 and 62 Board of Trade.—Louisville, both by reason of her excellent railway connections, river and terminal facilities, has become one of the leading points in the South for the receipt and handling of grain, while additional factors in building up her extensive trade in this line are the ample resources and enterprise of her leading merchants and receivers. In this connection prominent reference is made to the reliable house of Messrs. S. Zorn & Co., receivers and shippers of all kinds of grain. Mr. Zorn, who is sole proprietor, commenced business in this line in 1880, since which period he has built up a liberal and influential patronage, shipping largely wheat, oats, rye and corn to all sections of the United States. His connections are of a superior character, including leading consignees of grain all over the middle, western and northwestern states, while his facilities are strictly first-class, enabling him to promptly handle the largest consignments, advancing to any extent upon the same, and giving his patrons the benefits of the most favorable quotations on change. He is a native of Louisville, and his success in the grain trade has been achieved solely on the basis of a strict adherence to principles of equity. He is a director of the Short Line Railroad and is ex-vice-president and a member of the grain committee of the Board of Trade, and has given a cordial support to all measures best calculated to promote the permanent welfare of this important organization. He is also an active member of the Pendennis and Fine Caste Clubs, and is very popular in social circles.

H. W. RICHARDSON & CO.; Distillers and Wholesale Dealers in Kentucky Whiskies; No. 221 West Market Street.—The art of distilling in the United States, and notably in Kentucky, has made remarkable progress, and it is in this connection we make due reference in this review to the house of Messrs. H. W. Richardson & Co., the well-known distillers and wholesale dealers in Kentucky whiskies. This old established concern was founded by the late Mr. George D. Richardson in 1859, who retired in 1893, and was succeeded by his two sons, the present proprietors. The premises occupied consist of a substantial three-storied brick building, 25x100 feet in dimensions, utilized for office, duty-paid storage and bottling purposes. The distillery is situated in Meade County, and enjoys

All band saws six inches and wider are made from our Special Aluminum Steel, and are hardened and tempered by our special process, which none others possess.

the distinction of being one of the only three in the state, where the strictly old style sour-mash process is in operation, the output capacity being fifteen barrels of the celebrated old Richardson brand of whiskey daily, and attached to the distillery are two bonded and free warehouses with storage capacity for eight thousand five hundred barrels, cheaper qualities than the concern's specialty being carried in stock to meet the requirements of the trade, and the patronage of the house extends throughout Kentucky, Tennessee, Indiana, Illinois and Wisconsin, and under able management and a scrupulous maintainance of the high-class quality of the liquors made and handled, is annually growing in volume and value. Messrs. Richardson are natives of Meade County, where the family resides, exception being made in the case of H. W. Richardson, who manages the business in this city.

JACOB SEIBERT; Wall Paper, Window Shades, Etc.; No. 1306 South Side Market, between Thirteenth and Fourteenth Streets.—This is an age of decoration, and within a comparatively few years, it has been the subject of many improvements, the nature of which may easily be discovered by a visit to the Louisville establishment of Mr. Jacob Seibert, dealer in wall paper, window shades, etc. This business was established in 1860 by Mr. Seibert, who has since secured a liberal patronage in the city and state. The store is fully stocked with a superior assortment of the choicest imported and domestic wall papers, with dados and friezes to match, also window shades, mouldings, picture frames, table and floor oil-cloth, etc.,—gold and highly colored parlor and dining-room papers are shown here, while subdued and rich library paperings in imitation of leather, carved oak and walnut friezes to match are kept in stock, also felt papers of all grades and shades are displayed in bewildering variety. Mr. Seibert makes a specialty of paper hanging in all its branches, and has papered and decorated some of the finest residences, stores, hotels, etc., in the city, and his work is highly endorsed by experts for its elegance, finish and artistic beauty, while his prices are noted for their moderation. He was born in Germany in 1844, and came to Louisville with his parents in 1851, and is highly regarded for his artistic taste and strict probity, and those giving orders to him for paper hanging, etc., will secure the greatest satisfaction. During the civil war, Mr. Seibert served for three years in the Thirty-fourth Kentucky Volunteer Infantry, and was noted for his devotion to the cause of the Union. He is a prominent Freemason and an active member of the I. O. O. F., and was one of the building committee in the erection of St. Peters' Evangelical Lutheran Church, which is located on Jefferson Street, between Twelfth and Thirteenth Streets.

LOUISVILLE SEWER PIPE WORKS; P. Bannon, Proprietor; No. 421 West Jefferson Street.—One of the most progressive manufacturers of this city is Mr. P. Bannon, whose works are turning out the highest grade known to the trade of sewer pipe, drain tile, terra cotta, fireproofing and vitrified paving brick. Mr. Bannon is a native of County Down, Ireland, and has been a permanent resident of this city for the past forty-two years, and has now the entire confidence of his fellow citizens and numerous customers. In 1852 he started in the plastering business, and in 1868 commenced the manufacture of terra cotta, and in 1869 commenced the manufacture of sewer pipe. From a small beginning this has grown to be one of the most important industries of the kind in the United States.

The works for the manufacture of sewer pipe, terra cotta and fireproofing are situated at Thirteenth and Lexington Streets, and cover an area of four acres. The present plant was first erected in 1868, and goods are shipped direct in car lots to any point in the Union at lowest freight rates. The latest improved machinery has been introduced, and there are twenty-five large kilns in operation. All the standard sizes of vitrified salt glazed sewer pipe are manufactured here, from two to thirty inch diameters, also all the necessary bends, branches, reducers, increasers, taps, etc., and other staple lines produced here are fire clay flue and chimney linings, stove thimbles, fire clay stove pipe, chimney tops, etc., another specialty is Mr. Bannon's wall coping, a thoroughly vitrified fire clay tile, baked as hard as the granite rock itself, with surface smooth as glass and will last forever. Fire brick, boiler and grate tile and fire clay goods of every description are also manufactured, also terra cotta and fireproofing, which have been used extensively in the Louisville Trust Company building, to the extent of $15,000 worth, also in the immense Jackson Building in Nashville, Tenn., to the extent of $20,000; in the Kentucky National Bank building of this city, etc., etc. Mr. Bannon is also president and owns controlling interest in the Kentucky Vitrified Paving Brick Company, which was established three years ago, the plant being located on Magnolia Avenue, and covers an area of two acres. Mr. Bannon is universally respected as an enterprising and public spirited citizen. He is a member of the Board of Trade, and devotes close personal supervision to the important concerns controlled and owned by him. The office is centrally located, where orders can be placed and samples of his products be inspected. He is ably assisted by his son, Mr. M. J. Bannon, who is general manager not only of the Louisville Sewer Pipe Works, but also of the Fire Proof Construction Company. He was born in 1862, was educated at St. Xavier's College, this city, and graduated in 1878, and has general supervision of all the work of both companies.

THE J. M. CLARK PICKLE COMPANY; Nos. 136 to 142 Second Street. — This time-honored and flourishing concern dates its commercial existence half a century, it having been founded by Mr. Samuel Hyman in 1845. It was so conducted till the year 1880, when Mr. J. M. Clark succeeded to the proprietorship, he subsequently forming a co-partnership with Mr. Thomas L. Jefferson, and conducting the business under the firm style of J. M. Clark & Company. The concern became a corporate organization in accordance with the state laws in 1894, with a cash capitalization of $20,000, the personnel of the present executive management being as follows: John R. King, president; Wallace G. Miller, vice-president; R. E. King, secretary and treasurer. The premises occupied comprise a substantial three-storied and basement building, 104x248 feet in dimensions, admirably adapted for the purposes of the business as follows: basement, steam power and heating apparatus; first floor, general office shipping and ketchup mixing departments; second floor, bottling; third floor, sweet pickle packing and bottling of specialties. Here a force of twenty men and eighty-five girls is provided with constant employment, the range of production embracing Hyman sweet pickles, sweet cucumber mangoes, sweet cantaloupe and bell pepper mangoes, yellow cabbage pickles, "baby" gherkins, chow-chow, Spanish relish, East India chop, Mexican lillybot, Tamazula pepper sauce, pickled onions, Hyman's Worcestershire sauce, American and bluegrass tomato ketchup, French mustard, Spanish olives, pickled peaches, cider vinegar, English mixed and German dill pickles, sour kraut, etc., etc. The company operate a five hundred acre farm at Grovertown, Ind., four hundred acre farm near Knox, Ind., as also a farm in Mexico for the rearing of Tamazula peppers, each place being provided with brining houses, and the product therefrom being shipped to Louisville for bottling and general packing. Apart from an immense immediately local patronage, a large, lucrative and steadily growing trade is enjoyed which radiates broadly over the United States and Canada, irrespective of influential export connections, reared exclusively on the absolute merits and uniformly high standard of the pickles, sauces and condiments turned out from this old established and thoroughly representative concern.

LEAHY & SCANLON; Dealers in Coal; No. 355 Fifth Street.—It is safe to say that Louisville depends for its permanent prosperity upon the single article coal more than upon any other substance yielded us by a beautiful nature. It is not singular, therefore, that the Falls City should have become one of the principal coal centres of the United States, and one of the leading houses engaged in this business here is that of Messrs. Leahy & Scanlon, wholesale and retail dealers in anthracite and bituminous coal, whose office is located at No. 355 Fifth Street near Jefferson Street, and scales and yards on Kentucky Avenue, between Thirteenth and Fourteenth Streets. This business was established in 1870 by Mr. J. K. Leahy, who conducted it till 1883, when Mr. S. S. Gorham became a partner. Mr. Gorham retired in 1891 when Mr. D. Scanlon purchased his interest and was admitted into partnership, the firm being known as "Leahy & Scanlon." They get their supply of Kentucky coal from the celebrated Taylor mines, Ohio County, the product of which has been shown by analysis and by some tests to be one of the most economical and reliable fuels in the market. The Taylor coal is especially adapted for use in glass works, rolling mills, locomotives and for household and steam generating purposes. Orders for car lots of anthracite or bituminous coal are promptly filled at lowest rates, the firm quoting bottom figures to factories and dealers. The yard has a storage capacity of one hundred thousand bushels of coal and ten men and a number of teams are constantly employed. They are also sole agents in the Falls City for the widely known Princeton line, which is a general favorite with leading contractors and builders. Messrs. Leahy & Scanlon were born in Ireland and came to Louisville, the former in 1854 and the latter in 1868. Mr. Leahy first settled in Cincinnati, O., in 1847, and afterwards commenced business in Louisville, while Mr. Scanlon was previously, for twenty years, a master mechanic for the Louisville & Nashville Railroad. They are honorable business men and their success is as substantial as it is well merited.

JOSEPH COYNE; Railroad Contractor; No. 339 West Main Street.—The construction of a railway is the business of contractors, who execute the works by estimate, according to the plans and specifications of the engineers. A prominent exponent of this important industry in Louisville is Mr. Joseph Coyne, the widely-known railroad contractor. Born in Nashville, Tenn., he has from his first entry upon commercial pursuits, been closely identified with railroad construction and equipment, and during his twenty-two years of association therewith, has acquired a thorough practical knowledge of its special requirements, as also the necessities or essentials for street laying. He first engaged in the business at Jeffersonville, Indiana, taking up his headquarters in the Falls City some ten years ago. Since that period he has successfully completed a series of important contracts, notable among which may be mentioned thirteen miles of track work, for the Louisville and Nashville Railroad, elevated railroad on the Ohio River, portion of the masonry work on the Louisville and Southern Railroad, twenty-seven blocks of street laying for the city of Louisville during the past year, and he has just secured the contract to build the new connection between Shelbyville and Bagdad for the L. & N. Railroad Company. Mr. Coyne is ready to begin work on the new line immediately, and will start to work at an early date. The distance between Shelbyville and Bagdad is eight miles and one-half, and it will be well into the next winter or spring before the connection can be completed. No matter the magnitude of the commission, Mr. Coyne is ready to figure upon and bring to a successful termination, any railway contract, oftentimes employing one thousand men. Personally he is generally respected throughout municipal, financial and railroad circles—no commendatory comment these pages could bestow being capable of additional endorsement to his activity and enterprise throughout the Southwest.

L. D. PEARSON & SON; Funeral Directors and Embalmers; Nos. 220 to 224 Jefferson Street.—Among the leading representatives of the undertaking profession in Louisville, there is no concern more highly regarded and few enjoy a more liberal patronage than that of Messrs. L. D. Pearson & Son, the noted funeral directors and embalmers. This time-honored enterprise dates its existence back some forty-seven years, it having been founded by Mr. L. D. Pearson in 1848. The subsequent changes were primarily Pearson and Caudry, then Pearson and King, till in 1864, Mr. L. D. Pearson reassumed the sole control, twelve years later the present firm style being adopted on the admission of his son, Mr. F. C. Pearson to an interest in the business. The premises occupied comprise a substantial two-storied brick building, with a frontage of seventy-five feet on Jefferson Street, extending through to Green Street, augmented by commodious stables. The firm has constantly on hand in its warerooms a complete stock of everything required, embracing coffins and caskets, and all necessary articles pertaining to funerals—three hearses, twenty horses, and a series of carriages constituting the stable complement. Remains are taken in charge at any hour, embalming is effected according to the most approved processes, interments are procured in any of the city or suburban cemeteries, and funerals personally directed in first-class style—the charges being based on a scale of moderation. Mr. Pearson enjoys the distinction of being the first to introduce the popular metallic caskets in this section. Mr. Pearson, Sr., was born in Shelby County, Kentucky, and is a member of the Commercial Club, Knights Templar, and a thirty-second degree Freemason. His son, upon whom the active management of the business devolves, is a native of this city, and is president of the Falls City Funeral Directors' Association.

J. S. WALKER & CO.; Manufacturers of Burlap Bags, Etc.; No. 136 Fourth Street.—The great quantity of burlap and other bags, required for the transportation of grain, wool, etc., causes their manufacture and sale to be a most important industry in the United States. Prominent among the reliable houses in this line in Louisville is that of Messrs. J. S. Walker & Co., the widely-known manufacturers of burlap bags and twines. This business was established in 1876 by Mr. R. H. Robinson, who conducted it till 1886, when Mr. J. S. Walker became sole proprietor. Mr. Walker was born in Indiana, and came here with his parents when only six months old, and was formerly in the commission business with his father on Third Street. He is an able business man, who imports his burlaps direct from Calcutta, India, and turns out all kinds of bags, that are unsurpassed for quality of material, strength and finish. The premises occupied comprise a large three-story brick building 25x110 feet in area, the first floor being devoted to offices and salesrooms, while the other floors are utilized for factory and storage purposes. The factory is supplied with modern machinery, cutting and sewing machines, operated by electric power and seven thousand bags are turned out daily. Mr. Walker manufactures and keeps in stock all grades of twines and bagging, including oats, corn, wheat, peanut, collar and wool bags, also sugar bags, orchard grass bags and others, while he likewise handles burlap goods for furniture packing and other purposes, and the prices quoted in all cases cannot be discounted in this city or elsewhere. Orders are filled with dispatch, and the trade of the house now extends throughout all sections of Kentucky and Indiana. Mr. Walker is highly regarded for his strict integrity, and his success is as substantial, as it is well merited.

A. H. McATEE & CO.; Insurance; No. 709 West Main Street.—The insurance companies of the world must always take a prominent place as institutions beneficient and practical and indispensable to the present state of civilization. The large aggregate of capital, as represented in the property and shipping of Louisville has not only proved a fertile field for home institutions, but has encouraged many others in various

sections of the country, and also in England, to place their interests in the hands of gentlemen of large experience and undoubted reliability. One of the most able and energetic of these is Mr. A. H. McAtee, doing business under the firm name of A. H. McAtee & Co., with office at No. 709 West Main Street, corner of Seventh. Mr. McAtee is a native of Louisville, and has been identified with the insurance business since boyhood, acquiring a comprehensive and thorough knowledge of every detail of the business, which has caused him to become recognized as an authority upon all insurance matters, by our leading merchants, manufacturers and property owners. For eight years prior to the inception of his present house, he ably filled the position of secretary and manager of the underwriting department of the Falls City Insurance Company, and to his wise counsels and conservative underwriting, the company owed much of its success, and the principles advocated by him are still cherished and maintained by the successors to that company. As an agent he has long held a high reputation in the city, and controlled an influential and important business, placing policies in fire, marine, accident and plate glass insurance companies. The following are the companies represented by this house: London and Lancashire Fire Insurance Company, of Liverpool, England; the Lancashire Insurance Company, of Manchester, England; the Fidelity and Casualty Company, and the Agricultural and Continental Insurance Companies, of New York; the New Hampshire Fire Insurance Company, of Manchester, N. H.; the Michigan Fire and Marine Insurance Company, of Detroit, and the Union Insurance Company, of Philadelphia. The largest risks are promptly placed and distributed in a judicious manner, while the lowest rates of premium are invariably quoted, and a liberal and speedy adjustment and payment of all losses is guaranteed. Mr. McAtee is one of the most honorable underwriters in the city, and is a popular member of the Board of Trade and the Commercial and Pendennis Clubs.

W. L. LYONS & CO.; Stock and Bond Brokers, Etc.; No. 205 West Main Street.—The importance of Louisville as a great financial centre is generally recognized. She is in fact a most prominent mid-continental point for the disposal of miscellaneous securities, while the stock and bond business of the Falls City ranks second only to that transacted at but few other points west of New York city. It is in such connection we make but due reference in the pages of this industrial review to the well and favorably known firm of Messrs. W. L. Lyons & Co., brokers in stocks, bonds, grain, provisions and cotton, whose well appointed business office is centrally and eligibly located at No. 205 West Main Street. This business was organized in 1878 by Mr. W. L. Lyons, under the present firm style. His brother, Mr. H. J. Lyons, was admitted to an interest in its operations, in 1887. The firm deal largely in investment securities and stocks, and having direct communication by private wires with all the leading exchanges in the country, can buy or sell for cash or on margin any of the legitimately listed stocks, bonds or speculative shareholdings. Special telegraphic connections afford them, besides, the best advantages for buying and selling grain and provisions through the Chicago Board of Trade for cash or on margins, and for furnishing late and reliable information relative to the fluctuations of the markets. They deal in cotton through the New York and Southern Exchanges, and have superior facilities for promptly executing orders, and for carrying cotton at low rates of interest. The house is a sound, stable and responsible one, and has a superb patronage throughout the country. Both partners are natives of Louisville, where they are as popular in social as in commercial circles. Mr. W. L. Lyons is a member of the Commercial and Pendennis Clubs and a Knight Templar. He served eight years in the City Council and acted for several months as Mayor pro tem and was also for several terms chairman of the Finance Committee of the Council. Mr. H. J. Lyons, his brother and partner, is a popular member of the Kenton Club, and was formerly connected with the L. & N. Railroad, as city ticket agent.

R. H. DORN; Dealer in Malt, Hops and Distillers' Supplies; No. 119 Third Street.—The industries of Louisville are numerous and cover every branch of the commercial activity, and are ably represented here by enterprising merchants. Prominent among these is Mr. R. H. Dorn, dealer in distillers' and brewers' supplies. The premises occupied comprise a three-storied brick building, having a frontage of thirty feet on Third Street and extending back for one hundred and twenty feet, fitted up throughout with everything necessary for the successful prosecution of the business, elevator, etc. The choice grade of rye, barley, hops and malt carried, have been carefully selected to meet the requirements of the large trade of the house, which extends throughout this state and the South. Mr. Dorn, who was born in Italy, has resided here since his boyhood. He is a member of the Board of Trade, Odd Fellows and the Knights of Pythias, and is highly esteemed for his ability and integrity. His long experience in Louisville's commerce gives him peculiar advantages for this branch of trade, while his high character is a sufficient assurance that all transactions will receive faithful attention.

THE OUERBACKER-GILMORE COMPANY; Wholesale Grocers; Nos. 319 and 321 West Main Street.—There are some houses in this city whose long and steady career, heavy and extensive transactions make them landmarks in the history of the past, and prime factors in the commerce of the present. Of such the house conducted by the noted Ouerbacker Gilmore Company, wholesale dealers in groceries and provisions, is a prominent representative, by reason both of the extent of its trade and the force and energy displayed in its management. This concern was established in 1869 by Messrs. Ouerbacker, Gilmore & Co., they at that period restricting their operations to the handling of country produce. In 1880 the wholesale grocery and provision business was made the leading feature, and the trade was conducted as such under the original firm style till 1892, during which year Mr. A. T. Gilmore died. The interests of the deceased's estate are since sustained and the present trading title was assumed during January of the current year, the personnel of the present proprietorship being as follows: Samuel Ouerbacker, the surviving founder of the house, a native of Leavenworth, Ind., a director of the Louisville Board of Trade, and member of the Wholesale Grocers' Association; John Ouerbacker, Sr., his brother, born in Louisville; John Ouerbacker, Jr., son of the latter-named gentleman, a native of this city, and member of the Wholesale Grocers' Association and Commercial Club; George Ouerbacker, his brother, born at Leavenworth, also a member of the Commercial Club and Wholesale Grocers' Association; John H. Wilkes, native of Leavenworth, and now identified with the house for the past seventeen years; C. W. Inman, born at Elizabeth, Ind., a resident of New Albany, and now connected with the concern since 1885, also a member of the Board of Trade, and Daniel Hau, a native of this city, resident of Jeffersonville, Ind., now with the house since 1880, and a member of the Wholesale Grocers' Association. The premises occupied comprise a substantial four-storied and basement building, 45x200 feet in dimensions, fully equipped with elevators and modern conveniences. The stock covers every branch of staple and fancy groceries, provisions and food products, which are quoted at the lowest ruling market prices. The trade, apart from an immense local patronage, is brisk through all parts of Kentucky, Indiana and Tennessee, and steady employment is given to fifteen assistants in the warehouses, while a corps of ten traveling salesmen represent the interests of the house on the road. In a word, this progressive corporation contributes its full share towards maintaining the supremacy of Louisville as the great distributive commercial centre, south of the Ohio River.

JOHN W. & D. S. GREEN; Stock and Bond Brokers; No. 444 West Main Street.—The prominence of Louisville as a financial centre is sustained, not only by the great incorporated institutions, but also by private firms, that enjoy equally with them, the prestige that comes from years of honorable dealing as stock and bond brokers. Especially prominent among these is the firm of John W. and D. S. Green, the members of which have had a thorough training in financial operations. This business was established in 1868 by Messrs. Morton, Galt & Co., in which firm Mr. John W. Green was a partner, and in 1879 the latter gentleman purchased the business, and admitted his brother D. S. Green to an interest, under the present firm name. Finely appointed offices on the first floor are utilized, and here customers may rely upon receiving every attention and the most accurate information of the markets. The firm buy or sell on commission, for cash or on margin, stocks, bonds and investment securities of every description, together with real estate and commercial paper, and being themselves heavy operators, and having direct connection with the New York and Chicago exchanges, they are especially well qualified to give to the service of their patrons the benefit of their sound judgment and experience. They issue a monthly price list of the principal local and other bonds and stocks, and invite correspondence from investors and operators. Mr. John W. Green is a director of the Columbia Trust Company, and American National Bank, and the firm are prepared to render an especially valuable service, in the handling of the best class of standard investment securities.

JOHN COCHRAN & CO. (Incorporated); Distillers; Nos. 127 and 129 East Main Street.—The value of whiskey as a stimulant, tonic and actual curative agent in instances of exhausted vitality, is now universally recognized by physicians, and with its increased use has grown a demand for the best quality obtainable and also to secure brands surrounded by such records as to their history that shall be a satisfactory guarantee of their purity. This time honored but progressive and thoroughly representative concern dates its commercial existence back some sixty years, it having been founded by the late John Cochran in 1835. The business was subsequently conducted under the firm style of Jno. Cochran & Co., articles of corporation being secured in accordance with the Kentucky state laws in 1890. The premises here occupied consist of a spacious and commodious four-storied cellar and sub-cellar warehouse building, 25x210 feet in dimensions, giving ample accommodation for the handling and storage of stock and the general advantageous prosecution of the business. The distilleries of the concern are situate at Frankfort, Franklin County, this state, on the line of the Louisville and Nashville Railroad, and on the banks of the Kentucky River, and cover a large ground area. The machinery plant is one of the latest improved type, the storage capacity of the distillery warehouses being twenty thousand barrels, the grain consumption aggregating six hundred bushels per diem. A full force of skilled and experienced hands is provided with constant employment, and some criterion may be formed of the extent of the corporation's business, which radiates broadly over the entire United States, when the statement is made that the output for the past year reached five thousand barrels. The leading brands are the Spring Hill and Franklin handmade and all copper distilled whiskies, which are wholly free from added sugar, spirits or other foreign flavorings or artificial color. The company has an ample capitalization fund, and is ably officered as follows: G. H. Cochran president, a native of the Falls City, son of the founder of the house, and member of the Distillers' Association; Richard Morris, distillery manager, identified with the concern for the past sixteen years, and T. W. Cochran, secretary and treasurer, son of G. H. Cochran and member of the Louisville Board of Trade.

GABE A. JONES & SON; Livery, Boarding and Sales Stables; Nos. 518, 520 and 522 Center Street.—Of the many means of relaxation and recreation open to the people of to-day, few if any have that perpetual charm that characterizes driving. Therefore it is no wonder that driving is so popular and livery stables increase and multiply in all our principal cities. One of the largest and best known livery, boarding and sales stables in Louisville, are those of Gabe A. Jones & Son, which contain every modern arrangement as regards sanitation, ventilation, etc., and have a large capacity. Though erected in 1867 by the firm, these stables have been from time to time overhauled and every new device added, and to-day there is no stable in Louisville more complete. A general livery business is conducted, fine saddle horses kept for hire, and a general sales and boarding business done, and every care is exercised in all departments, and the excellent turnouts and liberal charges have given the house the extensive patronage it enjoys. In 1863 this concern was established by Mr. Gabe A. Jones, and from the outset, has proven an unqualified success. He was born in Shippin Port, now a part of Louisville, and is one of the oldest and best known livery men in this part of the state. He has always lived here and been closely identified with the city's interests, lending his aid to every project that tended to advance its welfare. In all circles he is highly respected, and takes rank among Louisville's most influential citizens. He buys and sells horses on commission and can give best of references. Terms reasonable.

CHRIST KRAEMER; Restaurant, Bakery and Confectionery; No. 518 Third Street.—One of the most important lines of business in all cities, is that of the baker and confectioner, and one of the leading houses in this line in Louisville, is that conducted by Mr. Christ Kraemer, which was opened by Mrs. H. P. Keisker several years ago, Mr. Kraemer becoming proprietor in 1891. The premises consist of a spacious and finely appointed store, where a full stock of choice confectionery, pies, cakes, etc., is carried, a bakery well equipped with every convenience, and also a restaurant. The last mentioned department is a model, and is finished in the most complete and up-to-date style, while the attendance upon customers is prompt and courteous. Complete satisfaction is guaranteed to the most critical patrons, and the stock carried is choice and extensive, including the best productions in the lines dealt in. Several assistants are employed, and the patronage is derived from all parts of the city and vicinity. Mr. Christ Kraemer was born in Germany in 1857, coming to this country five years ago and settling in Louisville in 1890. He is thoroughly conversant with every detail of this business and carefully supervises every department. He is a young man of ability, perseverance and enterprise, and is rapidly laying the foundations of an extensive enterprise, and the progress he has already made leaves no room for doubt as regards the future prosperity of his establishment.

PEARL LAUNDRY COMPANY; Nos. 250-252 West Jefferson Street.—In the washing and renovating of our daily attire, very excellent work is done by the Pearl Laundry Company. The establishment consists of a large two-storied building, 27x108 feet in dimensions, with a perfectly equipped plant, including all the latest improved laundry apparatus. Steam power is used and twenty skilled hands employed, who turn out the very best work in the city and a specialty is made of the finest domestic work, but orders from the trade are also executed. The business was founded twelve years ago by the present efficient manager, Mr. Glass. In 1894, the concern was reorganized and incorporated under the laws of Kentucky, the officers being H. A. Dudley, president, and Mr. L. B. Glass, manager. Mr. Dudley, who is a native of Richmond, Virginia, is one of our best known business men, and was previously secretary of the Board of Trade for a number of years. Mr. Glass was born in this city and has long been identified with the business, not only here, but also in Montgomery, Alabama. All orders by mail or telephone, (No. 1626) receive prompt attention, while all work is called for and delivered free of expense to all parts of the city.

F. I. BROCAR; Contracting House Painter; No. 804 West Jefferson Street.—One of the most reliable Louisville houses in its line, is that of Mr. F. I. Brocar, the widely known and successful contracting house painter and decorator. This extensive business was founded in 1866 by Messrs. Brocar & McKeldy, the latter retiring in 1868, when Mr. Brocar became sole proprietor, and has since continued alone. Mr. Brocar is a thoroughly practical designer and painter, possessing the happy facility of blending colors and shades, so as to produce an harmonious and artistic effect. He employs twenty-five skilled workmen, and promptly furnishes estimates and enters into contracts for all kinds of painting and decorations at the lowest figures consistent with superior work. The store is spacious and is fully stocked with a heavy and choice assortment of paints, oils, colors, painters' supplies, and Mr. Brocar also deals in superior graphite paint, pipe joint cement, belt dressing, etc., and promptly executes the largest contracts in a superior manner. He has lately finished several large contracts, including the painting of the Union Station, the Masonic Temple (three times), the Street Route Railway trestle work and all the bridges on the C. and O. Railroad, between Louisville and Paducah. He was born in New Albany, Ind., in 1844, and came with his parents to Louisville in 1857. During the civil war, Mr. Brocar served in the Thirty-fourth Regiment, Kentucky Volunteer Infantry, and was noted for his devotion to the cause of the Union. He rose to the rank of color sargent and is a popular member of the G. A. R., prominent Knight Templar, Freemason and a director of the Commercial Club, and is highly esteemed for his integrity, and was one of the first committee who went to Pittsburg, being the means of bringing the Grand Army to the Falls City.

J. SCHNEIDER; Harness, Saddles and Collars; No. 221 East Market Street.—An old established and representative saddlery house in Louisville, is that of Mr. J. Schneider, manufacturer and dealer in all kinds of harness, etc. This business was established in 1866 by Mr. John Schneider, who has since secured an influential patronage in this city and state. Mr. Schneider is one of the oldest and ablest saddlers and harness makers in the state, and is now assisted by his three sons, who are young men of superior ability. He was the originator and first maker of brass mounted harness in Louisville, and made the first set for Mr. Scott Newman, a well-known and esteemed citizen, in 1885, and since that period has forwarded similar harness to customers in Maine, California, New Orleans and Chicago. The store is commodious, and is fully stocked with a choice assortment of handmade coach, road and wagon harness of all descriptions, bridles, saddles, collars, whips, robes, etc., and all kinds of horse furnishing goods to customers at extremely moderate prices. Only the best leather and trimmings are utilized, and the harness manufactured by Mr. Schneider is not only unrivalled for its elaborate style and finish, but also for its strength and lasting durability. Mr. Schneider justly prides himself on his brass mounted harness, and employs only thoroughly competent workmen. He was born in this city in 1842, and learned his trade on the same block, where he has always carried on business. He is highly esteemed for his strict integrity, and justly merits the large measure of success secured in this useful industry.

LOUISVILLE OF TO-DAY.

PAUL WAGNER; Hardware; No. 2001 Eighteenth Street.—An important industry of every great commercial and manufacturing centre, which contributes greatly to its material prosperity, is generally the hardware trade. Prominent among the reliable houses in this section of Louisville actively engaged in this business which has gained a wide reputation for excellent goods and just dealing, is that of Mr. Paul Wagner, wholesale and retail dealer in hardware, house furnishing goods, etc. Mr. Wagner established this business in 1885, and has since secured a liberal patronage in the city and state. He was formerly for several years in the employment of the Rankine-Snyder Hardware Company, and has achieved success solely on the basis of reputable dealings, and the ability to secure and handle the best goods only at lowest rates. He owns and occupies a commodious two-story building, 30x75 feet in area, fitted up with every convenience for the accommodation of the well-selected and choice stock, the assortment including all descriptions of hardware, cabinet and builders' goods, cutlery, mechanics' tools, housekeeping articles, etc. He likewise keeps on hand screen doors and windows, window frames, wire cloth, spring hinges, etc., and parties desirous of putting up their own screens, can get all necessary materials, grooved sides, strips and mouldings from this house. Mr. Wagner is a native of Charlestown, Ind., but has resided in the Falls City many years, and his future success in the hardware trade seems well assured.

PFAFFINGER & COMPANY; Pork and Beef Packers; Nos. 922 to 930 East Market Street.—The diamond brand of hams, bacon and shoulders, as also of dried beef, has become deservedly famous in the southern states. This brand is that of the noted firm of Pfaffinger & Company, the extensive pork and beef packers of Louisville. The business was established in 1872 by Messrs. W. A. Hoiffing & Company, who were succeeded in 1877 by Messrs. J. Pfaffinger & Company. The decease of Mr. J. Pfaffinger occurred on May 21, 1884, since which period the business has been continued by the estate under the style of Pfaffinger & Company, with Mr. Wm. L. Pfaffinger as manager. The packing house is a three-story brick building, 30x210 feet in dimensions, with all conveniences and facilities at command. The slaughter house and sausage manufacturing department occupy a two-and-a-half story brick building on Quincy Street, 48x90 feet in dimensions. The firm's bologna, Frankfurters, Salmi and other standard sausage have enviable fame with the trade. The firm slaughters its own stock, and the curing of its hams, shoulders and bacon is conducted in the most skilful manner. The processes of smoking and curing are perfect, and the diamond brand of sugar cured hams, bacon, shoulders and dried beef stands unexcelled in the markets of America. Mr. William L. Pfaffinger, the manager, is a native of this city, and a business man universally respected. He is a member of the Butchers' National Protective Association, and the concern is one of the most important industries of our city.

MARTIN MARKENDORF; Pharmacist; No. 800 East Broadway.—If there is one drug house in Louisville worthy of, and which receives the fullest confidence of the public, it is that of Mr. Martin Markendorf, who established this business in 1879. His first location was at the junction of Twelfth and Delaware Streets, but in 1888, seeing a field open in the eastern portion of the city for a drug business, he removed to his present location. The premises occupied are elegantly appointed, the store being replete with everything that can render it attractive and convenient, while the laboratory contains the latest and most approved apparatus. The stock carried includes everything in the line of drugs and medicines, toilet articles, perfumery, rubber goods, etc., all of which are purchased direct from the leading sources of supply with which the house enjoys the most influential connections. Mr. Markendorf is the special agent here for the celebrated Oriental catarrh treatment and for Ranger's healing balm. The various preparations manufactured by the house, receive the highest endorsement of patrons for the different ailments for which they are designed. Forty-seven years ago Mr. Markendorf was born in Germany, but has resided in America since 1865. In 1876, he came to Louisville, and during his residence here of nearly twenty years, has won the highest respect in public and private life. His patronage is large and constantly growing, for to the people of Louisville the name of Martin Markendorf is synonymous with reliability.

J. RIEDLING & SON; Dealers in Flour, Hay, Grain, Mill Feed, Etc.; Nos. 737 to 741 East Main Street.—In presenting a reliable reflex of the representative business houses of Louisville, we take pleasure in submitting to our readers a brief sketch of the widely-known establishment of Messrs. Riedling & Son, wholesale dealers in flour, grain, hay, etc. This business was founded in 1865 by Mr. J. Riedling, who conducted it till 1892, when he admitted his son Mr. George Riedling into partnership. He has established influential connections in the best producing sections of the country, and is always prepared to offer substantial advantages to large buyers. The premises occupied are extensive, and are fully supplied with all modern conveniences for the handling and storage of flour, grain, hay, mill feed, etc. Prompt attention is given to all orders, and they are always enabled to quote the lowest current market rates, and to supply flour and mill feed of a quality that cannot be excelled anywhere in this country. The stock is valued at about $20,000. The business was first started at the northwest corner of Hancock and Market Streets, and afterwards removed in 1870 to the northwest corner of Hancock and Main Streets, and in 1892 to its present location. Messrs. J. and George Riedling are honorable and liberal business men, who are promoting the commerce of the Falls City with energy and success, and have gained the entire confidence of their numerous customers.

MERRICK BROTHERS; Tin, Iron and Slate Roofers; No. 917 East Broadway.—This flourishing industry was established four years ago by Mr. J. E. Merrick, two years later the style becoming Louisville Roofing Company, and in March, 1895, the present firm name of Merrick Brothers was adopted. They are tin, iron and slate roofers and architectural iron workers, manufacturing iron work for buildings, columns and beams, a specialty being made of derrick work. The premises occupied are spacious and well appointed, having an area of 80x25 feet. All work is done by hand and thoroughly guaranteed, and they contract for jobs of all kinds in their lines, promptly furnish estimates, etc. Though so short a time in existence they have executed several large contracts here, some of special note being the Finzer Tobacco Works, ornamental iron, and the roofing of R. C. Whaynes' residence, Henry Beaumister's residence, August Volz residence, Masonic Temple at Sixth and Walnut Streets, etc. All work has given the fullest satisfaction, and their best advertisers are those for whom they have executed contracts. The members of the firm are A. W. Merrick and J. E. Merrick, both of whom are men of great practical experience in their line, and are highly esteemed in the city. Mr. A. W. Merrick is a prominent Freemason, treasurer of the Old Glory Lodge, No. 26, Jr. Order of American Mechanics and otherwise prominently identified. He was formerly for eleven years in the employ of Snead & Co., Architectural Iron Works.

JOHN DIEBOLD & SONS; Dealers In Stone; Sixteenth Street between Maple and Arbegust Street.—It is a great convenience to builders to be able to secure dimension stone ready for the mason, consequently, the reliable dealer in this class of material is usually well patronized in large cities. Among the most prominent of those who have invested their capital and talents in this branch of business in the Falls City, is the firm of Messrs. John Diebold & Sons. This enterprise, known as the West Louisville Steam Stone Works, was established by Mr. John Diebold twenty-two years ago, he conducting the affairs of the concern alone till 1891, when his sons, Messrs. Andrew and John Diebold, Jr., were admitted to partnership. The premises have an area of 280x175 feet, the yards being provided with ample shedding; the machinery equipment embracing three traveling cranes, four sets of gang saws and kindred devices known to the stone cutting industry, operated by an eighty-five horse power steam engine. From thirty to fifty hands are employed cutting, and dressing rough, sawed and dressed stone for builders and contractors in Louisville and her environs. Among other contracts for the furnishing of stone satisfactorily completed by this firm may be mentioned the supplies of such material for the Louisville Medical College, Calvary Church, St. Anthony's Church, Christ Church, Kenyon Building, Louisville Trust Company's Building, First Presbyterian Church etc., etc. The senior Mr. Diebold was born in Germany but has resided in America forty years, thirty-three of which he has spent in this city, where his sons were born.

I. E. HABICH; Dealer in Groceries and Produce; Corner of Sixteenth and Southgate Streets.—Each section of Louisville has grocery houses which are conceded to be the leaders in their several lines, and so far as Southgate Street is concerned, this position must be given to the establishment conducted by Mr. I. E. Habich. This enterprise was established in 1876 by the present proprietor, and the undertaking has been steadily expanding since its inception. The store, which is owned by Mr. Habich, consists of a superior three-story brick building, 47x30 feet in area, and everything is supplied throughout that can in any way facilitate operations or add to the comfort and convenience of patrons. The stock carried consists of groceries of all kinds, from the choicest delicacies, to the staple products, butter, cheese, eggs and poultry, salt and smoked meats, and wines, liquors and cigars. In the rear of the grocery is a well appointed and conducted wine room, and here are sold the choicest wines, foreign and domestic brandies, whiskies, including the leading brands of Kentucky whiskies, ales and beer, a specialty being made of Senn and Ackermann's bottle and draught beer. The prices quoted are the most reasonable, and patrons have come to the conclusion that economy is infinitely better served in the long run, by trading at a reputable establishment like this. Mr. Habich is a native of Dulfs County, Md., and has resided here most of his life. He is a man of integrity, and ranks high among our influential citizens, and is prominently identified with several societies, among others being a member of the O. K. of A. and the Jefferson Benefit Association.

140 — LOUISVILLE OF TO-DAY. —

VALENTINE UHRIG; Bungs; No. 417 East Jefferson Street. An old established manufacturing industry in the Falls City, is that conducted by Mr. Valentine Uhrig, the widely-known manufacturer of compressed and cut bungs, faucets, taps, etc. Mr. Uhrig, who is a thoroughly practical wood turner, established this business in 1861, and his trade, which is steadily increasing, extends throughout the middle, western and southern states. The factory is a spacious two-story brick building, fully equipped with modern machinery, driven by a forty horse power steam engine, and fifteen skilled hands are constantly employed. This is the only bung factory south of the Ohio River, and its output amounts to about one hundred thousand bungs daily. Mr. Uhrig also manufactures faucets, taps, plugs, bushes, spiles, mallets, stair banisters, venel posts, base ball bats, dumb bells, Indian clubs, ten pins and balls for handles, etc., which are unrivalled for quality, finish and uniform excellence. He also attends carefully to all kinds of wood, stone and ivory turning, and promptly fills orders at extremely moderate prices, and numbers among his permanent customers the Pabst Brewing Company, Anheuser-Busch Brewing Company, Lemp Brewing Company, and many leading brewers, distillers and coopers in all sections of the country. Mr. Uhrig is ably assisted by his son Mr. Aug. V. Uhrig, who is a young man of great energy and promise, the former of whom was born in Germany, and the latter in the Falls City. They are highly esteemed for their strict probity, and justly merit the liberal patronage secured in this useful industry. Mr. Aug. Uhrig is prominently identified in musical affairs, and is an active member of Schnebter's Orchestra.

D. G. ROWLAND & CO.; Seeds, Agricultural Implements, Etc.; No. 329 East Market Street.—Louisville has long maintained a prominence in the trade of agricultural implements, etc., and in this connection special reference is made to the reliable firm of Messrs. D. G. Rowland & Co., manufacturers' agents and dealers, whose trade extends throughout all sections of Kentucky and the adjacent states. This business was established several years ago by Messrs. Colly & Snowden, who were succeeded in 1893 by Messrs. Colly & Rowland. Eventually, July, 1894, the present firm was organized by Messrs. D. G. Rowland and T. G. Truman, under the title of D. G. Rowland & Co. They are able business men, and represent in the Falls City the following noted companies, viz The Warder, Bushnell & Glessner Company, Springfield, O.; Champion mowing machines, reapers, etc.; P. P. Mast & Co., Springfield, O.; corn drills, cultivators, cider mills, Gale Manufacturing Company, Albion, Michigan; plows, harrows, hay rakes, etc., Silver Manufacturing Company, Salem, O.; feed cutters, etc. The premises occupied are spacious, and are supplied with every facility. They make a specialty of garden and field seeds, and can always supply the best and most reliable seeds at lowest market rates. They are honorable and reliable dealers and agents, who are very popular in trade circles. Mr. Rowland was born in Mobile, Ala., and was previously purchasing agent for several years for the Louisville and Nashville Railway, while Mr. Truman is a native of McCracken County, Ky., but has resided in the Falls City since 1849. Mr. Truman was interested largely in milling, and during the civil war was captain of Company C, Second Kentucky State Guard.

G. M. ALLISON & CO.; Remington Standard Typewriter and Columbia Cycles; No. 422 West Main Street.—The present era of progress has given birth to many mechanical inventions of great usefulness, none of which, however, exceed the wonderful typewriting machine. This leads us to present to our readers an account of the merits of the Remington Standard Typewriter, now conceded to be the best machine yet introduced to the public, and is now used extensively in the entire United States and Canada, and in fact all over the world. The Remington was the first typewriter invented, and is unrivalled for speed, perfect alignment, strength, uniform impression and durability. The Louisville office was opened in 1883 by Stanley B. Huber, who was succeeded by the firm of Huber & Allison, and on the retirement of Mr. Huber in January, 1894, Mr. G. M. Allison became sole proprietor. Here is kept a comprehensive stock of the famous Remington standard typewriters, Columbia cycles, and mimeographs, ribbons, carbon papers, copy holders and a full assortment of supplies and sundries, which are offered to customers at extremely moderate prices. This firm controls the business and sale of the Remington typewriters in Kentucky, Tennessee and part of Indiana. Mr. Allison is a practical typewriter, and is highly esteemed for his sterling integrity. The motto adopted by the makers of this unsurpassed piece of mechanism is "To save time is to lengthen life," and they have produced the most perfect typewriter in the world.

LOUIS FLEISCHAKER; Dry Goods, Etc.; Nos. 770 to 774 East Jefferson Street.—In "dry goods," a representative and prominent establishment in its line in Louisville is that of Mr. Louis Fleischaker, wholesale and retail dealer in dry goods, notions and shoes. This business was established in 1882 by Mr. Louis Fleischaker who was previously in partnership with his brothers and has since continued alone on his own account. The premises occupied comprise three large stores which have an area of 62 1-2x86 feet, elegantly fitted up and supplied with every convenience, handsome plate glass fronts, electric lights, etc. The stock carried is choice and comprehensive, embracing the newest styles of silks, satins, velvets, cashmeres, dress goods, of every description, linens, woolens, white goods, prints, domestics, ladies' and gents' furnishing goods, parasols, etc., which are unsurpassed for quality and are offered at prices that cannot be discounted by any other house in the city. Here is a large department for boots and shoes which are received direct from the most celebrated manufactures and are well adapted to the needs and wants of all classes. Ten competent clerks, saleladies, etc. are employed, who spare no effort to satisfy patrons. Mr. Fleischaker is a native of this city. He is highly esteemed for his strict probity, while he is constantly in receipt of the latest novelties and is thus enabled to offer extra inducements to his customers who include some of the leading families of the city and its vicinity.

J OHN B. STICKLER & SON; Gas Fitting and Plumbing; No. 417 Walnut Street.—Sanitary plumbing is now a specialty with many of our reliable plumbers and prominent among these in this section of Louisville is the firm of Messrs. John B. Stickler & Son. The business was established in 1877 by Mr. Jno. B. Stickler, who conducted it alone till 1891, when he admitted his son, Mr. John B. Stickler, Jr., into partnership. Mr. John B. Stickler, Sr., is a thoroughly practical and experienced sanitary engineer, who has done a large amount of plumbing, gas and steam fitting on some of the finest buildings in the city and its vicinity, to the entire satisfaction of patrons. The store is commodious, and here is kept always a full and choice stock of plumbers', steam and gas fitters' supplies, chandeliers, globes, brackets, brass and bronze goods, water closets, wash basins, bath tubs, etc., a specialty being made of brass and chandelier finishing and also arranging piping and executing work for soda water manufacturers and the fitting up of fountains. They also attend carefully to sanitary plumbing and gas fitting in all branches, and enter into contracts for the complete fitting up of buildings. Only first class workmen and the best materials are employed, and all work is turned out in a very superior manner at reasonable figures. Both partners are natives of this city, and are highly regarded for their skill and strict rectitude, and are popular and active members of the Master Plumbers' Association.

M. SHEEHAN; Grocer; Nos. 1854 and 1856 Portland Avenue.—Prominent among the leading grocery houses of this section of Louisville is that of Mr. M. Sheehan, which has achieved a high reputation for fair dealing and for handling only strictly reliable goods. Twenty-five years ago Mr. Sheehan established this business and his career has been a most successful one. Twenty years ago he erected his present commodious building and has occupied it since that time. It is a three-story structure, 25x210 feet in area and is specially adapted for the grocery and liquor business. The stock carried includes the choicest and fancy groceries, flour, feed and produce, while a specialty is made of wines and liquors for family use. The goods are unrivalled for purity and freshness and the house caters strictly to high-class trade. Four experienced assistants are employed and Mr. Sheehan strenuously strives to satisfy every patron. Mr. Sheehan was born in Ireland but has lived in America the greater part of his life, coming to Louisville when a young man. In commercial circles he is widely known.

H. SANDFORT; Dealer in Groceries, Feed, Meats and Vegetables; No. 1118 Seventh Street.—Few establishments in Louisville are better qualified to serve the interests of the public, than Henry Sandfort, dealer in groceries, feed, meats and vegetables, wines, liquors and cigars, etc. He established this business in 1878, at the corner of Centre and Broadway, but moved to the present location in 1880. From the start, Mr. Sandfort has built up a large and remunerative trade. The premises are provided with all modern conveniences, and the store is finely fitted up and furnished. Here is kept a comprehensive and well selected stock, embracing a full line of staple and fancy groceries, teas, coffees, spices, condiments, sugar, syrups, molasses, fresh meats and vegetables, the purest and best wines, liquors, cigars, tobacco, and in fact everything a well equipped store should contain. Mr. Sandfort was born in Germany in 1848, and came to Louisville in 1866. He is an honorable and energetic business man, who is very popular in social as well as in commercial circles, and his future success is well assured.

C. OPDEBEECK Leaf Tobacco Broker; No. 745 West Main Street.— Among the representative houses, which of late years have contributed largely to secure to the Falls City the ever-growing benefits of this trade, is that of Mr. C. Opdebeeck, the widely-known tobacco broker. Mr. Opdebeeck was born in Antwerp, Belgium, and came to the United States in 1866, and to Louisville in 1874. He formerly resided in New Orleans, and is now vice-president of the Louisville Tobacco Exchange. He buys extensively for the export trade, and ships to Great Britain, Ireland, Canada and Europe. He brings great practical experience to bear on his business, and is recognized as one of the best judges of seed leaf in this country, and a test by him is always sufficient to finally fix the quality and value of any particular lot. He has established influential connections in the best producing sections of the country, and is highly esteemed in trade circles for his sound judgment, business principles and strict integrity, while his superior facilities enable him to place on the European market, a class of American leaf tobacco, that is eagerly sought after by foreign manufacturers and dealers.

THE J. T. BURGHARD COMPANY; Wholesale and Retail Dealers in Carpets, Lace Curtains, Portieres, etc.; Corner of Brook and Market Streets.—A prominent establishment in Louisville is that carried on under the title of The J. T. Burghard Company, wholesale and retail dealers in carpets, oilcloths, lace curtains, rugs, etc. This business was founded in 1860 by Mr. J. T. Burghard, who continued it till November 1890, when it was incorporated under the laws of Kentucky with a capital stock of $100,000, of which $60,000 have been fully paid up, the executive officers being Mr. J. T. Burghard president, Mr. A. W. Meyer vice-president, and Mr. A. W. Elwang secretary and treasurer. They import direct from the most celebrated European houses, and are constantly on the alert to secure the latest novelties, which are offered to customers in this city at the same time as they are for sale in New York, Philadelphia or Chicago. The premises occupied comprise a spacious five-story and basement building, which has an area of 25,000 square feet, the basement being filled with matting and oilcloths, the first floor being utilized for offices, lace curtains, rugs and upholstery goods, the second for ingrain carpets, while the third floor tapestry brussels and the fourth floor for cocoa matting, linoleums, etc., and the fifth floor to moquette and velvet carpets. The stock includes all the leading novelties in carpetings, the latest designs in moquettes and body brussels, tapestry brussels, art squares, portieres, lace curtains, linoleums, mattings, oilcloths, rugs, etc., which are unsurpassed for quality and uniform excellence, while they are offered to patrons at extremely low prices. Orders are filled with care and dispatch, and the trade of the company extends not only throughout the city and its vicinity, but also to the principal cities of Kentucky, Indiana and Tennessee. Mr. Burghard was born in Germany and also Mr. Meyer, while Mr. Elwang was born in Louisville. They are merchants of ability and integrity, and are active members of the Commercial Club. Messrs. Meyer and Elwang have been identified with this house for the past ten years, the former of whom is a popular member of the Knights of Pythias, I. O. O. F., and he is also a director of the Y. M. C. A.

HENRY GAUSS; Pharmacist; Baxter and Highland Avenues.—Next to the physician, the druggist is one of the most necessary professional men in any community, and it is imperative that he should be a man of intelligence and reliability. Among the younger members of this important profession in Louisville, is Mr. Henry Gauss. The Highland Pharmacy was established in 1880 by Mr. P. Bender, and successfully conducted by him until 1891, when Mr. Gauss became proprietor. The premises occupied are elegantly appointed, and the stock is one of the choicest in the city, consisting of drugs and chemicals of the purest quality, toilet articles, patent medicines, druggists' sundries, etc. Mr. Gauss makes a specialty of compounding prescriptions, and anything of this kind can be entrusted to him without fear as to the result. Among the valuable proprietary medicines and compounds manufactured by him, are his Savoring extracts, known as Gauss' Flavours, being pure fruit extracts, containing neither ether, chloroform or any adulterous preparation. The trade of the house is first-class, and extends to all parts of Louisville and vicinity. Mr. Gauss is a young man, and a native of Indianapolis, Ind. In 1876, he removed to Louisville, and now ranks among the best known of her professional men. He graduated with high standing from Louisville College of Pharmacy, and the ability shown while attending that institution, has developed by experience, and placed him among the foremost druggists of the city. In private and public life he is held in the highest esteem.

JOS. BECKMANN; Manufacturer and Grinder of Shears, Scissors and Cutlery, Tanners' and Curriers' Tools, Etc.; No. 536 West Market Street.—A branch of industry of a most useful character in the city of Louisville, is the manufacture of shears and cutlery of all kinds. In this connection reference is made to Mr. Joseph Beckmann, the widely-known manufacturer and grinder. This business was established in 1875 by Messrs. A. Himerdinger and Joseph Beckmann, who conducted it till 1875 when Mr. Himerdinger retired and Mr. Beckmann continued the business. He is a thoroughly practical cutler, who also makes a specialty of grinding, repairing and polishing. The works are fully equipped with special tools, grinding and polishing machinery, etc., and only really first-class workmen are employed. He manufactures all kinds of shears, scissors, cutlery, tanners' and curriers' tools, and also deals in concave razors, pocket knives, etc., which are offered to customers at very moderate prices. All cutlery and shears are made of the best steel and are unsurpassed for reliability and have no superiors in the market. Mr. Beckmann was the pioneer in this industry in Louisville and is highly esteemed by the community for his mechanical skill and strict probity. His shears, cutlery, etc., are quite equal if not superior to the best imported from abroad. Mr. Beckmann was born in Germany in 1845, and came to Louisville twenty-four years ago, and is one of our progressive citizens.

ROBERT LECHLEITER; Feed and Fresh Meat; Corner of Fifteenth and Maple Streets.—It is a noticeable fact that no branch of commerce exercises such an important influence in the welfare of a city as the grocery trade, and the Louisville establishment conducted by Mr. Robert Lechleiter, has secured an enviable reputation for the superiority of its staple and fancy groceries, and has built up a first-class patronage. It is a model grocery store, and its proprietor is known to employ only honest business methods, for he is a man who never misrepresents his goods, and his reputation for integrity is irreproachable. In addition to groceries, wines, liquors and cigars of the best brands are carried, a sample room, with separated entrance from Maple Street, being conducted, and here foreign and domestic wines, brandies, whiskies, ales, porters, cordials, beers, etc., are kept, the stock including the finest grades of Kentucky whiskies and the celebrated beer of Senn and Ackermann. The house was established in 1876 at Twenty-second and Walnut Streets, removal being made to the present quarters in 1891, on account of the growth of the business. Mr. Lechleiter was born in Germany. He came to Louisville in 1847, and has resided here ever since, and is a member of the uniform rank of the Knights of Honor and otherwise prominently identified.

BOURBON EXCHANGE; Jacob Henry, Proprietor; Wines, Liquors and Cigars; Northeast corner Johnson and New Main Streets.—One of the best conducted saloons in this section of Louisville, is the Bourbon Exchange, of which Mr. Jacob Henry is the popular proprietor. Mr. Henry first engaged in the business five years ago at the corner of Clay and Madison Streets, removing to the present more commodious quarters in 1893. He occupies a spacious ground floor, elegantly equipped, while the saloon is close to the Bourbon Stock Yards, making it a favorite rendezvous of the leading stock raisers and shippers who here transact business, attracted naturally by the high-class quality of the wines, liquors and cigars kept in stock. Here can be obtained first-class Kentucky rye and bourbon whiskies, the best brew of lager beer, etc., and the attendance upon patrons is all that can be desired. Mr. Henry is a native of the Falls City and prior to engaging in this occupation was favorably identified with the express business; he is a member of the I. O. O. F. Encampment, the Order of Free and Accepted Masons, and a prominent member of the Mutual Protective Association.

F. CURRAN & COMPANY; Wholesale Liquors; No. 212 First Street.—A representative, and one of the most noted houses in Louisville in its line is that of Messrs. F. Curran & Company, wholesale liquor dealers, which was established by Messrs. F. Curran, Edward G. Williams and J. J. Curran in 1882, and by honorable dealing has built up an extensive patronage throughout Kentucky, Indiana, Tennessee and the eastern states. The premises occupied comprise a substantial three-storied and basement brick building, 50x100 feet in dimensions, fully supplied with every convenience. The stock embraces the finest brandies, wines, gins, rums, Scotch, Irish, bourbon rye and wheat whiskies, champagnes, clarets, cordials etc. A leading specialty is made of Curran's Glen Lea Bourbon whiskey, which has few equals and no superiors. The members of this progressive firm are natives of the city. Mr. Williams is the traveling representative of the house, Messrs. Curran attending to the duties of the home office. They are actively engaged with the American Distillers' and Wholesale Liquor Dealers' Association, Mr. Williams being likewise a prominent member of the Order of Elks, and J. J. Curran is a prominent member of the Knights of Honor.

PETER SCHANZENBACKER; Leaf Tobacco; No. 1217 West Market Street.—Louisville is the largest leaf tobacco market in the world, and as a leading exponent of this important branch of commerce, we make due mention in these pages, of Mr. Peter Schanzenbacker, the widely-known broker, who established this business in 1865, and has since succeeded in rearing an extensive trade. The premises occupied consist of a substantial three-storied warehouse and office building, rising two stories in rear, such structure being utilized for drying and sorting purposes, the various processes being operated by steam power, and presenting a model of system in every feature of its equipment. Mr. Schanzenbacker is of German nationality, but was raised and educated in this city, where to-day he ranks among our progressive business men. He is a member of the Leaf Tobacco Exchange, secretary of the Louisville German Mutual Fire Insurance Company, a director of the Falls City Hall Market Company, the Farmers' Tobacco Warehouse Company, and a stockholder in the German Bank.

FRED. BAUER; Manufacturer and Dealer in Stoves, Tin, Copper and Sheet Iron Work; No. 1104 Market Street, Eleventh and Twelfth, South Side.—An important industry in Louisville is the manufacture of tin, copper and sheet iron work, and one of the most reliable houses actively engaged in it, is that of Mr. Fred. Bauer, the widely-known roofer, etc. Mr. Bauer was born in Germany in 1844, and came to the United States with his parents who settled in Floyd County, Indiana, in 1846. He was only three years old when his parents died, and eventually he came to Louisville in 1859, since which period he has resided and carried on business in the same block. He is an expert metal worker, who makes a specialty of roofing, guttering, spouting, etc., and also deals largely in stoves, ranges, holloware, cutlery, etc. The roofs constructed by him have met with the hearty approval of architects, builders and owners. The store is spacious, and Mr. Bauer also keeps on hand a complete assortment of tin, Britannia and Japanned ware, step ladders, bird cages, toilet sets, etc., and is sole agent in this city for Moore's air tight heater. Mr. Bauer is the only manufacturer of carriage lamps in Louisville, and is highly esteemed for his strict integrity. He is an active worker, and was one of the organizers of the Royal Templars of Temperance.

JACOB DAUTRICH; Cigar Box Manufacturer; No. 1405 Shelby Street.— Prominent among the leading manufacturers of cigar boxes in Louisville, is Mr. Jacob Dautrich, who established this business in 1879, and has since secured a liberal patronage, not only in Kentucky, but also in the adjacent states. The factory is a large two-story frame building, fully equipped with the latest improved machinery, saws, etc., operated by steam power, and a number of skilled hands is employed. Only carefully selected lumber is utilized and the boxes produced are unexcelled for finish and workmanship, while the prices quoted for them defy competition. Mr. Dautrich uses large quantities of Spanish cedar lumber monthly, which is obtained from New York city, while he likewise consumes large quantities of veneered cedar and poplar, which is received from Cincinnati, O. He was born in Germany in 1829 and came to Louisville in 1854. He is an honorable business man, and is ably assisted by his son, who has a thorough knowledge of the business, and is highly respected by all who know him.

EXCELSIOR NOVELTY WORKS; Electric Works of all Kinds; No. 616 Fourth Avenue.—In April of this year the Excelsior Novelty Works were founded, and has so far proved a most successful departure. It is a corporation formed under Kentucky laws with a capital of $5000 paid in, and the officers are president and treasurer, G. F. Porter, J. R. Jackman, Jr., secretary and Mr. J. P. B. Stinger, manager. The factory is a spacious structure, modern and complete in its appointments. All the most approved machinery and tools are provided and electricity furnishes the motive power. The output consists of electric work of all kinds, bicycle repairing, rubber stamps, etc., some of the specialties being tins, railroad badges, cutting and shoe dies, embossing dies, stencils, dating stamps, etc. The company also attends to electrotyping, stamping and press work on medals, society, club, picnic and ball badges, etc. The company's products have no superiors, and already a large patronage is derived from all parts of the city and vicinity. The company strenuously aims to satisfy every patron through the excellence of their product and the fairness of their charges. Mr. G. F. Porter was born in Manchester, N. H., but has lived here for twenty years. He is a G. A. R. man, having served during the late war as corporal in the First California Volunteer Infantry, and is a

LOUISVILLE OF TO-DAY.

member of Geo. H. Thomas Post, G. A. R. and of the Union Veteran Legion. Mr. J. R. Jackman, Jr., was born in Bardstown, Nelson County, Ky., and was for some years machinist for the Bellmont Distillery Company. Mr. J. P. B. Stinger is a native of Cincinnati, O., He is a practical electrotypor of wide experience and ability, also served in the late war and is a member of John A. Logan Post, G. A. R., St. Louis.

SCOTT & SNYDER; Interior Decorators; No. 507 Walnut Street.—We are indeed living in an age of progress, and with the more refined tastes of the people has come a demand for more artistic productions in home decorations. A representative house in this connection is that of Messrs. Scott & Snyder, whose establishment is illustrative of the extent to which this business has been carried. The elegantly appointed store is 30x75 feet in dimensions, and by ingenious devices a most bewildering variety of exquisite patterns in all descriptions of paper hangings is displayed, and the house carries a heavy stock, and employs fifteen experienced workmen, and executes everything in the line of decorative paper hanging, etc. The skill and taste of this house are proverbial in the trade, and the extensive patronage represents the most desirable city and suburban custom. The members of the firm, Messrs. C. B. Scott and Chas. M. Snyder are both gentlemen of experience and practical knowledge of the business, with which they have long been prominently identified. Mr. Scott supervises the execution of all orders, directing his force of employees personally in their work, thus insuring to patrons the best possible results, Mr. Snyder looking after the office and salesroom. Both gentlemen are natives of this city, and are highly esteemed in business circles as men of probity, whose successful attainment is a fitting reward to their zeal and energy.

JAMES A. CLARK & CO.; Whiskies; No. 131 Third Street.—An old established and representative Louisville house in its line is that of Messrs. James A. Clark & Co., wholesale dealers in whiskies. This house dates its existence back some thirty-eight years, having been founded by Mr. James A. Clark in 1857. Since that date several changes have taken place, resulting in 1891 by Mr. Clark reassuming the business under the present firm style. The premises occupied comprise a substantial four-story brick building, 25x100 feet in dimensions, fully supplied with every convenience, and the trade extends throughout Indiana, Illinois, Michigan, Iowa, New York and Pennsylvania. The specialties bottled by the house include the noted Oak, Ashland, Anderson and Woodford brands of pure Kentucky whiskies, and these liquors are mellow and delicious, and are sold free or in bond at extremely moderate figures under guarantee to give perfect satisfaction. Mr. Clark is a native of Massachusetts, and enjoys the highest of reputations alike in the social as in the financial and commercial circles of the Falls City.

WM. GNAU; Groceries, Provisions and Feed; Nos. 300 and 302 Adam Street.—Mr. Gnau, who is a native of Germany, came to this country forty years ago, and being a mechanic for a number of years, worked at the trade. He established this grocery business in 1870 at Story Avenue and Ohio Street, and being successful, in 1875 built his present premises. The store is well equipped with all the conveniences necessary to carry on the extensive and fast growing trade. The stock includes a superior assortment of staple and fancy groceries, provisions and feed, and these goods are fresh and desirable in quality, received direct from first hands and are sold at uniformly low prices. No house in the city that deals in the miscellaneous commodities of the grocery industry handles a higher standard of goods. Mr. William Gnau was born in 1842, and is one of the oldest grocerymen in this locality. He has a large remunerative trade, and is highly esteemed by the community for his integrity and just dealing, and those giving orders here will obtain advantages very difficult to be duplicated elsewhere.

E. H. HUESEMANN; Groceries, Liquors, Cigars, and Tobacco; Corner Fifteenth and Kentucky Streets.—Louisville is well supplied with grocery establishments, and prominent among those which lead in this line, we wish to draw special attention to that of Mr. E. H. Huesemann, which was established by the present proprietor. The store has an area of 24x100 feet, and in appointment and equipment, is a model of convenience. The stock carried consists of all kinds of staple and fancy provisions and general produce, wines, liquors and cigars. These goods represent the finest products of the best known producers, for the house caters only to a first-class trade, a specialty of fine old Kentucky whiskies being made. Three assistants are employed, and all orders, large or small, are filled with the utmost care and promptness, goods being delivered, free of charge to all parts of the city. Every advantage is afforded to patrons, the house owing its success, largely to the liberal methods always employed. Mr. Huesemann was born in Ripley, Indiana, and after receiving his education at Dearborne County, he came to Louisville in 1876, three years later embarking upon his present venture. He is highly esteemed for his integrity, and the success which has attended his enterprise is but the merited reward of his ability and industry.

F. J. DOHN; Groceries and Produce; No. 1701 Fifteenth Street.—One of the most prominent houses in its line in this section of Louisville is that of Mr. F. J. Dohn, dealer in groceries and produce. This business was established twenty-five years ago by his father, who conducted it till 1893, when he retired in favor of his son the present proprietor. Mr. Dohn handles a superior variety of goods, dealing in choice groceries of all kinds, produce and wines and liquors, the assortment being composed of both staple and fancy articles, carefully selected expressly for family use, from the most reliable sources of supply. Foreign and domestic wines, brandies, whiskies, ales and beers are handled, and among these specialties are made of Senn & Ackermann's celebrated beer and the best Kentucky whiskies. Competent assistants are employed, and Mr. Dohn assures prompt and polite attention to every customer at lowest current market rates. The premises

F. J. DOHN.

occupied are spacious and thoroughly modern in appointment and equipment, the ground area being 25x100 feet. Mr. F. J. Dohn was born in Louisville, and ranks among the most progressive of his younger business men. He has always been identified with this business, and thoroughly comprehends its every detail, while the qualifications he possesses, assures a bright future for this old and reliable house. His father still has an interest in the business. He is one of Louisville's best known and influential citizens, and has always taken an active interest in everything pertaining to her welfare. Though born in Germany, he has resided here for forty-three years. During the late war he saw four years of active service, being for three years under General Curtis in the Fourth Missouri Cavalry, and the rest of the time in the Fourth Kentucky Infantry, and his sterling characteristics have made him popular in both business and private life.

S. P. GRAHAM; Lumber and Shingles; No. 810 Magazine Street.—Occupying an important position in the lumber trade of Louisville is the old established house which was founded by the late Mr. John Graham, in 1854. The business was subsequently conducted from 1863 till the date of Mr. John Graham's decease in 1886, under the firm style of John Graham and Son, the latter succeeding to the sole proprietorship at that period. The premises cover an area of 230x230 feet, where is constantly carried several hundred thousand feet of lumber, chiefly under cover and of a quality to commend itself to the confidence of the most critical buyers. Mr. Graham enjoys advantageous relations with lumbermen in the best timber regions of the country and is thereby enabled to fill the orders of contractors, builders, and large consumers, promptly and at lowest prices. His business radiates south to the Gulf of Mexico and is broadly distributed throughout Indiana and Illinois. Mr. Graham enjoys the distinction of being the largest handler of cedar, cypress, white pine, poplar and chestnut shingles in the city, his sales for 1894 aggregating fifteen million shingles, irrespective of large quantities of doors, sashes, etc. He is a native of Louisville, well and favorably known in business circles, a prominent member of the Board of Trade and Commercial Club, and has acquired his prominence by a strict observance of the ordinary principles of equity in all transactions.

G. VAUGHAN & CO.; Dealers in Leaf Tobacco and Strips; No. 1026 West Main Street.—A representative and one of the oldest houses in its line in Louisville, is that of Messrs. G. Vaughan & Co., dealers in leaf tobacco and strips. This time honored house was established by the father of its present proprietors in 1848, he at that period operating in tobacco in Ballard County. In 1866 removal was made to this city, and the present firm style was adopted. From 1880 to 1893 it was a state corporate organization, reversion being made to individual business proprietorship during the latter year. In 1879 the founder of the house died, and the firm, as now constituted, consists of Messrs. J. P., E. W. and Q. D. Vaughan. They operate in strips and leaf tobacco, factories being located at Louisville, Henderson, Owensboro and Paducah, Ky. The different plants are equipped with all the latest improved devices for stripping, re-drying, etc., and they handle in the interests of manufacturers.

dealers and exporters, fifteen hundred to twenty-five hundred hogsheads of tobacco per annum. Messrs. Vaughan are all natives of Montgomery county, Tenn. J. M. Vaughan, son of J. P. Vaughan, is buyer for the Louisville house. Mr. J. P. Vaughan is a Freemason and has lived in Louisville since 1866. Mr. E. W. Vaughan is also a Freemason and resides at Paducah. Mr. Q. D. Vaughan, it might be remarked, served with distinction in the defence of the Southern rights in the ranks of the Confederate army, under General Forrest, and further personal comment on the standing of this staunch old Southern house we deem would be superfluous.

ADOLPH HALLENBERG; Architect; No. 424 West Main Street.—A representative member of the architectural profession is Mr. Adolph Hallenberg, a native of Louisville, who brings to bear the experience of many years study and practical application of the science of the skilled architect, and has evinced marked originality and great executive ability in dealing with difficult problems. He has been identified with this business for fifteen years, and has designed and erected many of the handsome buildings and fine residences in Louisville. He is a young, energetic and industrious man, studied in Paris, France, at the Ecole Beau Arts, and is a member of the Massachusetts Institute of Technology. He is well versed in general architecture and plans, and specifications are furnished promptly. He superintends all his own work, and does a large business, which proves very satisfactory.

G. LAYER; Wholesale and Retail Dealer in Fresh Meats; No. 13 Second Street Market.—There is no dealer in meats in Louisville, more widely known and reliable than Mr. Gottlieb Layer, who, thirty-five years ago established this business, his first location being in the Citizens' Market, removing to his present quarters some twenty-eight years ago last April, 1895. The store is well fitted up and a model of neatness, while the slaughter house is complete in its appointments, and thirty-five head of cattle are slaughtered weekly. Six assistants are employed, the trade being wholesale and retail, extending to all parts of the city and its vicinity. The stock carried consists of fresh meats, corned and dried beef, tongues, etc., and an idea of the sales in these commodities may be gleaned from the fact that he supplies the City Hospital, the House of Refuge, the Galt House, Vienna Bakery and Restaurant, and numerous other public and private houses. Mr. Layer was born in Guttenberg, Germany, but has lived in Louisville for thirty-five years, and is one of her most influential citizens. He is president of the Baby Carriage Company,

president of the Southern Malting Company, a member of the Board of Park Commissioners, a member of the I. O. O. F., and A. K. T. and B. A. Mason.

M. EDELMUTH; Cigars and Tobacco; No. 433 West Market Street.—There are some manufacturers who adhere strictly to honorable methods, and prominent among the reliable cigar manufacturers of the Falls City, ranks Mr. M. Edelmuth, proprietor of the noted "Roxy" cigar factory. This house has a widespread reputation as a supply depot for fine and medium grade cigars, well worthy of the good opinion of critical smokers, at moderate prices. The business was established by Mr. Edelmuth, twenty-four years ago, who by just dealing, has since succeeded in rearing an extensive trade throughout the South and West, irrespective of an immense local patronage. The premises occupied are spacious, and employment is given to about thirty-five skilled hands, the output aggregating two million cigars per annum. The leading brands manufactured are Roxy, (5c.), M. E. Crook, (5c.), Cottage, (5c.), El Juno, (10c.), and M. E. Best, (10c.) These goods are conscientiously maintained at the highest standard of excellence, and in fine quality challenge comparison with any productions in the country.

M. EDELMUTH.

Mr. Edelmuth is of German nationality, and prior to settling in Louisville was for eight years identified with the cigar industry at Jeffersonville, Ind. He is an expert in the selection of leaf, and is placing his goods upon the market at prices which are satisfactory to the most critical buyers.

KIS-ME-GUM COMPANY; No. 137 Third Street, and Nos. 237 and 239 Washington Street.—We desire to make prominent mention in this review to the Kis-Me-Gum Company, manufacturers of the celebrated Kis-Me chewing gum. This company was incorporated in May, 1895, with a capital of $60,000 and the management is vested in the able hands of J. M. Clark, president, and T. L. Jefferson, secretary and treasurer, and Dr. A. C. Montenegro, vice-president and chemist. The premises utilized as office and storeroom comprise a three-story brick structure, 22x96 feet in dimensions, and the factory 25x100 feet on Washington Street, is equipped for every department of the business. The laboratory shows that it is in charge of a chemist of the highest order. Kis-Me chewing gum is made only from the purest ingredients, in all flavors and is recognized as the most delicious article of the kind upon the market. Its flavor and aroma are more lasting than any other, and exercise a most salutary effect in sweetening the breath and cleansing the teeth and the whole mouth. It also promotes the health of those using it in a marked degree, by stimulating the flow of that natural digestive fluid, saliva, which in these days of strong teas, coffees and other beverages, is a valuable preventative of dyspeptic attacks. The trade in this delicacy has grown to such proportions, as to necessitate the establishment of agencies in New York, St. Louis, Pittsburg, Cincinnati and other large centres, and to tax the company's manufacturing capacity to the utmost. The Kis-Me gum has been manufactured for a number of years, and the business was conducted by J. M. Clark & Co., until May 15th, 1895, when the parties interested incorporated the Kis-Me-Gum Company. Mr. J. M. Clark is one of our most prominent business men, and holds in addition to his position as president of this company, the presidency of the Louisville Lead and Zinc Mining Company, manager of the Kentucky Soda-Ash Company, and the Missouri Mining Company. Mr. Jefferson is a director and the vice-president of the Bank of Louisville, president of the Southern Warehouse and Transfer Company, and treasurer of the Masonic Home for Widows and Orphans.

PETER ELLWANGER; Raiser and Shipper of Early Vegetables; Bowles' Market.—The raising and shipping of vegetables, constitutes one of the important branches of industry. The name of Ellwanger has been associated for years in the Falls City in this line, Mr. John Ellwanger having established this business in 1844. His gardens were located where the City Hospital now stands; and also on the ground of the old Preston Wood. Twenty-five years ago his son, Mr. Peter Ellwanger succeeded him, and his gardens are now situated at Crescent Hill. This is the largest piece of ground undivided in the city. Gardening is carried on here upon approved methods, and a large staff of assistants being employed, and there is no vegetable house in the city that enjoys the patronage this does. It is the oldest stand in the market, being the only remaining one of those that occupied space in the building when it first opened. Associated with Mr. Peter Ellwanger, are his brothers, John and Victor, both of whom are men of wide experience and marked ability. These two gentlemen have charge of the gardens, while Mr. Peter Ellwanger attends to the sales. In addition to the gardening business, Mr. Ellwanger conducts a large grocery store, and is also an extensive raiser of fine stock. The Messrs. Ellwanger are natives of Louisville. Financially this house ranks high, the proof of this statement being its references;—the German Security Bank and the Union National Bank.

THEO. RECTANUS; Druggist and Chemist; Corner Market and Preston Streets.—Prominent among the reliable members of the druggists' profession in this section of Louisville is Mr. Theo. Rectanus, the popular pharmacist. This pharmacy was opened in 1870 by Mr. Taffel, who was succeeded by Mr. G. Lilly, and eventually in 1891, Mr. Theodore Rectanus became the proprietor. He is an able chemist, and a popular member of the Pharmaceutical Society of Kentucky and Botanical Club of Louisville. The store is finely fitted up, and is fully stocked with a superior assortment of pure, fresh drugs and chemicals, pharmaceutical preparations, proprietary medicines, mineral waters, druggists' sundries, a specialty is made of compounding physicians' prescriptions in a reliable and accurate manner at very reasonable prices. The stock carried is valued at about $8,000, and Mr. Rectanus also compounds the famous Rex blood purifier and original headache powders, of which he now sells large quantities in all sections of the United States. He is highly esteemed for his strict integrity, and his pharmacy is one of the most popular in the city.

FRED. GAUSMANN; Dealer in Groceries, Dry Goods and Notions; No. 1801 Bank Street.—One of the most successful representatives of the retail grocery trade of Louisville is Mr. Frederick Gausmann, who deals largely in groceries, produce, dry goods, liquors and tobacco. Mr. Gausmann was born in Germany in 1847, and came to Louisville in 1867. He has had long experience in the grocery trade, and throughout his career has secured the esteem of his patrons. He is a careful business man, and has ever aimed to supply all dealing with him with groceries of a superior quality. He established this business in 1877, and in 1891 came to his present location. He has an excellent store building, and a complete stock of the best of goods. He also deals largely in country produce, butter and eggs, patent flour, coffee, teas and sugars, etc., and makes a specialty of Kentucky whiskies, cigars, etc. He was a member of the building committee that built the St. Peter's Evangelical church, one of the best church edifices in the city. He is highly esteemed for his sterling integrity, and is a leader in benevolent work, and always ready to further any measure intended for the city's welfare. He was formerly president of the John Simms Furniture Manufacturing Co., whose factory on Eighth Avenue and Main Street was destroyed by fire in 1876, when the company was dissolved.

F. X. SCHIMPELER & SONS; Distillers and Jobbers of Kentucky Whiskies; No. 230 West Market Street.—In the handling of pure Kentucky whiskies, and the wholesale importation of wines, no house is so thoroughly representative in Louisville, as that of Messrs. F. X. Schimpeler & Sons, which was established in 1862 by Mr. F. X. Schimpeler, who in 1880 admitted his son Charles, and in 1891 another son, Fred Schimpeler to partnership. The premises utilized comprise a four-story brick building, 30x200 feet in dimensions, equipped with every convenience. They are largely interested in the famous Cloverleaf distillery, Nelson County, Ky., the entire output of which they handle, and a specialty is made of that popular brand of whiskey, "Old Clover," high grade hand-made sour-mash, which is to be found at all the leading hotels, restaurants and saloons throughout Kentucky, Ohio, Indiana and Tennessee. Other well-known brands, emanating from this distillery are "Old Clover Pure Rye" and "Kentucky Senate" sour-mash, while the firm are also the proprietors of the "F. X. S. Kentucky bourbon. They also carry a choice stock of famous champagnes, ports, sherries, etc., together with brandies and liquors of every description, and are sole agents for the Sunnyside Vineyard Co., of California. The sales amount to $200,000 a year. The partners are natives of Kentucky, and are popular members of the Commercial Club.

TROST BROTHERS; Distillers and Wholesale Liquor Dealers; No. 127 Third Street.—Prominent among the representative houses engaged in Louisville in the distilling and wholesale trade in fine whiskies, is that of Trost Brothers, who first commenced business some years ago in Columbus, Miss., and in July, 1892, removed to this city. The firm utilizes a substantial four-story brick structure, 30x100 feet in dimensions, fitted up with every convenience, and the trade extends throughout the South and East, the sales amounting to $100,000 annually. The firm's special brands of whiskies, Good Cheer, Elgin Club and Sultana, have been received with high favor by leading connoisseurs everywhere. The partners, Messrs. William and Harry Trost are natives of Columbus, and prominent members of the National Wine and Spirits Association.

GERMANTOWN BREWERY; Nos. 1361 to 1367 Shelby Street.—Twenty years ago the Germantown Brewery was established by its present proprietor, Henry Huber, and has proven in every sense of the word, an unqualified success, and the output is on draught in the best saloons and hotels in the city and its vicinity. The brewery proper is a massive four-story structure, 90x180 feet in area, equipped with every modern device and appliance that can in any way facilitate operations. Adjoining the brewery is the malt house with a storage capacity of twenty thousand bushels, and the output amounts to thirty thousand barrels annually. The beer has no superior in this market, and this is entirely due to the fact that from the very outset the management has employed only the purest materials, and though there are breweries making a larger quantity than this one, none make a better quality. Mr. Henry Huber was born in Germany, the home of lager beer, and there learned the first rudiments of this important business. In 1869 he came to America, locating the same year in Louisville. He is a man of ability and energy, and the success which has crowned his undertaking, is but the natural reward of his industry.

BELLE OF NELSON DISTILLING COMPANY; Bourbon and Rye Whiskey; No. 123 East Main Street.—Ten years ago, under the laws of Kentucky, the Belle of Nelson Distilling Company was incorporated with a capital of $150,000. The same year business operations were begun and no sooner were the goods of the company placed upon the market than they met with great favor. Time has only served to strengthen their popularity, and to-day their various brands find ready sales in all parts of the United States. The plant is located at New Hope, Tilford Switch, Kentucky, and covers in all eight acres of ground. The distillery is splendidly constructed and is, in equipment, a perfect model of up-to-date convenience and completeness. Machines and appliances of the most approved device are provided throughout and the distilling capacity is seven hundred bushels a day. Large storehouses are also provided, their capacity being twenty thousand barrels. The very best rail and other facilities are at hand. Upwards of thirty skilled workmen are employed, while eight salesmen represent the company through the territory covered. The officers of the company are, president, Robert J. Tilford; general manager, C. M. Tilford; secretary and treasurer, David Bartley.

ALBERT H. LEONHARDT; Groceries and Produce; Southeast corner Nineteenth and Walnut Streets. The grocery and produce trade of Louisville has no more conspicuous representative than Mr. Albert H. Leonhardt, who has been successfully engaged in this line of trade for the last twenty years and has gained a reputation and a patronage second to none in the city. Starting in business thirteen years ago at the corner of Fourteenth and Market Streets, he removed eleven years ago to his present commodious quarters, where he occupies the ground floor and basement each 20x80 feet in area admirably arranged and adapted for the convenient handling of the great variety of goods always carried in stock. These include a full line of staple and fancy groceries, canned goods, table delicacies, imported and domestic, fresh meats and vegetables, all at the lowest market prices and of the best quality, and an especially fine line of choice liquors. These comprise the best brands of Kentucky whiskies which are guaranteed of absolute purity and are supplied to the very best trade, the Nadorf Brewing Company's beer and the Betz cream beer. Four trained assistants are regularly employed to attend to the numerous customers and two wagons are kept busy in the delivery of orders, the regular patronage covering a wide extent of territory. A native and life-long resident of Louisville, Mr. Leonhardt has always been actively identified with all that concerns the best interests of Louisville and is well known as an enterprising and public spirited citizen. He is a director of the Nadorf Brewing Company and the Kentucky Trust Company.

CALIFORNIA FIG SYRUP COMPANY; No. 1222 Lexington Avenue.—The primary mission of medical science is not to cure sickness but to prevent it. Remedial agents would, of course, never be needed, if by means of antidotes taken in advance, all disorders could be averted. This, of course is impossible,—we consider, nevertheless, that if successful experience goes for anything, that the syrup of figs, as prepared from the private formula of the California Fig Syrup Company, comes nearer to the standard of perfection as a first-class family preventive medicine than any other similar specific now in use. Nor is this all that can be said of this grand preparation, for it likewise is an actual remedy for that long list of ailments which arise from a constipated habit of the bowels. The company is a regular organized corporation, has an ample cash capital, and is ably officered as follows: R. E. Queen, president and general manager; George A. Newman, general agent of the Eastern Department. Thoroughly appointed laboratories are conducted at San Francisco and Louisville, while a branch office is also operated in New York. The premises occupied in the Falls City consist of a substantial four-storied and basement brick building, thoroughly equipped in every way, employment being here provided for a force of forty assistants. Mr. Queen is a native of Owensboro, this state, but resides in San Francisco, while Mr. Newman was born near Philadelphia. He is a graduate of the Philadelphia College of Pharmacy, and a director of the Louisville Banking Company, the Fidelity Trust and Safe Deposit Company, the Louisville Gas Company and the Louisville Electric Light Company.

LOUISVILLE OF TO-DAY.

THE J. J. DOUGLAS COMPANY; Distillers; No. 122 Second Street.—The J. J. Douglas Company, of Louisville, is a thoroughly representative concern in the distilling and handling of whiskey, having achieved a permanent success. The business was established many years ago by Mr. J. J. Douglas, and was incorporated under the laws of Kentucky in 1886, with ample capital, and an executive composed of Mr. J. J. Douglas, president, and Mr. J. Bloch, vice-president. The warehouse consists of a three-story brick building, 26x110 feet in dimensions, utilized for office purposes, salesrooms, bottling department and storage. The company are proprietors of the famous old style handmade Yosemite sour-mash, Woodford County, Kentucky, whiskey, and the Jim Douglas handmade sour-mash old style Kentucky whiskey, brands that are in extensive demand, both east and west, and are to be found in all the leading hotels, saloons, drug houses, etc., in all parts of the country. These whiskies are aged, off the highest grade and of delicious flavor and body, and are prime favorites among connoisseurs. Whiskies are sold either in bond or free, and are put up to suit the trade, in barrels or cases. Ten experienced travelling salesmen are employed, and the sales amount to $250,000 annually. Mr. Bloch supervises the sales department, and is highly regarded for his strict probity. Mr. Douglas is a native of Kentucky, a gentleman of excellent business qualities and is recognized as an authority upon all the details of this important business.

VALENTINE WEBER; Grocer; No. 1435 Washington Street.—There is no merchant in Louisville engaged in the handling of groceries and liquors more favorably known than Mr. Valentine Weber, who for nearly a quarter of a century has conducted a prosperous business at his present location. Mr. Weber was born in Germany, but has resided here since 1865, and for four years was employed by the old Kentucky Woolen Mills Co. He opened his present store twenty-four years ago, and the large trade which he soon acquired has steadily grown until to-day his patronage is among the best in the city. He occupies a corner store on the ground floor, having an area of 60x50 feet, fitted up with every convenience. He always carries in stock a full line of fancy and staple groceries, feed and produce c. the lowest market prices, and has a well established reputation for the prompt and accurate filling of all orders. His stock of liquors is large and carefully selected, and includes all the leading brands of Kentucky whiskies and Frank Fehr's celebrated I. X. L. lager beer. Mr. Weber is a deservedly popular gentleman, a member of the Independent Order of Odd Fellows and the Knights of Honor, and a trustee of the German Orphans' Home.

BONNIE BROTHERS; Distillers and Wholesale Liquor Merchants, No. 120 West Main Street.—A representative and noted firm in the wholesale liquor trade of Louisville, Ky., is that of Messrs. Bonnie Brothers. This firm was established twenty-five years ago by F. W. Bonnie. At subsequent periods the firm was strengthened by the addition of R. P., W. O. and E. S. Bonnie, who at this time are the sole owners of this business, by reason of the retirement from the firm of the senior member, Mr. F. W. Bonnie. Possessed of thorough experience, ample capital and controlling influential connections, this firm by strict attention to business, coupled with honorable dealings, have built up an extensive patronage throughout the United States. The premises occupied comprise a four-storied building with two sub-cellars 25x200 feet in area, equipped with every convenience, in which is stored probably the largest stock of tax paid whiskey held by any firm in the United States. The firm are extensive wholesale dealers of high grade bourbon and rye whiskies, making specialties of their famous Bonnie bourbon, Bonnie rye, Joel B. Frazier and Nelson Club brands that are favorably known from Maine to California. These whiskies are mild and delicious in flavor, and are well adapted for first-class club, hotel, saloon or drug trade. They are sold tax paid or in bond at lowest figures, under a guarantee of perfect satisfaction. A prompt reply will always be given to every inquiry for prices. The Messrs. Bonnie Brothers are members of the Board of Trade and of several Protective Associations that have been formed for the protection of the whiskey interests throughout the United States.

152   ◆   LOUISVILLE OF TO-DAY.   ◆ ◆

A. **A. EMLER**; Wholesale Produce and Commission Merchant; No. 415 Preston Street.—As the metropolis of the state of Kentucky, Louisville necessarily forms a very important market for the sale of produce, fruits and vegetables, and prominent among the reliable houses in this line is that of Mr. A. M. Emler, the popular wholesale produce commission merchant. Mr. Emler established this business in 1882, and has since secured a liberal patronage, not only in Kentucky, but also in the adjacent states. He has influential connections in the best producing sections of the country, and deals extensively in produce, making a specialty of car lots of potatoes, apples, onions, etc. Having a quick market, he is enabled to handle the largest consignments, advancing liberally, when required on the same, while he never fails to make prompt returns to shippers. He always realizes highest market rates for consignments. Mr. Emler was born in Germany, in 1856, and came to Louisville in 1875, where he is highly esteemed for his strict integrity. He is a prominent Freemason, and refers by permission as to his financial standing and responsibility, to the German National Bank, Germania Safety Vault and Trust Company, and also to Dun's and Bradstreet's Commercial Agencies.

L. **L. PFISTER**; Stoves and Tinware; Nos. 1723 Portland Avenue and 2506 West Market Street. Prominent among Louisville's leading business houses in its line, is that of L. Pfister, dealer in hardware, cutlery, paints, oils, stoves and tinware. Mr. Pfister is a native of Germany, but came to Louisville in 1869, when but fourteen years of age. In 1876 he established the present business and has since secured a permanent and influential patronage. He occupies spacious and well appointed premises. In 1892 the rapid development of affairs made it advisable to enlarge the facilities and accordingly the house at No. 2506 Market Street was opened as a branch house, to supply the customers in the west end. The stock carried includes everything in the line of stoves and ranges, tinware, hardware, oils, paints, glass, copper and sheet iron ware, and in short everything in the line of house furnishing goods and builders' supplies, specialties being made of copper and sheet iron ware and roofing, guttering and spouting. The stock carried represents the finest products of leading manufacturers, with whom the house enjoys the most enviable connections. Mr. Pfister has the sole agency here for the celebrated cooking ranges, and quotes prices that cannot be discounted in the city. He takes rank among the most progressive and prominent citizens of Louisville, and in society work he takes an active interest, being prominently identified with the Knights of Honor, A. O. U. W. and the Oriental League. He is also the proprietor of the well-known Pfister Hall, southwest corner of Twenty-Fifth and Market Streets.

O. **O'NEIL COAL AND COKE COMPANY**; Corner Third and Main Streets.— The mid-continental centre of the American trade in coal and coke is admittedly Louisville, and in this connection, special attention is directed in this statistical review to the representative Oneil Coal and Coke Company. This business was originally established by Messrs. Oneil & Co., thirty years ago, and became a corporate organization under the existing trading title in 1888. The company has an ample cash capital, and is ably officered as follows: James O'Connor, president; W. W. Oneil, vice-president; Chas. O'Connor, secretary, and S. M. Merwin, treasurer. They are extensive shippers of and dealers in Connellsville furnace, gas and crushed coke, Pittsburg, Raymond, parlor cannel and anthracite coal, disposing of some one and a half million of bushels of these grades of fuel per annum. They own and operate extensive storage yards at Floyd and Washington Streets, where thirty hands and twenty-five teams are employed, filling orders for steam users, retail dealers and large consumers in the city and suburbs, shipments in car and cargo lots being made from the mines when desired. The greatest care is exercised by this company in preparing its fuel for the market, and consumers will consult their own interests by making a thorough trial of the famous coal and coke handled by it before placing their orders elsewhere. The officers of the company are all prominent and popular members of the Board of Trade.

J. **J. SCHWARZWALDER & SONS**; Beer Casks, Kegs and Tanks; Seventeenth and Gallagher Streets.—One of the largest and oldest houses in the country, devoted to the manufacture of cooperage stock of all kinds is that of J. Schwarzwalder & Sons. In 1853 Mr. J. Schwarzwalder established this business and in 1870 he admitted his sons into partnership. The members of the firm now are H. Schwarzwalder and E. H. Herb. The headquarters are in New York city, and there they occupy a spacious four-story brick factory and warehouse and twelve years ago the Louisville plant was erected. This covers an area of 300x375 feet and the various buildings in their equipments are perfect models of up-to-date completeness. Machinery and appliances of the latest design are utilized operated by a one hundred and seventy-five horse power steam engine, and two hundred skilled hands are employed, the output consisting of beer casks, kegs and tanks, twelve hundred beer kegs being turned out daily, which are unsurpassed for finish and durability. All goods are shipped on order from the New York house, and the product is in great demand in all parts of the country, many large lager beer breweries getting all their supplies in these lines here. Mr. J. Schwarzwalder, the founder died in 1880. Messrs. H. Schwarzwalder and E. H. Herb reside in New York. The management of the Louisville house devolves upon Mr. John Bickelhaupt, whose wide experience and ability are doing much to advance the establishment. He is a native of New York city, and has been identified with the house for twenty-two years. Two years ago he was appointed manager in Louisville.

TROSS & SPAHN; Horseshoers, Blacksmiths and Wagon Builders; No. 218 Twelfth Street.—There are many people in Louisville who believe in the old plan of putting only first-class materials and the best hand work in the wagons they turn out. Among these in this important industry in the Falls City is the firm of Tross & Spahn, builders of wagons, blacksmiths and horseshoers. This business was established twenty years ago by Mr. John Tross, who was succeeded by the firm of Tross Brothers. Mr. John Tross died in September, 1880, and was succeeded by his brother Mr. Fred. Tross, who eventually admitted Mr. Henry Spahn into partnership. Both partners are thoroughly practical blacksmiths and wagon builders, who have since secured an influential patronage in the city and its vicinity. Only the best materials and first-class workmen are employed, and the wagons are unexcelled for strength, finish, workmanship and durability. The workshops are well equipped and all work is strictly handmade, while the prices quoted for all wagons, repairs, etc., are extremely moderate. They also attend carefully to horseshoeing, and thoroughly understand this important industry. Mr. Tross is a native of this city, while Mr. Spahn was born in Germany, but has resided here the greater part of his life. They are highly regarded for their skill and strict probity, and fully warrant all their work to be equal to any in the country.

GEO. NAGEL & SON; Dealers in Groceries, Produce, Meat and Vegetables; Corner Eighteenth and Kentucky Streets.—Of the business houses in Louisville, whose careers furnish us with illustrations of rapid development through perseverance, none take higher rank than that of George Nagel & Son, dealers in groceries, etc. Mr. George Nagel's first business venture was made thirteen years ago, when he embarked in the confectionery business on Green Street, and after conducting it successfully for some time retired, only to begin afresh upon his present venture in 1887. The premises occupied are commodious, having a ground area of 20x60 feet, and their appointments are models of the up-to-date business house. Everything that can facilitate operations or add to the convenience of patrons, has been provided and several expert assistants are employed. The stock consists of all kinds of staple and fancy groceries, provisions, smoked, salt and fresh meats and wines and liquors, a well conducted sample room being maintained. The groceries, etc., represent the finest products of the leading sources in their various lines, while the stock of liquors includes the choicest foreign and domestic wines, brandies, whiskies, ales, beers and cordials. The members of the firm are George Nagel and his stepson William Selke. Mr. Nagel has resided in Louisville upwards of twenty-five years. He is a stockholder in the Union National Bank, a prominent member of the K. of P., and is held in high esteem for his sterling probity. Mr. William Selke has been a member of the firm four years and has greatly aided in successfully developing it. He is a native of Louisville, and one of the most prominent of her younger citizens, being also an active Freemason.

PATRICK HYLAND; Grocer; No. 1434 Twelfth Street.—A progressive business house in Louisville, is that conducted by Mr. Patrick Hyland, dealer in groceries and provisions. Twenty-five years ago, Mr. Hyland established this business, and no grocery in this section of the city holds a high place in popular favor. The premises occupied are neatly appointed, while the goods include a choice assortment in the line of teas, coffees, sugars, syrups, canned goods, meats and general staple groceries, all gotten from the best sources of supply. Competent assistants are employed, and the patronage comes from various parts of the city. The growth of the house has been steady from the outset, and the best recommendation that it can be given, is the fact that some of its best customers to-day, began dealings here when the business was first inaugurated. Mr. Hyland was born in Ireland, but lived in America for forty-six years, twenty-five of which have been spent in Louisville. Upon coming to America, Mr. Hyland first located in Cleveland, Ohio, from which place he went to Kansas City and from there to Louisville. He is popularly known and esteemed in this city, taking an active interest in everything pertaining to her welfare.

E. G. DUCKWALL; Commission Merchant; Nos. 154, 156 and 158 Fourth Street. No house stands higher in popular favor in this section of Louisville, than that conducted by E. G. Duckwall, wholesale dealer in flour, feed, hay and grain. In 1851, D. and W. A. Duckwall founded this business and were succeeded by D. Duckwall & Son, the present proprietor coming into possession in 1889. The premises occupied comprise a substantial three-story building, equipped with every convenience, while the stock carried is extensive, including the very best products in the commodities dealt in. In addition to the above building, large warehouses are maintained at Nos. 129, 131, 133 and 135 Bullitt Street. Mr. Duckwall is a commission merchant and wholesale dealer in hay and grain, flour and mill feed, these goods being shipped to them direct from the leading sources of supply, thus enabling them to offer inducements to the trade, that smaller houses cannot think of duplicating. The trade of the house, in the commodities mentioned above, is largely confined to Louisville and the surrounding country, but in addition to this he makes a specialty of supplying distilleries, and in this capacity, he makes extensive shipments to all parts of the South. Supplies are largely received from Kentucky, Indiana, Illinois, Missouri, Kansas and Nebraska, and an idea of the extent of the operations may be gained from the fact that from four to five thousand car loads are handled annually. Mr. Duckwall is a son of the late D. Duckwall, the founder of this extensive enterprise, and one of Louisville's prominent citizens, whose lamented death occurred in 1892. Mr. Duckwall is a young man of wide experience in this line, and in addition to this the exceptional business qualifications he possesses, gives him rank among the foremost of the city's successful and progressive citizens.

E. G. DUCKWALL.

THE BADGLEY & HOERTER COMPANY, (Incorporated); Photographic Materials and Supplies; Nos. 351-353 West Jefferson Street. —This company was incorporated November 1st, 1894, with ample capital under the laws of Kentucky as The Badgley & Hoerter Company, Mr. Samuel F. Badgley being the president; Mr. Jo. A. Hoerter, the secretary and treasurer. Both Messrs. Badgley and Hoerter bring great practical experience to bear on the business, and were previously for several years prominently connected with Mr. W. D. Gatchel in the same line in this city. The premises occupied comprise a spacious first floor 25x100 feet in area, fitted up with every convenience for the accommodation and display of the extensive, choice and valuable stock which is unsurpassed in the city or elsewhere. Messrs. Badgley and Hoerter are noted for their enterprise in securing everything of the latest improved character, so that the best results and the most perfect pictures can always be obtained. Mr. Badgley was born in New Jersey, while Mr. Hoerter is a native of Indiana. They are progressive, liberal and honorable business men, who solicit orders and guarantee to give prompt and careful service, and we predict for them a rapidly increasing patronage, not only in this city, but also in all sections of the southern states.

D. H. BALDWIN & CO.; Pianos and Organs; No. 236 Fourth Avenue; A. A Van Buren, Manager.—The trade in musical merchandise is in a flourishing condition in Louisville, and in this connection we make prominent reference to the noted house of Messrs. D. H. Baldwin & Co., wholesale and retail dealers in pianos and organs, with headquarters in Cincinnati, and branch warerooms in all the leading cities of the South and Southwest. The firm's interests in Louisville are ably looked after by Mr. A. A. Van Buren, while the parent house was established by Mr. D. H. Baldwin thirty-eight years ago. The premises occupied consist of a four-storied and basement structure, supplemented by three floors of the adjoining building, and a capacious warehouse on Fourth Street, three stories high. Here is carried the largest stock of pianos and organs in the state, including the Estey and Hamilton organs, the noted Decker, Baldwin, Ellington, Haines, Fischer and Valley Gem pianos, etc. Mr. Van Buren is the resident partner of the firm here, with which he has been identified for the past twenty-five years, controlling their extensive business from this centre which radiates to all points south of the Ohio River and west to Missouri. He is a member of the Board of Trade and the Commercial Club.

J. W. RECCIUS; Sporting Goods; No. 327 Fourth Avenue.—The leading sporting goods house in Kentucky is the old and reliable establishment of Mr. J. W. Reccius, who has had a distinguished success in this line of trade. Mr. Reccius started in business for himself in 1879 at

LOUISVILLE OF TO-DAY.

No. 1633 Market Street, and in 1886 he sold out to his brother and opened a new store himself at No. 361 West Jefferson Street. In 1892 he removed from there to his present convenient and commodious premises where he has a well appointed store which occupies the first floor of a substantial four-story brick building with a front of twenty feet and a depth of eighty feet. Here he carries a full line of athletic and gymnasium goods, games and novelties and has the leading headquarters for baseball supplies and general sporting goods. He handles a trade of large and growing magnitude, and customers always find his goods the most reliable and his prices the lowest. He employs three competent assistants and patrons always receive prompt and courteous attention. Mr. Roscius is a native and lifelong resident of Louisville and is a popular member of several social clubs.

FBENDER; Druggist; Corner Wenzel and Jefferson Streets.—Mr. Bender is one of Louisville's leading druggists and his store, which is well known is neat in all its appointments and its proprietor possesses in the highest degree the art and ability of making it attractive. He carries a full line of drugs, chemicals and medicines, standard proprietary goods, toilet articles, sundries, cigars and everything usually found in a first-class drug store. A courteous and competent clerk assists the proprietor in satisfactorily serving the wants of the numerous customers. Special attention is given to the careful and accurate compounding of physicians' prescriptions, in which materials of absolute purity are exclusively used, and the store has a large proportion of the best family trade. Mr. Bender is one of the best known and most respected men in Louisville. He is a member of the State Board of Pharmacy and College of Pharmacy and belongs to various fraternal and social organizations, including the Masons, Odd Fellows, Knights of Pythias and Knights of Honor. Mr. Bender also conducts a store at Clifton, being in charge of competent clerks under his supervision.

WD. GATCHEL & SONS; Photo. Goods and Picture Frames; Nos. 343 and 345 West Jefferson Street.—This extensive business was established in 1865, by Mr. W. D. Gatchel, who is now assisted by his sons A. D. and F. E. Gatchel, young men of great energy and business ability. They are active managers of the business, which is the oldest of the kind in Louisville. In 1890, Mr. A. D. Gatchel opened a branch at Birmingham, Ala., at No. 214 Twenty-first Street. The salesrooms in this city comprise a spacious first floor 25x100 feet in area, fitted up with every convenience for the accommodation of the extensive and valuable stock, where both the professional and amateur can best select what will meet their requirements. Here can be obtained all sizes of cameras, lenses, dry plates, posing chairs, photo paper, field outfits, picture frames, etc. Orders are carefully filled and the trade of the house which is steadily increasing, extends from the Allegheny Mountains to the Mississippi River, and from the Ohio River to the Gulf of Mexico. Mr. W. D. Gatchel was born in New York state, and has been in this business both at Cincinnati and Louisville. The members of the firm are honorable and liberal business men, who are fully alive to the progress of the photographic art, and their success in this artistic industry is as marked, as it is well deserved.

EDWARD ZOELLER; Band and Orchestral Instruments; No. 210 Jefferson Street.—The leading dealer in this part of the country in band and orchestral instruments of every description is Mr. Edward Zoeller, who has been in business here in this line since 1884, starting on Third Street and removing in 1891 to his present location, where he has a commodious store on the ground floor with a ground area of one thousand square feet, where he carries a large and carefully selected stock of musical instruments of the very best foreign and domestic make. Mr. Zoeller is an acknowledged expert in all kinds of musical instruments as well as a repairer of same and he has a carefully selected corps of trained assistants while his superior facilities enable him to equip entire bands or orchestras, or to furnish single instruments at the most reasonable terms. A native of Germany, Mr. Zoeller has resided in Louisville since six years old and is widely known and respected as a genial gentleman and a thoroughly reliable man in all his business dealings.

MISS E. CLUFF; Millinery Parlor; No. 319 West Jefferson Street.—A largely patronized and first-class millinery establishment in Louisville is the representative one of this section, namely the attractive store of Miss E. Cluff. Miss Cluff established this business in 1865, and has ever enjoyed a large and fashionable patronage, while she is always the first in Louisville to introduce the latest Paris, London and New York fashions. The premises occupied comprise a spacious first floor 60x165 feet in area, the front being devoted to the salesrooms. All the latest novelties in imported bonnets, hats and trimmings are here displayed in perfect accord with the prevailing fashions, also ribbons, plumes, flowers, silks, satins, velvets, etc. A number of skilled milliners are employed, and orders are filled and delivered at short notice at extremely moderate prices. A specialty is made by Miss Cluff of bridal outfits and mourning millinery, who is unremitting in her attention to customers and numbers among her permanent patrons the most fashionable ladies of the city and its vicinity. Miss Cluff is highly esteemed for her strict integrity and her millinery parlor is the oldest in the Falls City, and we strongly recommend it as one justly meriting the patronage of a first-class trade.

F. E. LONG: Proprietor Tenth Street Planing Mill; No. 808 Tenth Street.—The latest mechanical devices in planing mill machinery, are to be found in the old established Louisville Planing Mill, the present proprietor of which is Mr. F. E. Long, the well-known builder and contractor. This business was founded in 1855 by H. J. Lewis & Bro., and the resources of the establishment have kept pace with the progress of mechanical ingenuity. The original proprietors were succeeded in 1859 by Taylor and Montgomery, and still later by M. M. Taylor, who sold out to Mr. F. E. Long in May, 1895. Under the present proprietor the establishment represents the very highest development of planing mill and wood finishing machinery. The premises occupied cover an area of 125x165 feet. The mill proper is a two-story brick and frame structure, covering a ground space 60x100 feet in area, and has a full equipment of the latest improved woodworking machinery, operated by a forty horse power engine. Twenty skilled hands are employed and a large trade is supplied, the principal patronage being from builders and contractors in the vicinity and the city. The product includes sash, doors, blinds, mouldings, weatherboards, flooring, brackets and general planing mill work, all of which is executed in a superior manner, while all the lumber used is thoroughly seasoned. Mr. Long is a native of Kentucky, and has for many years been engaged in business here as a contractor and builder, earning an enviable reputation for just dealing. As proprietor of this old mill, he proposes to maintain the previous high standard of its equipment. He stands high in the esteem of the community, is a member of the Independent Order of Oddfellows and enjoys the entire confidence of his numerous customers.

A. GERST: Dry Goods and Notions; Corner Twelfth and Walnut Streets.—One of the most reliable dry goods and notion concerns in this section of Louisville, is that of Mr. A. Gerst, who succeeded to the control in 1877. This has been a store in this line of trade for several years, and was occupied at one time by Frank Eschrich, who opened it in 1868. When the business was first established here, there was no other dry goods store in this locality. The premises occupied are spacious, and are fitted to repletion with a choice and well selected assortment of fancy and staple dry goods and notions, fancy goods, hosiery, etc. Mr. Gerst is an enterprising and active business man, who brings to bear every possible qualification for success in catering to the wants of the public. His perfect knowledge of the business has attracted a large and remunerative country trade, while he has also a flourishing patronage in the city. The lowest prices prevail, and orders are promptly and carefully filled. Mr. Gerst is a native of Ohio, and previous to coming here, was a traveling salesman. He came to Louisville in 1872, and has resided here ever since. During the late war he served with credit in the Fifth Ohio Volunteer Infantry. He is greatly respected for his integrity and many excellent qualifications, and stands high in business circles.

DEERING HARVESTER COMPANY: Manufacturers of Harvesting Machinery and Binder Twine; No. 215 West Main Street.—Special prominence is given in this volume to the Deering Harvester Company, which is represented in this city by Mr. J. W. Zollars. Were we to devote every page of our work to a description of the Deering Harvester Plant in Chicago, of its agricultural implements and of its enormous annual output, we could but do partial justice to this mammoth institution. Since the establishment of the business in 1880, under the firm name of Mr. William Deering & Co., there has grown up an industry that every American citizen should be proud of, in as much as its products have gone into every portion of the civilized world, and wrought a revolution in agriculture, that has done more than anything else to demonstrate the superior mechanical genius of the American inventor and artisan. The plant of the Deering Harvester Company, in Chicago, has an area of fifty-one acres, employing three thousand men and turning out one machine a minute. From the extreme limits of Siberia, to the southern confines of the Torrid zone, the Deering Harvesters, reapers, mowers and binders are steadily and persistently working out the great problem of economic agriculture. For fifteen years, this concern has been conducting an immense business in the Southwest, of which Louisville has been the great supply depot. From the immense warehouse of the company are shipped annually large numbers of the Deering Harvesters, binders, etc., to all parts of the South, especially, Kentucky and Indiana. Mr. J. W. Zollars was formerly at the head of the Sioux Falls, S. D. branch, and in January, 1895, assumed the management of the Louisville branch, whose business is rapidly increasing under his able methods.

CHARLES TELLMAN: Grocer; No. 266 East Green Street.—One of the leading grocery establishments in this section of Louisville, is that of Mr. Charles Tellman, who started in business eleven years ago. He has a large share of the best patronage of Louisville, which he has gained by persistent endeavor, enterprise and uniformly reliable dealing, together with a careful and intelligent study of the wants of his numerous customers. His store to-day is recognized as a model establishment by the public. Situated on the ground floor with a front of twenty feet and a

LOUISVILLE OF TO-DAY.

depth of sixty feet, the main store carries a large and comprehensive stock of staple and fancy groceries of the best grades, all of which are fully warranted as to purity and quality, while the long experience of the proprietor as a buyer and his close relations with the most reliable sources of supply enable him to offer the very best goods at the most reasonable prices, while a competent force of careful and courteous assistants are employed. The choice stock of liquors carried includes all the leading brands of the famous Kentucky whiskies, and the lager beer of Frank Fehr and the Phoenix Brewing Company,—goods which are acknowledged excellent and well merit the extensive popularity they enjoy. Mr. Teilman, who is a native of Germany, has long been a resident of Louisville, where he is popular as a citizen as well as prominent as a merchant, and he is a leading member of the St. Boniface Society.

RUTH BROTHERS; Furniture Manufacturers; Twenty-seventh and Grayson Streets,—Though comparatively one of the youngest manufacturing concerns of the city, there is no industrial establishment of Louisville that has shown more progressiveness, than that of Ruth Brothers, manufacturers of furniture. They occupy a spacious two-story building, 75x200 feet in area, which was erected by the firm in 1887, specially for their business. The different departments are fully equipped with modern tools and machinery, operated by a fifty-four horse power engine. A large number of skilled workmen are employed, and the output consists of furniture of all kinds, the specialties being kitchen safes, tables, etc. These goods have no superiors in the market, and wherever introduced meet with ready sales. The goods have met with great favor and already an extensive patronage is controlled through Indiana, Kentucky, Ohio, Alabama, Georgia, Mississippi, Tennessee and Florida. Sales are made exclusively to the trade, and a large stock is always kept on hand. In 1889 this house was established by its present proprietors. The Messrs. Ruth are natives of Lawrence County, Indiana, and twenty-seven years ago they came to Louisville and attained employment in the line they now follow.

J. T. SULLIVAN & COMPANY; Wholesale Produce and Commission; No. 319 Second Street.—The handling of food products on commission forms an important factor in the commerce of Louisville, and among the most enterprising merchants engaged in it is Mr. J. T. Sullivan, who handles not only produce, but makes a specialty of cocoanut and creamery butter. Mr. Sullivan is a native of this city, and spent his early life in Kentucky, afterwards removing to Cincinnati, Ohio. In 1892 he opened an office in this city, and has built up an extensive trade in butter, etc. The premises occupied comprise a first floor and basement, each 20x30 feet in dimensions, admirably adapted for the business. Producers should see that their consignments are shipped to J. T. Sullivan & Company, if they wish to obtain the best results, and receive the largest returns and the most prompt and courteous treatment. Mr. Sullivan is also the agent for the state of Kentucky for the sale of the new cocoanut butter, a hygienic substitute for lard, in frying, cooking, dressing broiled meats, pastry making and cake baking. This preparation is the chemically pure refined oil, extracted from the white meat of the cocoanut, and has the endorsement of the medical fraternity everywhere, as an invaluable agent in cooking, especially calculated to aid digestion. The proprietors are The Pure Food Product Company, of Chicago. This cocoanut butter is highly recommended by James J. Hearne, chief steward, Joseph Seyl, head cook and Herman Weinman, head pastry cook of the Palmer House, Chicago, and is spoken of in flattering terms in the United States Health Report Journal, May 14, 1895, and is the sweetest and best substitute for butter yet introduced.

H. H. SYMMES & CO; Contractors for Asphalt, Asbestos and Granitoid Work; No. 215 Fifth Street.—The gentleman whose name heads this sketch is a leader in this particular line of business. He is well and favorably known in building and commercial circles, and sustains an excellent reputation for integrity and reliability. He was formerly of Osborne, Symmes & Co., established 1887, and later of H. H. Symmes & Co., who were succeeded by Bates, Symmes & Co., subsequently he was head of the Symmes Roofing and Paving Co., and has been in business alone since January, 1895. Mr. Symmes is contractor for asphalt, asbestos and granitoid work, also applies the "Symmes Cloth Bound Asphalt Roof" guaranteed for ten years, and is a dealer in roofing and building material. He gives particular attention to asphalt floors for stores, warehouses, breweries, distilleries, stables, etc., and has a large trade in and out of town, and does work of a very superior character, and can refer to numerous structures, including public buildings, institutions, hotels, theatres, bank and office buildings, mills, factories, breweries, distilleries, manufacturing plants of various kinds, warehouses, etc., throughout the city and state. Mr. Symmes executes orders on short notice, and employs twenty experienced hands, and has two teams in service. He was born and brought up here in Louisville, and is a man of energy and enterprise and of varied experience.

JOHN BARTMAN & SONS; Wholesale and Retail Dealers in Lumber.—There is no business carried on to-day in the United States that is more distinctively and radically American, than the trade in lumber and timber, and in this important staple Louisville is well represented by several reliable and representative houses. Prominent among these is that of Messrs. John Bartman & Sons, wholesale and retail dealers in all kinds of lumber and wood finish for buildings. This business was founded in 1874 by Mr. John Bartman, who eventually admitted his sons, Messrs. William and George and Jacob Bartman into partnership. Mr. John Bartman is one of the oldest and best judges of lumber in the city, and was born in Germany in 1830, and came to Louisville in 1853, while his sons who are energetic and able young business men, are natives of this city. Only the best grades of lumber and building materials are handled, and the trade of the firm, which is steadily increasing extends throughout all sections of the city and state. The business was formerly conducted at Hancock and Main Streets, but in 1891 was removed to its present location, corner Campbell and Broadway. Messrs. John Bartman & Sons are highly regarded for their strict integrity and are very popular in trade circles, and dealings once entered into with them are sure to result profitably to all concerned.

WHITEHEAD & CO.; Groceries, Fresh Meats and Vegetables; Northeast corner Eleventh and Grayson Streets.—One of the leading concerns in Louisville engaged in the handling of staple articles of food is Whitehead & Co., who are dealers in staple and fancy groceries, fresh meats and vegetables, fine wines, liquors, cigars and tobacco. This business was started three years ago by Taylor Whitehead. The main store is 20x75 feet in area and there is a separate saloon entrance from Eleventh Street. The stock is most complete in every way and includes a full line of staple and fancy groceries, fresh country produce, choice meats and table delicacies and canned goods. The stock of liquors is exceptionally fine and is selected with particular care. It includes all the leading brands of Kentucky whiskies, in which the age and purity is guaranteed, the Phœnix Brewing Company's famous beer and all kinds of reliable table liquors. Also a choice line of cigars which includes the best brands in Havana and domestic tobacco. This store caters to an A1 trade and is most eligibly situated for conveniently serving a first-class permanent patronage. Mr. Whitehead himself is still in the employ of the J. M. Atherton Distilling Company, and he thus gained a **practical experience** which now enables him to select the choicest liquors. **He is an active Freemason** and is personally popular.

THE GOLDEN RULE STORE; C. E. Overstreet & Co.; Dry Goods, Trimmings, Notions, Etc.; No. 238 Fourth Avenue.—The attention of our many readers is directed to the unique dry goods concern of Messrs. C. E. Overstreet & Co., better known as "The Golden Rule Store." The members of this representative firm, Mr. C. E. Overstreet and Mr. D. C. Walker, have by their untiring industry, coupled with a thorough knowledge of the requirements of the public, built up a most substantial trade among the best people of Louisville and the dealers in the surrounding towns. Their store is a handsome three-storied brick building with basement, having a frontage of forty feet and a depth of one hundred and ten feet. The main salesroom occupies the entire first floor. Their extensive stock embraces everything desirable in the lines of silks, satins, velvets, dress goods in all the new textures and shades. A specialty is made in ribbons, a complete assortment of all widths and shades being always carried. The house, it need hardly be added, deals only in the finest goods. The patrons include the oldest families in this city, but by no means are confined to the wealthiest classes. The immense business centred here was originally founded June 12, 1876, by the present energetic head partner, Mr. C. E. Overstreet. Mr. D. C. Walker being admitted into the concern in 1889, when the present firm was formed. Both partners are natives of this state and are recognized as merchants of rare business energy and ability and enjoy the highest of reputations in commercial circles.

OWEN TYLER; Building Material and Supplies; No. 338 West Main Street.—Mr. Owen Tyler established this business in 1891 and the undertaking has proven an unqualified success. He is a dealer in building material and supplies and the yards are at Third and River Streets and Floyd and River Streets. These are spacious, provided with the best facilities for receiving and shipping by rail or water, and contain large storage sheds, and the trade extends to all parts of Kentucky, the leading builders and contractors being included among the patrons. Mr. Tyler represents the following celebrated companies: St. Louis and Findlay Hydraulic Press Brick Company; the Mack Manufacturing Company, vitrified brick; Bostwick Fire proof Steel Lath Company, of Wheeling; Kintear & Gager Company, of Columbus, Ohio, manufacturers of steel ceilings, fire shutters and rolling steel blinds; Beatric Manufacturing Company, of St. Louis, etc. He is sole agent here for these and a heavy stock of their products is carried, including vitrified, press and ornamental brick, wood moulding, steel ceilings, corrugated iron, etc. Every inducement is offered to the trade as regards prices, and Mr. Tyler's name is **in business circles**, a synonym for integrity. Mr. Tyler was born in Louisville and is a member of the firm of Davis & Tyler, manufacturers of signs of all descriptions; a member of the Kenton Club, Elks, etc.

JOHN SACKSTEDER & SON; Proprietors of the Mount Eden Vineyard, Native Wines; No. 716 East Green Street.—The steadily growing popularity of native wines has given a great impetus to the trade and a widely known native wine house in Louisville is that of Messrs. John Sack-

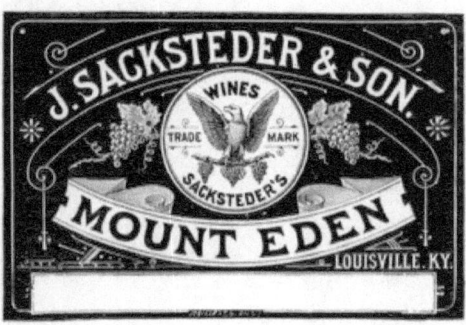

steder & Son, wine growers. This business was established forty years ago by Mr. John Sacksteder, who conducted it till 1884, when he admitted his son, Mr. Louis G. Sacksteder, into partnership. The partners have had long experience and their trade extends throughout the southern, southwestern and northern states. The premises occupied are spacious and the cellars in this city have a capacity of storing fifteen thousand gallons of wine. The Mount Eden Vineyard, near Leavenworth, Ind., containing thirty acres in fine grapes, produce their principal brands, these being known as "Sweet Muscader," "Ives Seedling," "Sweet Sack," "Dry Sack," "Mount Eden," and "Riesling." Their wines are unsurpassed for purity and quality and they also produce sacramental wines for church purposes and fill orders at extremely moderate prices, either in bulk or bottles. Mr. John Sacksteder is a pioneer in the wine industry of Kentucky and was born in Germany, but has resided here for the past fifty-six years, while his son, Mr. L. G. Sacksteder, is a native of this city. They are honorable business men and this is the only exclusive native wine house in the Falls City. Mr. John Sacksteder, previously to settling here, operated vineyards in Germany as far back as 1835, and is recognized as the oldest wine grower in this country.

THOMPSON & COMPANY; Wholesale Produce Commission Merchants; Nos. 236 and 238 Jefferson Market.—The oldest established and one of the most noted houses in this line in the city, is that of Messrs. Thompson and Co., the popular wholesale produce commission merchants. This business was established in 1838 by Mr. A. Thompson, who conducted it till 1876 when the present firm name of Thompson and Co., was adopted, the co-partners being Messrs. J. H. and S. S. Thompson, and E. H. Stallcup. Mr. J. H. Thompson is a son of the founder, and Mr. S. S. Thompson is a nephew of Mr. J. H. Thompson, the present senior partner. They are constantly receiving consignments of produce from the southern, western and southwestern states, also fruits etc., from Florida and California. Messrs. Thompson and Co. deal largely in produce, and make a specialty of early Southern vegetables and fruits. Liberal advances are made on consignments, which are disposed of promptly at highest market rates, while they never fail to make immediate returns to shippers. Orders and consignments are solicited and in winter they transact a large business in eggs, poultry and butter, and in the summer season in fresh fruits. The premises occupied comprise a spacious three-story brick building 50x90 feet in area, extending to Green Street, equipped with every convenience. The partners are natives of Louisville and are active members of the National League of Commission Merchants of the United States. They refer by permission to Dun's Mercantile Agency and the Bank of Commerce, of Louisville, as regards their financial standing and responsibility. Mr. Stallcup has been identified with this house several years, and is an active Freemason and prominent member of the Knights of Pythias.

J. WM. MILLER; Dealer in Groceries and Produce; Nos. 1715 & 1717 Seventh Street.—One of the oldest established concerns in this section of Louisville, is that of Mr. J. Wm. Miller, dealer in groceries and produce, fresh meat and vegetables. This flourishing business was established in 1869 by Mr. Soane, who carried on a large trade until 1879. He was succeeded by Mr. Miller, who has since built up an extensive and remunerative trade. He occupies a spacious store, fully equipped and furnished with all modern improvements, making it well adapted to business purposes. Mr. Miller is an active, enterprising man, who started in business with a small capital, but by a close and careful attention to business, and a thorough knowledge of every detail of the business, has now one of the largest and best stores in this part of the city. From the time he first commenced business, he has aimed to meet the wants of those who patronize him, and that he has been successful in his efforts to furnish the best class of goods at popular prices, is shown by the large substantial custom he has secured. Mr. Miller was born in this country, near Louisville in 1801, and has always lived in or near the city, and has been councilman from the eighth ward six years.

G. A. HIKES & BROTHER; Meat and Vegetables; Corner Seventh Street and Broadway. Among the best firms in the grocery business of Louisville, is that of G. A. Hikes & Brother, who also have a meat and vegetable market. This flourishing business was established about 1866 by a Mr. Gaulbert at the same location. After some changes in 1883, the present firm was organized under the name of G. A. Hikes & Brother, who have built up an extensive trade, which is constantly increasing. The store is convenient and a large and choice line of staple and fancy groceries, canned goods, table delicacies, teas, coffees, sugars, spices, fresh vegetables, meats, etc., is always on hand. Mr. G. A. Hikes is a native of Illinois, but came to Louisville in 1869. He was born in 1846, and Mr. W. L. Hikes was born in Jefferson County, Kentucky, in 1857. They are both active, energetic and enterprising business men, who carefully look after the interest of their customers, and by their promptness and fair dealing, they have rapidly built up a large and first-class trade.

BRAUN BROTHERS; Wooden and Willow ware; Nos. 405 to 409 Brook Street.—Among the useful branches of trade in Louisville, that of the sale of all kinds of wooden and willow ware is one of considerable value. In this connection reference is made to the newly established house of Messrs. Braun Brothers, wholesale dealers, etc., who established this in 1894 and have already secured a liberal patronage not only in Kentucky, but also in the southern and western states. Mr. George Braun was previously for 13 years, engaged with the house of Messrs. Myer, Bridges & Co., wholesale dealers in wooden and willow ware. His brother, Mr. Frank Braun, was formerly in the butchering business. The premises occupied are spacious and are fully stocked with a choice assortment of wooden and willow ware, paper, paper bags, brooms, baskets, brushes, etc. Only the best goods are handled and a specialty is made of paper sacks and bags while the prices quoted for all goods cannot be discounted by any other house in the country. Mr. George Braun was born in Louisville in 1857 and Mr. Frank Braun in 1862, and have always resided on Baxter Avenue. They are honorable and popular merchants and we predict for them a successful career in this useful business.

A. BOHLSEN; Groceries and Meats; Oak and Fifth Streets.—One of the most reliable grocery stores of the Falls City is that conducted by Mr. A. Bohlsen, which he established in 1872. From its inception the establishment found favor with the public and increased rapidly in patronage and popularity. The stock carried comprises the choicest staple and fancy groceries, imported teas and coffees, creamery and dairy butter, fresh eggs, canned goods, etc., all being of the purest and freshest quality. Meats and vegetables are also extensively dealt in, in fact Mr. Bohlsen makes a specialty of these commodities, and all goods are purchased direct from the best sources of supply, with which the house enjoys advantageous connections. The establishment is 27x80 feet in dimensions and is well adapted for the business and has been occupied by Mr. Bohlsen since 1894, his location, previous to that time, being at Sixth and Walnut Streets. The store is elegantly equipped and no house in the city is better prepared to meet the wants of its patrons in this particular line. Mr. Bohlsen, who is a native of Germany has lived in America the greater part of his life.

GUS. AUSBECK; Grocer; Nos. 1614-1622 Seventh Street.—In 1868, with a limited capital, but an extensive supply of perseverance and enterprise, Mr. Gus. Ausbeck established this grocery store in Louisville. The store has a ground area, 40x80 feet, and in point of equipment, is a model of up-to-date convenience. The stock carried embraces everything in the line of fancy and staple groceries and provisions of all kinds, the goods being kept at the highest standard of excellence to meet the wants of the trade, which is emphatically first class. Mr. Ausbeck's wide experience and superior connection with the trade, enable him to buy to the very best advantage, the keenest discrimination being displayed in all matters, while the heavy patronage makes the constant replenishing of the stock necessary and hence the goods are always fresh. Three clerks are employed, and the trade comes from all parts of the city and surrounding territory. Mr. Ausbeck was born in Germany, and is an excellent representative of that sturdy and prosperous race. He came to Louisville in 1858, and since that time has actively asserted himself in advancing her interests. When the battle cry startled the country in 1861, he readily took up arms, serving under Colonel Harlan in the Tenth Kentucky Infantry. In Freemasonary, Mr. Ausbeck is an active worker, and in the city enjoys the highest regard of his fellow citizens.

CHARLES RAMSER; Dealer in Stoves, Tinware, China and Hardware; No. 603 West Broadway.—A representative and reliable Louisville house in its line, is that of Mr. Charles Ramser, dealer in stoves, tinware, etc. Mr. Ramser, who is a thoroughly practical roofer and sheet metal worker, established this business in 1884, since which period he has secured a liberal patronage in the city and state. The premises occupied, which are owned by Mr. Ramser, are spacious and well equipped and are fully stocked with a superior assortment of stoves, ranges and heaters, radiators, tinware, china and hardware of every description, which are offered to customers at very moderate prices. Only first-class goods are handled. Mr. Ramser also attends carefully to roofing, guttering and spouting, general jobbing and repairing, and makes a specialty of the Barker patent chimney top and ventilator, which is a sure cure for smoky chimneys, and is a general favorite wherever introduced, owing to its efficiency and utility. Mr. Ramser was born in Louisville in 1858. He is a liberal and honorable business man, and all goods purchased at this establishment are guaranteed to be exactly as represented in every particular, and his future success seems well assured.

C. J. COMSTOCK; Lumber Dealer, Office and Yard; Nos. 2030 to 2036 Lytle Street.—A representative house in this section of the city in its line, is that of Mr. C. J. Comstock, wholesale and retail dealer in lumber, etc., who established this business nine years ago, and has since secured a liberal patronage, numbering among his customers many leading contractors and builders. He has been identified with the lumber trade since 1879. The yards and sheds at Nos. 2030 to 2036 Lytle Street, have an area of 105x135 feet, and are supplied with every convenience. Here Mr. Comstock keeps a heavy and choice stock of southern lumber, etc., also building material and builders' hardware, doors, sash, blinds lath, shingles, etc., which are offered to customers at the lowest ruling market rates. He sells over three million feet of lumber annually, and makes a specialty of car lots. Mr. Comstock is a native of this city, and as a business man is prompt and honorable, while he is also very popular in trade circles.

D. S. MILLS & CO.; Commission Merchants; Nos. 210 and 212 West Main Street.—Louisville has long maintained a prominent position in the grain, hay and produce trade, and among the representative houses in this line is that of Messrs. D. S. Mills & Co., commission merchants and wholesale dealers. This business was established in 1868 by Mr. D. S. Mills, who is sole proprietor, possessing long experience in the grain trade, and is largely endowed with the elements that lead to success in any undertaking. The premises occupied are spacious, and every facility is at hand for handling consignments of grain, seeds, hay, grain bags and produce. Mr. Mills has influential connections in the surrounding states and the West, and with dealers and the trade throughout the South and is well prepared to render entire satisfaction to consignors. He is constantly receiving consignments, and is always able to offer superior inducements to buyers, making also liberal advances when required on shipments, guaranteeing at all times quick sales and immediate returns. Mr. Mills has resided in Louisville since 1866, and is highly esteemed for his strict probity, and is an active member of the Board of Trade.

PAUL A. NEFF; Grocer; Northwest corner Seventeenth and Rowan Streets.—To the average family the choice of a grocer is not so much the question of the lowest prices, as it is of the one who handles the most reliable goods. Prominent among the reliable houses of this section of Louisville is that of Mr. Paul A. Neff, who has secured a high reputation for dealing and for handling only strictly first-class goods. Mr. Neff established this business in 1866 and has built up a liberal patronage. The premises occupied have been specially erected for this business by Mr. Neff and are supplied with every convenience. The stock carried includes the choicest and freshest staple and fancy groceries, including the finest teas, coffees, spices, sugars, canned goods, condiments etc., etc. These are purchased from the very best sources of supply and represent the purest of productions for the house caters strictly to a high-class trade. Several assistants are employed, while "quick sales and small profits" is the motto of this establishment. In 1837, in Germany, Mr. Paul A. Neff was born and settled in Louisville in 1856, and started in business in 1866. He is highly regarded for his strict probity and is one of our popular and influential citizens.

PETER BITZER; Grocer and Dealer in Feed; No. 701 Twelfth Street.— No house in Louisville has enjoyed a longer career of uninterrupted success than that of Peter Bitzer, the widely-known grocer. John Bitzer established this business thirty-five years ago, and under his able management it steadily advanced until 1880, when at his death, it passed into the hands of his son, the present proprietor. The premises occupied consist of a three-story and basement building, substantially built of brick, 40x100 feet in area. This is occupied for salesrooms and storage, the salesrooms being elegantly appointed, while the stock carried embraces everything in the line of staple and fancy groceries, flour and feed, wines and liquors, all of which represent the very best products in these lines, and are purchased direct from the leading sources of supply, with which the house enjoys most advantageous business relations, enabling it to quote prices that lesser houses cannot think of duplicating. The wines and liquors carried are especially choice, representing the best foreign and domestic productions, among the latter being included the most celebrated brands of Kentucky whiskies. The trade comes from all parts of this locality, and four competent assistants are employed. Liberality characterizes all business transactions of the house. Forty-six years ago, Mr. Peter Bitzer was born in Germany. When eleven years of age he came to Louisville with his parents, and has ever since resided here, his every interest being identified with the city, and to advance her interests, his assistance is never withheld.

LOUISVILLE GIRTH AND BLANKET MILLS; Corner Preston Street and Burnett Avenue.— It is only three years since the Louisville Girth and Blanket Mills were established, but so immediate was their success, that to-day they enjoy a patronage which is far in advance of many similar concerns that have been catering to the public for more decades than this enterprise has had years. The factory is a massive brick structure, 50x100 feet in area, fully equipped, with special machinery and appliances, cards, spinning machines, twisters, pickers, hand looms, etc. The building is lighted throughout by its own electric dynamo, and is in every respect a model of the up-to-date factory. The output consists of saddle girths and saddle blankets, the output of the former alone amounting to upwards of two hundred dozen a week and over. Forty operatives are employed and the trade comes from all parts of the United States and Canada, the goods always finding ready sales wherever introduced, and being pronounced the most perfect productions of the kind upon the market. A large stock is always carried, and sales are made exclusively to the trade. The proprietor of this enterprise is Mr. William D. Heiling, one of the progressive and influential citizens of Louisville. In financial and industrial life he is widely known, being identified with such extensive industries such as the Crystal Spring Distilling Company, of which he is secretary, and the Louisville Iron, Lead and Zinc Mine and Smelting Company.

JNO. T. BARBEE & CO.; Whiskies; No. 132 Second Street.—The whiskey industry constitutes no inconsiderable factor in the sum of trade in all the great centres of business activity in the United States. This is more particularly true of Louisville, which unquestionably possesses some of the leading concerns engaged in the trade in the country to-day. Among the prominent establishments in this line, should be mentioned that of Messrs. Jno. T. Barbee & Co. This establishment was founded under the present trading title some four years ago by Mr. Jno. T. Barbee, who has since secured an extensive patronage. The premises here occupied consist of a substantial three-storied and basement building, 22x86 feet in dimensions, giving ample accommodation for the storage and preservation of the valuable stock. The distillery of the concern is situated at Versailles, Woodford County, Ky., and is equipped with all the latest improved machinery known to this branch of industry, the output capacity averaging fifteen hundred barrels of whiskey per annum, storage accommodation being provided for some ten thousand barrels. The grain used is selected with great care, while the fact may not be generally known that the water used, from its softness and springlike purity, has been characterized by experts as the best ever known to attain the highest perfection in the process of distillation, the result apart from other noted grades, being the production of the famous Old Barbee handmade sour-mash whiskey. This standard whiskey holds a foremost position strictly on its merits, while the public and the trade, quick to discern what is the best, patronize those dealers who keep in stock a full supply of the Old Barbee brands of sour-mash whiskies. Mr. Barbee is a Virginian by birth, now resident here for some time past, and was previously for four years a member of the wholesale liquor firm of Messrs. John G. Roach & Co.

SOUTHERN HEATING COMPANY; Nos. 218 and 220 Third Street.—The use of steam and hot water for warming buildings has become so well understood, and during the last few years has made such rapid advances in public favor, that it seems unnecessary to prove their superiority over all other modes of heating. In connection with these remarks, special attention is directed in this review of the commerce and industries of Louisville to the Southern Heating Company, whose well appointed offices and warerooms are located at Nos. 218 and 220 Third Street. This company was incorporated under the laws of the state of Kentucky in 1894, and is ably officered as follows: Walter E. Mellinger, president and treasurer; David A. Gorman, vice-president and superintendent, and M. H. Mellinger, secretary. The premises occupied comprise a substantial three-storied brick building, the first floor being devoted to office purposes and the exhibition of apparatus in operation under steam, the upper floors being relegated generally to the storage of stock. The company are extensive handlers of all kinds of heating specialties, boilers, engines, smoke consumers, radiators, registers and ventilating apparatus, and are prepared to submit estimates and complete contracts for the entire steam heating and ventilating of buildings of any dimensions on moderate terms. They act also as general consulting engineers, and are representatives of the following well-known companies: J. H. McClain Company, Canton, O.; Buffalo Forge Company, Buffalo, N. Y.; Powers Regulator Company, Chicago, Ills., and the Deane Steam Pump Company, of Holyoke, Mass. A visit to the warerooms of the company, where a splendid stock of these inventions is constantly carried, will satisfy the most skeptical that here can be obtained the finest steam, water and fan heating and ventilating apparatus in this section of the country.

WM. JETTER; Manufacturer of and Dealer in Boots and Shoes; No. 460 South Side Market Street.—The boot and shoe trade has many able and enterprising exponents in the city of Louisville, and none that enjoys a more deserved popularity, than the establishment of Mr. Wm. Jetter. This business was established many years ago by Mr. Fred. Boss, who conducted it till 1882, when Mr. Jetter succeeded to the control. Mr. Jetter is a thoroughly practical shoemaker, whose goods are highly esteemed by an appreciative public. The store is commodious, and the stock embraces full lines of footwear for all ages and both sexes, from the dainty kid ball slippers to stout shoes for boys' wear. Every pair sold in this establishment is warranted to be as represented, and all work to order is guaranteed to render entire satisfaction, as to fit, finish and materials. Repairing is promptly and neatly done, and a heavy supply of home made and eastern boots and shoes is always on hand, while the prices quoted for all foot wear, cannot be discounted in the city or elsewhere. Mr. Jetter was born in Germany in 1844, and came to Louisville in 1872. He is highly regarded by the community for his strict integrity, and is an active member of the A. O. U. W., Knights and Ladies of Honor, Harmonia Society, and also of the Schwaben Aid Society.

CHAS. A. WEBER; Fancy Groceries and Delicacies; No. 302 West Market Street.—There is no grocery house in Louisville, that occupies a higher place in public favor, or contracts a larger or more select patronage than that of Chas. A. Weber. In 1861, under the style of A. and G. Gelfius, this house was established, one year later coming into the sole possession of George Gelfius. He conducted it until 1893, when at his death his nephew, the present proprietor succeeded. Mr. Weber, who is a young man, and a native of Louisville, is thoroughly experienced, and under his guidance, the old and enviable reputation has not only been maintained, but greatly added to. The premises consist of a three-story brick structure, 20x75 feet in area, fully supplied with every convenience, and the stock consists of everything in the line of fancy groceries and delicacies, specialties being made of imported and domestic cheese and Italian Spaghetti. The leading sources are drawn on for supply, and nowhere in this or any other city, can a choicer or more complete stock of these commodities be found. Several assistants are employed and the trade comes from all parts of this and neighboring towns and country. Goods are delivered free of charge, to all parts of the city. Mr. Weber is one of the most esteemed and influential of Louisville's younger sons.

GEORGE W. CORBIN; Sign Writer; No. 923 West Market Street.—Among the leading exponents of the sign writing art in Louisville, is Mr. George W. Corbin, whose practical knowledge and excellent taste have won for him a high reputation. He established this business in 1887, and occupies a spacious first floor as office and workshop. Mr. Corbin attends to everything coming within the scope of the advertising sign

164 — — LOUISVILLE OF TO-DAY. — —

writer and painter, executing pictures and caricatures in any style and of any size, emblems and signs in embossed gilt, bronze, glass, script, block and ornamental brass and copper, canvas, netting and wire, these being executed in the highest style of the art, by skilled and experienced workmen of whom ten are usually employed. Careful attention is also given to printing on paper, metals, etc., and to rural advertising, including board, sign and dead wall work on railroad, steamboat or highway routes, in any part of the United States. Mr. Corbin's work in all departments is noted for the attractiveness and beauty of his productions, and he also owns a patent for manufacturing flags, etc. He is a native of Indianapolis, and has traveled over every part of the United States as a journeyman, and has also made two trips to Europe. He is a popular member of the G. A. R. and the Sons of Veteran.

E DMUND L. MEYER; The Eagle Boot and Shoe House; No. 350 East Market Street.—A representative house which has risen to prominence in the Falls City, is that of Mr. Edmund L. Meyer, the popular dealer in fine boots and shoes. This business was established in 1885 by Messrs. Meyer & Wolf. Mr. Wolf retired in 1891, when Mr. Meyer became sole proprietor. He is an able business man, who numbers among his permanent patrons, some of the leading families of the city and its vicinity. The premises occupied are spacious, and are fitted up with every convenience, the stock is one of the finest of the kind in the city, including a superior assortment of medium and fine grade boots, shoes, slippers and rubber goods, for gentlemen, ladies, misses, boys and children. These goods are purchased direct from the most celebrated manufacturers, and are quoted at extremely moderate figures, while they are unsurpassed for style, durability, fit and finish. Custom work is also done here in the highest style of the art, hand-sewed shoes for tender feet being a specialty. Every pair of boots and shoes sold in this establishment is warranted to be as represented. Mr. Meyer is an honorable business man, and an expert in catering to a critical trade, and we strongly recommend this store to our numerous readers, as one fully meriting their continued support and patronage.

F. W. JOHANBOEKE & SONS; Wholesale Hats, Caps, Etc.; No. 641 West Main Street.—Prominent among the reliable houses actively engaged in the wholesale handling of hats, caps, gloves, umbrellas etc., is that of Messrs. F. W. Johanboeke & Sons, which was established by Messrs. F. W. & H. R. Johanboeke, under firm style of Johanboeke Brothers in 1864. Mr. F. W. Johanboeke and his sons, Messrs. A. L. and W. H. Johanboeke, succeeding to the control in 1887. The present eligible quarters were secured in 1890, and consist of a spacious four-story and basement building 20x175 feet in dimensions, equipped with every facility for the accommodation of the immense stock of hats, caps, straw and fur goods in season, gloves and umbrellas, the output of the most celebrated manufacturers in this country. The house does a large and steadily increasing trade, which radiates broadly throughout Kentucky, Indiana and Tennessee. First-class retailers are aware that supplies received through this house can invariably be relied upon, while the figures quoted are extremely reasonable. Special attention is paid to mail orders, and in this branch of the business they have succeeded in giving general satisfaction to the trade.

C HAS. EGGERS; Merchant Tailor; No. 357 Market Street.—This business was established in 1860 by Mr. Henry Eggers, who conducted it till 1876, when he died after an honorable career. He was succeeded by his son, Mr. Chas. Eggers, the present proprietor. Mr. Eggers is an able cutter and tailor, and since he has been catering to the wants of the citizens of Louisville has gained a prominence, placing him in the front rank of the leading merchant tailors of the city and state. The store is finely fitted up, and is fully stocked with a choice assortment of suitings, broadcloths, cassimeres, overcoatings, etc., in all the latest styles of seasonable goods of foreign and domestic manufacture. Mr. Eggers gives personal attention to each customer, and the garments made by him are perfect in fit, style and artistic workmanship, while his prices are noted for their moderation. He was born in Louisville in 1856, and is highly esteemed for his strict integrity. Among his permanent customers are many of Louisville's best dressed citizens, and he allows no garment to leave his establishment, that does not come up fully to the highest standard of excellence.

V AL. KRAUSHAAR; Grocery and Saloon; Southeast corner Twenty-fifth and Market Streets.—A favorite resort for commercial and business men in this section of Louisville is the West End Exchange, of which Mr. Val. Kraushaar is the popular proprietor. Mr. Kraushaar is a business man of experience and integrity, and his sample room is one of the best conducted in the city. He commenced business in 1878 on the opposite corner and eventually in 1889 built his present substantial building. The saloon is finely fitted up with mahogany fixtures, etc., and the stock of imported and domestic wines, liquors, whiskies and cigars is quite equal to those of any other house in the city. Mr. Kraushaar caters to a good class of trade and a visit to the West End Exchange is well repaid at all times by the pleasant associations and prompt service. Mr. Kraushaar was born in Germany forty-eight years ago and came with his parents to Louisville when very young. He makes a specialty of handling the finest rye and bourbon whiskies, which are absolutely unexcelled in the city for purity and flavor and this is one of the few saloons in the city that still charges ten cents for whisky. Mr. Kraushaar was also previously engaged in the grocery business but retired from that trade in 1892.

S. REIS; Wholesale Horse Collar Manufacturer; No. 126 Second Street. —A representative house in its line in Louisville is that of Mr. S. Reis, wholesale dealer in and manufacturer of horse collars, who established this enterprise in 1870, and has since secured a liberal patronage, his trade extending throughout the entire United States. He is a thoroughly practical collar maker, who personally supervises all operations of the factory, so that no collar can leave the establishment that is not perfectly made and fully up to the standard. The premises occupied comprise a spacious four-story and basement building, 30x125 feet in area, which is utilized for factory purposes and storage of stock. Only carefully selected materials are utilized, and all sizes and qualities of horse collars are produced, while twenty skilled hands are employed. Mr. Reis' horse collars are recognized standards with the trade and have no superiors in the market, and are offered to retailers at very moderate prices. He is the owner of several useful patents relating to horse collars, and is constantly on the alert and striving to improve and maintain the quality of his goods. Mr. Reis was born in Germany, but has resided in Louisville many years, where he is greatly respected for his strict integrity. He is a large real estate owner, and is one of our public spirited and influential citizens.

A. J. SPURRIERS' SONS; House and Decorative Painters; No. 210 Second Street.—A widely known and reliable house engaged in the painting and decorating trade in Louisville, is that of A. J. Spurriers' Sons. This business was established in 1858 by the father of the present proprietors. They execute all kinds of plain and ornamental painting, graining, sign painting, etc., in the most artistic manner, and have lately finished the interior work in Fousdee & Gaollert Co's. Building, St. Joseph's Infirmary, Sts. Mary's and Elisabeth's Hospitals, Strauss' dry goods store, etc., also exterior work on many prominent buildings in the city. They make a specialty of the decoration of private residences and guarantee the utmost satisfaction in every instance. Fifteen to twenty-five skilled workmen are employed, and they promptly furnish estimates on all kinds of work. Messrs. Spurriers are natives of this city, and members of the Master Painters' Association, while Mr. Edward Spurriers is also prominent in Odd Fellow circles. By honorable methods, they have secured a permanent trade, and are recognized as leading exponents of this branch of skilled industry.

W. C. & S. M. NONES; Wholesale and Retail Dealers in Vehicles; Nos. 443 and 445 West Main Street.—A representative house in this section of Louisville in its line is that of Messrs. W. C. & S. M. Nones, wholesale and retail dealers in vehicles of every description. The premises occupied comprise a spacious five-storied and basement double building, 50x150 feet in area, equipped with elevator, etc. The stock embraces all kinds of vehicles, from a farm truck to a four in hand coach, the firm acting as sales agents for such noted concerns as the Ohio Buggy Company, of Columbus, O.; H. H. Babcock Company, of Watertown, N. Y.; Morris Woodruff, of Dayton, O.; James and Mayer Buggy Company, of Lawrenceburg, Ind.; W. S. Frazier & Co., manufacturers of sulkies, Aurora, Ind.; Fenton Metallic Manufacturing Company, of Jamestown, N. Y., manufacturers of the celebrated Fenton bicycles; McFarlain Carriage Company, of Connersville, Ind., and the Kentucky Wagon Manufacturing Company. The trade of the house is chiefly of a local character, and under energetic guidance, is annually increasing in volume. Mr. W. C. Nones, the senior partner is a native of Hartford, and has been a respected resident of Louisville for the past forty years. He is president and general manager of the Kentucky Wagon Manufacturing Company. Mr. S. M. Nones, his son, was born in the Falls City. He is a young man of great energy, upon whom devolves the entire active management of this enterprise, which has now been in prosperous existence for the past four years.

C. P. BARNES & BROTHER; Jewelers and Opticians; Nos. 504 and 506 West Market Street.—One of the oldest established and most popular jewelry establishments in the city of Louisville, is that so ably conducted under the firm style of C. P. Barnes & Bro., which was founded by Mr. C. P. Barnes in 1858. The business has been for a quarter of a century conducted under the firm style, as at present. Business operations were primarily commenced at No. 319 Third Street, removal being made to the present commodious quarters in 1892, where they occupy the entire first floor. Here is likewise carried one of the heaviest and most reliable stocks of jewelry, watches, etc., in town. The assortment embraces the finest grades of American made and imported watches, clocks, silverware, diamonds, optical goods and the usual complement of the strictly first-class establishment of this type. Ten assistants are employed, and the trade of the house extends throughout Louisville and the southern and western states. The policy of this house has ever been one of equity, the strict avoidance of misrepresentations and the giving of good value for money received. Mr. Barnes is a Kentuckian by birth, and a prominent member of the Order of Free and Accepted Masons, Oddfellows and Knights of Honor.

WILSON EAR DRUM COMPANY; Louisville Trust Company Building.—For centuries, scientific men have sought in vain for some artificial methods to relieve those suffering from deafness, which is one of the greatest afflictions of the human race. At last Mr. George H. Wilson, of Louisville, Ky., invented and patented a device in 1892, known as Wilson's common sense ear drums, which are simple in construction and wonderful in results. Mr. Wilson from infancy suffered from deafness, caused by risings in both ears. He was treated by a number of our famous aurists without receiving relief, and was told that there was no cure for his infirmity. Mr. Wilson, driven by stern necessity, began experimenting on himself, and after eight years of labor succeeded in perfecting his common sense ear drum, which he now wears with perfect comfort and ease, day and night. In order to introduce this remarkable invention to the general public, the Wilson Ear Drum Company, was organized January 10, 1893, with ample capital, Mr. David H. Wilson being the manager; and the company now has branch offices in Toronto, Ont.; Chicago, Ill.; Boston, New York, also in Great Britain, and Australia. The company's home office is located in Louisville, where a full stock of Wilson's common sense ear drums is always on hand. These ear drums are made of the finest Para rubber, and are so delicate and pliable, that they cannot be felt in the most sensitive ear, while they cannot be seen when in the ear, and have no wires, etc., to annoy the wearer. They are sold in pairs, the price being only $5.00. Hundreds of flattering testimonials have already been received from those afflicted with deafness, who highly commend these unrivalled devices. These drums together with fine nickel forceps and drum inserted are forwarded to any addresses by registered mail, on receipt of price, the company guaranteeing their delivery, and also guarantee a perfect fit.

J. DOLFINGER & CO.; Importers and Dealers in Queensware; No. 316 West Market Street.—The firm of J. Dolfinger & Co. was founded in 1862, and has always been conducted under the present style. In 1892, the death of Mr. J. Dolfinger, the founder, occurred, and since then the business has been conducted by Messrs. Edward and Frank Dolfinger. The building used is a substantial structure, four stories in height, 30x200 feet in area, with basement devoted to storage. This is the most extensive concern in its line in Louisville, and carries a heavy and choice stock, embracing brilliant cut glass and pottery, novelties in decorated china and glass, lamps, onyx tables, dinner sets, chamber sets, fine table cutlery, etc., a specialty being made of the finest grades of goods. They import their queensware direct from England, china and novelties from France and Germany, while the American goods are bought direct from the most noted manufacturers. They have an unrivalled collection of goods in every department, and the trade is wholesale and retail, extending throughout Indiana and Kentucky. Sixteen assistants are employed, and several salesmen represent the house on the road. Reliable and liberal dealing has always characterized the firm, while all goods are sold at most reasonable rates. Messrs. E. and F. Dolfinger were born in Louisville, and are regarded as among her progressive citizens, and have won success by justly deserving it.

GEO. H. KETTMANN & CO.; Importers and Jobbers of Watch Materials and Jewelers' Supplies; No. 547 West Market Street.—In the business of the importation and jobbing of watch materials and jewelers' supplies in Louisville, the house of Messrs. George H. Kettmann & Co., has achieved an enviable reputation for the judgment displayed in the selection of its stock. This prosperous enterprise was established by Messrs. Kettman and Kersting in 1888, five years later, Mr. George H. Kettman assuming the sole proprietorship, and continuing the business under the existent trading title. Business operations were first commenced at the corner of Fourth and Jefferson Streets, removal being made to the present commodious quarters four years ago. They comprise two spacious floors, each 25x80 feet in area, giving ample accommodation for the display of the exceptionally well selected lines of goods carried. The stock embraces everything comprehended under the term of watch materials and jewelers' supplies, supplemented by a choice assortment of watches, clocks, jewelry and optical goods. Ten assistants are employed, while the interests of the house are ably looked after on the road by traveling salesmen, the trade extending throughout the entire southern states, Texas, the Carolinas, Alabama, Tennessee, Mississippi, Illinois, Indiana, Arkansas and Missouri. Mr. Kettmann is a native of Memphis, Tennessee, where prior to engaging in this business, he was identified with the watch making industry in all its branches. He is a popular member of the Louisville Board of Trade, the Commercial Club and the Liederkranz Society.

DOW WIRE WORKS COMPANY; Eighth and Market Streets.—The leading factory in the South, devoted to the manufacture of counter railings, fine scroll and brass work, etc., is the celebrated Dow Wire Works Company of this city. This industry was established in 1876 by Mr. A. G. Dow. In 1887 the concern was incorporated under the present title, with a paid-up capital of $50,000. The machinery and appliances of the factory are of the latest improved type, run by steam power, and from fifty to sixty hands are employed. Only the highest grades of iron and steel wire, brass wire, etc., are used, and a specialty is made of the celebrated Greyhound bicycle wheels, which have rapidly become popular with manufacturers and wheelmen alike. For durability, tensil strength, lightness and beauty of finish, they are unsurpassed, and among the goods produced here may be mentioned, wire cloth, poultry netting, plain and fancy counter railings and guards for banks and offices in a great variety of patterns, fine scroll work in bronze, black and brass, metal elevator cabs and enclosures, weather strips, wire mats, fenders, etc. Flower stands and wire foundations for floral designs are produced here of the most elaborate character. In iron bedsteads the company has long maintained a national reputation as to price and quality. An article new in general use and exclusively manufactured here, is Dow's coil door springs. They are sole United States agents and manufacturers of the Kirker Bender fire escape, the only safe and practical escape in existence, and a novelty that would pay any asylum, hospital, hotel or school to investigate, endorsed by firemen and building inspectors everywhere. We fence the world, is the company's appropriate motto, while its trade mark of a wire fence encircling the globe, is forcibly indicative of the progressive spirit of enterprise which animates the management.

GEO. DEHLER, JR.; Hardware and Cutlery; Nos. 404, 406 and 408 East Market Street.—It would be extremely difficult to name a branch of business of more importance at the present day, than that of the general hardware trade. This business is well represented in Louisville by many reliable houses, and prominent among the number is that of Mr. George Dehler, Jr., wholesale and retail dealer in hardware and cutlery. In 1881 Messrs. Dehler and Berle established this business, and after successfully conducting it for two years, Mr. Dehler became sole proprietor.

The premises occupied consist of a massively constructed three-story and basement building, 40x120 feet in area, thoroughly modern in its appointments, while the stock includes hardware and cutlery, wagon materials, agricultural implements, farmers' tools, etc. This house is agent for the celebrated Brinly plows and Capewell horse nails. These goods represent the very best products of the largest home and foreign factories, and the excellent trade relations maintained with these, as well as the extensive scale of operations (this being the largest retail store in the city), enables Mr. Dehler to offer inducements which smaller houses cannot think of duplicating. Several assistants are employed, and the trade comes from all parts of the city and state. Mr. Dehler is an able and energetic business man, who has gained a wide reputation for superior goods, and possesses an accurate knowledge of the needs and requirements of a critical trade. A special honor has been conferred upon this house, its windows having been selected for the purpose of displaying the various relics and momentoes of the late civil war, during the G. A. R. Encampment in this city in September. Many firms have desired this honor, but Mr. Dehler's own popularity told strongly in his favor, and his store was the unanimous choice of the committee appointed to select a place for the display. Mr. Dehler was born in Louisville, and is one of her most esteemed and influential citizens. He has for years followed this line, having been identified with the firm of W. B. Belknap & Co., and with Jacob Schmitt before embarking upon his present venture.

- - LOUISVILLE OF TO-DAY. - -

GEORGE RAMSER; Stoves and Tinware; No. 1027 Third Avenue.—An industrial establishment in Louisville that has for years been largely patronized, is that conducted by Mr. George Ramser, dealer in stoves and manufacturer of tinware. Mr. Ramser first established this business in 1860, and after a couple years gave it up, to accept a lucrative position in the same line. In 1870 he again embarked and this time the venture proved permanent. He occupies two spacious floors, where is carried a full line of stoves, ranges, etc., of the best makes, tinware and kitchen utensils of all kinds. The workshops are fully equipped, and the house makes a specialty of guttering, roofing and spouting, and has a large patronage in these lines. Several assistants are employed in the different departments, and the trade comes from all parts of the city and surrounding country. The career of this house has been ever characterized by a strict adherence to honorable methods, and to this fact its success may be attributed. Mr. Ramser was born in France, coming to Louisville in 1856.

FRED. BRINKE; Dealer in Staple and Fancy Groceries; Corner Fifth and Chestnut Streets.—In 1884 Mr. Fred. Brinke opened his present establishment, and is meeting with marked success. The premises occupied consist of a substantial three-story brick structure, equipped in the most modern manner. Staple and fancy groceries of all kinds, including the choicest teas and coffees, spices, sugars, fruits, canned goods, produce, etc., are found here, the very best sources of supply being drawn upon to secure them. Several competent assistants are employed, and all orders are executed with precision and dispatch, all customers being treated in the same impartial manner. Everything is done to promote the interests of patrons, and the prices quoted are the most reasonable possible, consistent with the high grade of goods carried. Mr. Brinke was born in Germany, but came to Louisville in 1874. He is thoroughly conversant with every detail of the business, and his upright methods in all transactions, have won him the esteem of the city's business circles.

KOERTNER & BURKEL; Cafe, Billiard and Pool Room; Nos. 336 and 340 West Jefferson Street. One of the best conducted saloons in this section of Louisville, is that of Messrs. Nick Koertner & Jake Burkel, or as the house is popularly dubbed "Nick and Jake's." The saloon is spacious and elegantly equipped with every facility and convenience, and contains a choice stock of foreign and domestic liquors, ales, beer, cigars, etc., which have no superior for purity and excellence. This saloon is unanimously declared the headquarters for base ball players and their adherents, those participating or attending races, theatrical companies, etc. Several courteous barmen are employed, who promptly supply the demands of patrons. Mr. Koertner was born in Germany in 1846, and came to Louisville in 1858. For eight years he was employed at Willard's Hotel, and left there to enter the business he now so successfully is engaged in. Mr. Burkel came to Louisville in 1864 from St. Louis, Mo., and was for a time in the liquor business on Fourth Avenue. Both are active and honorable men, and fully merit the popularity and success to which they have attained.

ED. D. BEATTY; Tin Roofing, Spouting, Guttering, Etc.; No. 824 West Main Street.—A reliable house in its line in Louisville is that of Mr. Ed. D. Beatty, tin and sheet iron worker, and dealer in cooking and heating stoves, etc. The business was established in 1865 by Messrs. Beatty & Shalies, who conducted it till 1875, when Mr. Ed. D. Beatty became sole proprietor. He is a thoroughly practical sheet metal worker, who utilizes only the best materials and employs first-class workmen. The premises occupied are spacious, and all work is strictly handmade, and the roofs constructed by Mr. Beatty have always met with the approval of architects, builders, and owners. Mr. Beatty has roofed some of the finest buildings in the city, and his prices in all cases are extremely moderate. He was born in Louisville, and his father was elected mayor of the city in 1844.

ALEX. MYERS; Broker; No. 329 and 331 West Market Street.—Mr. Myers commenced business in 1865. The premises occupied comprise a spacious three-story brick building, 25x180 feet in dimensions, fitted up with every convenience for the successful prosecution of the business. Mr. Myers' merchant tailor misfit parlor is in the rear, and all business transacted is strictly confidential. He promptly lends money on the deposit of collateral as security, advancing liberally on jewelry, watches, diamond goods, clothing and other valuables, all business being conducted in an honorable manner without fear of publicity or embarrassment to borrowers. Mr. Myers has also on hand a superior assortment of watches, jewelry, and a large stock of diamonds, which he offers to customers at extremely moderate prices. He was born in Baltimore, Md., but has resided in Louisville for the last forty-two years, and is highly esteemed by all classes for his sterling integrity. He is a popular member of the Commercial Club.

LOUISVILLE OF TO-DAY. 169

G. A. SCHUSTER & SONS; Grocers; Nos. 649 to 655 Third Street.—One of the most reliable grocery houses in this section of Louisville, is that of Messrs. G. A. Schuster & Sons. This business is one of the oldest of the kind in the city, and is conducted on the old Bohlsen stand. It was established many years ago by Mr. Bohlsen, who was succeeded by Mr. Evers, and eventually in 1887 by Mr. G. A. Schuster, who admitted his sons, Messrs. Frank and Charles F. Schuster into partnership. Mr. G. A. Schuster died in 1891, and his sons are still continuing under the old firm name of G. A. Schuster & Sons. The premises occupied are spacious, and the stock carried at all times is one of the freshest and choicest in the city, including full lines of groceries, teas, coffees, spices, canned goods, fresh and salt meats, provisions, oysters, fish, game, fruits and vegetables, also feed, lime and cement. The store is a model of neatness and cleanliness, and the lowest market prices prevail. Messrs. Frank and Charles F. Schuster are natives of this city, and are honorable business men, and number among their permanent customers, many of the leading hotels, restaurants and private families of this section of the city.

SAMUEL BOOKER & CO.; Mammoth Stables; First Avenue, between Market and Jefferson Streets.—Louisville is well supplied with superior livery stables, and prominent among the number are those known as the "Mammoth Stables," of which Mr. Samuel Booker is proprietor. He opened these stables in 1885 and has since built up a liberal patronage. The premises are thoroughly drained, properly ventilated, and have excellent accommodations for one hundred and sixty horses. Mr. Booker has some of the finest equipages to be found in the city and a stock of superior horses, which can be hired on very reasonable terms, and a specialty is made of supplying light livery for families. His stables are also headquarters for the sale and purchase of fine farm, buggy and saddle horses and he likewise boards horses by the week or month. He is an honorable and liberal business man and was previous to embarking in this enterprise a prosperous farmer in Shelby County, Ky.

J. L. STAIB & COMPANY; Produce Commission Merchants; Nos. 124 and 126 Fourth Avenue.—A prominent and representative house in the produce commission trade of Louisville, is that of Messrs. J. L. Staib & Co., which was established in 1885, by Mr. J. L. Staib, who has since secured a liberal patronage. He occupies a spacious three-story brick and basement building, 30x135 feet in area, fully equipped with every convenience. He has influential connections in Kentucky, Indiana, Illinois and Tennessee, and deals largely in butter, eggs, poultry, grain, hay, also in potatoes, apples, etc. Liberal advances are made when desired on consignments, while quick sales at highest market rates, and immediate returns are guaranteed. Mr. Staib transacts a large business supplying retailers in Louisville and its vicinity, and he also deals and keeps on hand a choice stock of pine, poplar and cypress shingles. During the season Mr. Staib runs the steamer, Falls City, of which he is manager and owner, semi-weekly trips being made up the Kentucky River to Frankfort, Shaker's Ferry and intermediate points from Louisville. He is a native of this city, and is highly esteemed for his strict integrity, and is a popular member of the Commercial Club.

CHARLES DECKEL; Grocer; No. 901 East Jefferson Street.—A trustworthy grocery establishment in this section of Louisville, is that of Mr. Charles Deckel, which was established forty-five years ago by the Messrs. Funcks, who were succeeded by Stoke & Manneman and afterwards by Benj. Schaup. In 1886 Mr. Charles Deckel became the proprietor and has since greatly developed the business with a choice assortment of fresh crop teas, coffees, spices, sugars, canned goods, etc., while a specialty is made of flour, fresh butter and eggs. Only the finest groceries are handled and popular prices prevail. Mr. Deckel was born in Louisville, in 1863. He is an energetic and honorable business man who is very popular with all classes.

A. SEEKAMP; Wines and Liquors; Nos. 846 and 848 West Main Street.—This wholesale liquor business was founded in 1871 by Messrs. John Seekamp & Brother, who conducted it till 1887, when Mr. A. Seekamp became sole proprietor. He brings great practical experience to bear, coupled with influential connections, and imports wines and brandies direct from the most celebrated European houses. The premises occupied are spacious, and here is kept always a heavy and choice stock of imported wines and liquors, while a specialty is made of the finest grades of Kentucky bourbon and rye whiskies, the principal brands handled being known as Cane Spring, Cumberland and T. B. Ripy. Orders are filled with dispatch, and the wines and liquors handled are admirably adapted for a first-class hotel and club trade, and the patronage the house now has, extends throughout all sections of the city and state. Mr. Seekamp has resided in Louisville for the last thirty-four years, and is highly esteemed in trade circles for his strict integrity, and is always prepared to offer substantial advantages in prices to retailers and others, while all representations as to age, purity, etc., can always be implicitly relied on.

PAXTON & THOME; Merchant Tailors; No. 342 West Market Street. —One of the most prominent tailoring establishments of the city of Louisville, is that formerly conducted by Griffin and Winn, which was established several years ago and was conducted by them until September, 1892, when Messrs. Paxton & Thome succeeded, the members being W. E. Paxton and Clarke Thome. In 1893, the present spacious modern quarters were taken and they are 20x80 feet in area, and fully supplied with every convenience, elegant cabinets, electric lights, etc. The stock carried includes the finest domestic and foreign woolens, worsteds, suitings, etc., all carefully selected and representing the latest ideas in design and material. Ten expert assistants are employed in the house, as well as a large number on the outside, and the trade comes from all parts of the state, some of our best dressed citizens being included among the permanent patrons. Despite the fact that nowhere in this or any other city, can one get better materials, better workmanship or more perfect fit, the charges made by Paxton & Thome are exceedingly moderate. Mr. W. E. Paxton was born in Shelby County, Ky., coming to Louisville eleven years ago to accept a position as salesman with Julius Winter & Co. Mr. Clarke Thome is a native of this city and was for some years identified with the firm of Stratton & Terstedge. Possessed of exceptional business qualifications, these gentlemen are only meeting with the merited reward of their efforts, in the success which they have attained, and are highly regarded in social and business life.

H. C. BRUNER & SON; Produce Commission Merchants; Nos. 325 and 327 Second Street.—The excellent transportation facilities and central location of Louisville, have made it prominent as a market for the handling at wholesale of produce and fruits, the business engaging the attention of a number of firms of importance. Among these one of special note is that of H. C. Bruner & Son. In 1884 this business was founded by H. C. Bruner and M. Tracy. Mr. Tracy withdrew from the firm in 1892, and Chas. W. Bruner, son of the senior member, was admitted into partnership, and the style of H. C. Bruner & Son, was adopted. The premises occupied consist of a substantial three-story brick structure, 25x180 feet in area, and are equipped with every convenience. Several assistants are employed, and the trade though largely local is by no means confined here, shipments being made to Cleveland, Boston, Buffalo and other large cities. A specialty is made of butter, eggs, cheese, poultry and fruits, and these commodities are received direct from the leading sources of supply in Indiana, Tennessee, Kentucky and neighboring states. Consignments are solicited, sales being effected upon the most favorable terms and prompt remittances made. The firm is strictly reliable, and its reference in this city is the Western Bank. Mr. H. C. Bruner was born in Bucks County, Pa., and has resided in Louisville since 1882. Previous to that time he was in business in Hayden, Indiana, for some years, and is a member of the I. O. O. F. Mr. Chas. W. Bruner was born in Indiana, coming here with his father in 1882. Both partners are members of the Produce Exchange.

JOHN GARGAN & CO.; Coppersmiths; No. 138 Fifth Avenue.—One of the most notable houses in its line in Louisville is that of Messrs. John Gargan & Co., coppersmiths, which stands second to none in this part of the country. The business was established in 1859 when a small plant was started by the firm of Gargan & Corcoran, composed of John Gargan and Martin Corcoran. In 1868 Mr. Corcoran died and the firm style was changed to John Gargan & Co. Mathew Corcoran was admitted to partnership in 1880 and now is the only active member of the firm, the death of Mr. John Gargan having occurred March 15th. The factory is a spacious structure 32x150 feet in area and the equipment is in every respect modern and complete. Large coke furnaces are in operation and fifteen skilled workmen are employed. The output consists of copper stills, soda fountains, beer and candy kettles, while all kinds of steamboat distillery, brewery and factory work is executed. The firm has supplied all the distillers of Louisville and surrounding country with pipes, worms, stills, etc., as well as many throughout the United States and Canada, and from the outset success has crowned the efforts of this house. Reliability and liberality have characterized the efforts of this firm and its productions are unrivalled for quality and workmanship. Mr. Corcoran was born in Dublin, Ireland, but lived here since 1850, thirty-two years of that time having been passed with the firm. He is an honorable business man and in the city ranks among influential and popular citizens.

A. M. RAMSAY; Plumber; No. 806 West Market Street.—In the mechanical arts, there is no branch more important than sanitary plumbing and gas fitting. Among those who have gained an excellent reputation in this line in the Falls City is Mr. A. M. Ramsay, the widely-known sanitary plumber. Mr. Ramsay established this business in 1888, and has always made it a rule to do nothing but first-class work. He occupies a spacious store and basement, each 20x100 feet in dimensions, fitted up with every convenience and facility. Here is kept always a choice assortment of plumbers' steam and gas fitters' supplies, bath tubs, boilers, water closets, sinks, traps, hydrants, brackets, chandeliers, globes, also the most reliable sanitary devices. A specialty is made of sanitary plumbing, ventilation and drainage, and Mr. Ramsay has fitted up and done a large amount of work on the finest buildings in the city and its vicinity, while his prices in all cases are noted for their moderation. From fifteen to twenty expert journeymen are employed, and estimates are cheerfully furnished. Mr. Ramsay is a native of this city, and is highly regarded in trade circles for his skill and strict probity. He is an active member and president of the Master Plumbers' Association. Among the many contracts for plumbing and gas fitting that Mr. Ramsay has filled during the past few years are those for the Cave Hill Cemetery Company, K. W. Smith (Insurance agent), National Building and Loan Association twelve houses, Hale Brothers & Malone twenty-five houses on Second Street, and Louis Keller, builder. Mr. Ramsay is on the most friendly terms with all the leading architects of our city and his work is highly commended by experts.

WILLIAM STILZ; Wholesale and Retail Dealer in Seeds, Produce, Etc.; No. 213 Market Street. Among the most active merchants in Louisville engaged in handling garden and field seeds and produce is Mr. William Stilz. This enterprise was founded by Messrs. Stilz and Caster in 1883. Two years later the firm having dissolved Mr. Stilz assumed control, and under his energetic management the influential trade already built up has been greatly increased, extending throughout Kentucky and the southern states. The premises occupied are spacious, affording facilities for wholesale and retail sales, and cold storage for perishable consignments. Orders either by mail or telephone receive prompt attention, while prices are invariably controlled by the market. Mr. Stilz, who was born in this county, is highly regarded for his ability and probity, and is very popular in trade circles.

GEO. LOOMS; Manufacturer of Fine Carriages, Buggies, Phaetons, Etc.; Nos 322, 324 and 326 First Street.—Louisville can boast of a number of enterprising manufacturers of fine carriages, but few if any stand more prominently before the public than does Mr. George Looms, who established this business in 1883, and has since succeeded in retaining an extensive patronage in the city and state. Business operations were primarily commenced at No. 116 West Main Street, removal being made to the present more commodious quarters ten years ago. They consist of a substantial three-storied brick building, 102x102 feet in area, the first floor being devoted to office, blacksmith shop and storage, second floor, painting and woodworking departments, third floor, surplus stock. Twenty-three skilled hands are employed, and fine carriages, buggies, phaetons, surreys and road wagons of every description, all hand work and of the best character, are promptly made to order. The carriages here manufactured are especially noted for their strength, lightness, ease of draught and elegant finish, and are prime favorites in this city and vicinity, the annual sales of the same aggregating some $45,000. Prompt and skilful attention is given to both new work and repairs, smithing, painting and jobbing, and the proprietor of the house enjoys a wide popularity by reason of his upright business methods, his liberality of terms and prices and the uniform reliability of his products. Mr. Looms is an Ohioan by birth.

FRANK HENRY'S EXCHANGE; Wines, Liquors, Etc.; No. 309 East Market Street.—A prominent house engaged in the sale of wines and liquors in the Falls City, is that so ably presided over by Mr. Frank A. Henry, Sr., popularly known as Frank Henry's Exchange. This well-managed concern was established by Mr. Henry in 1869 and he has always conducted the business in this immediate neighborhood, and has occupied his present commodious quarters for the past thirty years, which are handsomely appointed and supplied with every modern convenience, electric lights, fans, etc. The business is conducted on strictly first-class lines, card playing, dice throwing, gambling in any form and the use of profane language being strictly prohibited. The stock carried embraces the finest wines of noted vintages, old French brandies, sparkling Rhine wines and champagnes and rich Kentucky rye and bourbon whiskies, conspicuous among the latter is exhibited a rare stock of the renowned McHennie rye—Mr. Henry's leading specialty—a bland, ripe and delicious whiskey, that has few equals and no superiors. In malt beverages, here can be procured the famous Bass' ale and Guinness' stout, Frank Fehr's celebrated lager beer being at all times on draught, while

Frank Henry.

the smoker's appetite can here be regaled with a Rose Perfecto, a Henry Clay or any of the leading brands of imported or domestic cigars. Mr. Henry is of German nationality, but has long made Louisville his home and the scene of his business operations. He is a member of the Mutual Protective Association, Knight Templar, Thirty-second Degree Royal Arch Mason (Louisville Commandery), A. O. U. W. (Falls City Lodge), Knights of Honor (Daniel Boon), Knights of Pythias (Grand Lodge), and the Hermann Society and Liederkranz Signing Societies. Mr. Henry is also a popular comrade of the Grand Army of the Republic, and served during the late war with the Twenty-eighth Kentucky Infantry, holding the rank of captain in that regiment.

W. P. COLE & CO.; Manufacturers' Agents and Jobbers; No. 134 Second Street.—Among the leading business houses of Louisville, none stands higher, or controls a larger patronage, in their particular line, than the firm of W. P. Cole & Co., manufacturers' agents and jobbers in fine carriages. In 1891 this house was established, and its prosperity has been as permanent as it was immediate. From the very outset, patronage began to flow in from all sides and this has only been augmented as time passed. Each year the trade limits have expanded, the trade volume increased, until to-day sales are made to all parts of Kentucky, Tennessee, Indiana and other states, several salesmen representing the house through this territory. The salesrooms are fully stocked with a superior assortment of buggies, surreys, phaetons, spring wagons, carts, etc., the finest products of the leading factories of the country, for which the firm acts as agents. Many orders are filled from here, but the larger ones are shipped direct from the different factories. Mr. W. P. Cole, the sole proprietor, has resided for some years in Louisville. He is a young man, possessing superior ability, and is fast taking a leading place among the prosperous citizens of the Falls City.

G. ALBERDING; Cigars and Tobaccos; No. 206 West Market Street.—There are some houses in Louisville that make and handle only genuine cigars, and among such may be mentioned that of Mr. G. Alberding, manufacturer of fine cigars and wholesale dealer in manufactured tobaccos. Mr. Alberding, who is an experienced cigar maker, established this business in 1859 and has since been the recipient of a liberal patronage, his trade extending throughout Kentucky and the adjacent states. From the start he determined to put on the market none but honest goods and that he has adhered strictly to this determination is well evident by the popularity of his favorite brands, "**Pride of Louisville**," and "Little Spanish" cigars. His other brands, which are known as "Tom Bowling," "Odense," as well as several more, are general favorites and always command a ready sale. Mr. Alberding's brands are handled largely in many of our popular cafés and restaurants and are offered to the trade at extremely moderate prices. He was born in Germany in 1834 but has resided in Louisville since 1856 and he is an honorable business man and very popular in trade circles.

SWANN-ABRAHAM HAT COMPANY; Nos. 601 and 603 West Main Street.—A representative Louisville establishment is that conducted by the Swann Abraham Hat Company, manufacturers and jobbers of fine hats, straw goods, gloves and umbrellas. Mr. T. M. Swann was connected with the house of Pollard, Prather & Smith in 1859 and following on down till the present firm was organized. The affairs of the company, however, were reorganized in 1890, and the business incorporated with a capital of $150,000 with Messrs. W. J. Abraham, president, T. M. Swann, vice-president, and H. E. Harris, secretary. The Swann brand of hats have a high standard of excellence in the trade, and the house maintains a reputation in mercantile circles, second to none in the business, and is the largest house of the kind in the Southwest. The premises occupied comprise a five-storied brick building, 35x210 feet in area, admirably fitted up, the different floors being reached by means of elevators. This is one of the largest houses in its line in the South and Southwest. An exclusively wholesale business is done, and fifteen traveling salesmen are employed, and the trade of the house extends throughout Kentucky, Illinois, Tennessee, Georgia, Indiana, Arkansas, Louisiana, Texas, Virginia and West Virginia. The president of the company, Mr. Abraham, is also a director in the Louisville Gas Company.

GEORGE HESS & BRO.; Undertakers; No. 353 Market Street.—Among the leading representatives of this useful and indispensable profession, the undertaker, few are better known in Louisville or more highly regarded than the firm of Messrs. George Hess & Bro. This business was established in 1847 by Mr. George Hess, Sr., who died in 1860, his widow continuing the enterprise till 1869, when Messrs. George Hess & Bro., assumed control. **Mr.** George Hess, Jr., died in 1888 and the business became the property of **Mr. Henry C.** Hess, who is still carrying it on under the old firm name of **George Hess** & Bro. He brings great experience to bear, and caters to the needs of all classes of the population, furnishing everything requisite for the plainest or most imposing funerals. The premises occupied are well equipped, and the warerooms contain a carefully selected stock of coffins, caskets, burial cases, shrouds, trimmings and all kinds of funeral goods. Remains are taken charge of at any hour of the day or night and prepared for burial, while interments are procured in any of the city or suburban cemeteries, and funerals are superintended in a careful manner to the entire satisfaction of bereaved friends and relatives. This house has ever made it a rule to charge only moderate prices, and Mr. Hess also promptly supplies hearses and carriages. Mr. Hess is an honorable and energetic business man, who has achieved success by honestly deserving it. Embalming when desired is scientifically performed, and Mr. Hess is noted for having at present the finest hearses in the city.

P. E. BONKOFSKY; Importer of Millinery; No. 419 Fourth Avenue.—Foremost among the milliners of Louisville is Madame P. E. Bonkofsky, a lady of exquisite taste and ability. The premises occupied are eligibly located and fitted up in a tasteful manner, with plate glass front, handsome show cases, etc. The fine stock carried of imported and domestic millinery goods, includes genuine French artificial flowers, ostrich and other feathers, ribbons, laces, straw, felt and other hats, bonnets trimmed and ready for immediate use, and untrimmed shapes of the latest and most fashionable styles and particular attention is paid to the designing and making up to order, mourning bonnets and hats. Many of the goods used are imported through New York and Philadelphia houses, while the samples of the leading styles are made specially for Madame Bonkofsky in New York and Paris. Twenty hands are constantly employed, altering, trimming and making up materials for the numerous patrons of this popular establishment. During the twenty years, Madame Bonkofsky numbers among her permanent customers, many of the wealthiest and most fashionable ladies in Louisville, and it is safe to say that the reputation of the house both for the character of the work done, and the quality of the materials used is second to none in this city or state.

THE KNADLER PICKLING AND PRESERVING COMPANY; No. 111 Third Street.—An old established house, that has achieved a widespread popularity throughout this entire section of the country for the superiority of its product, is that of the well-known Knadler Pickling and Preserving Company. This concern dates its existence back twenty-nine years, it having been founded by Mr. H. G. Knadler in 1866; the business was subsequently conducted under the firm style of Messrs. Knadler & Stilz, the present trading title being assumed in 1890. The premises occupied comprise a substantial three-storied building, 44x36 feet in dimensions, giving ample accommodation for the storage of stock, etc., while the factory is supplied with the latest improved machinery and appliances. A force of fifteen skilled hands is employed, and the range of production includes mixed pickles, chow-chow, lilyhot and Gherkins, pickled onions, sweet, mixed or plain, pepper sauce, Saratoga Club sauce, white wine, extra apple and pure grape vinegars, salad dressing and tomato sauce, olives, olive oil, horseradish, catsup, Worcestershire sauce, French mustard, Royal Poinciana baking power, extracts of all kinds, etc. All of the company's goods are prepared with scrupulous care and neatness, the Knadler brands being general favorites with the trade and consumers. Quality has ever been the first consideration with this honorable house, and its goods are absolutely unrivaled. The proprietorship of the business is vested in the hands of Messrs. H. G. and John M. Knadler, both natives of the city, where they are esteemed and respected alike in social as in mercantile circles.

THE BATES & SONS COMPANY, (Incorporated); Contractors for Roofing, Asphalt, Cement, Granitoid Paving, Floors and Driveways. —No. 149 West Main Street.—In the roofing of all kinds of buildings, a representative concern in this section of the Falls City, is that known as The Bates & Sons Co. This concern was founded in 1850 by the late John H. Bates, who died April 7th of the current year. In 1880 business was conducted under the firm style of Messrs. John H. Bates & Son, state corporate **charter** being secured in 1895. The company has a cash capital of $10,000, the executive officers being as follows, (no president having been elected since the decease of the founder of the house who originally filled that office); W. H. Bates, secretary and treasurer, James Bates, general manager. The plant covers an area of 25x160 feet, and includes ample shedding, etc., for the storage of stock. The company are contractors for roofing, asphalt, cement, granitoid paving, floors, and driveways, asbestos, sectional pipe and boiler covering. A special feature is likewise made of the restoration of old leaky tin and iron roofing, and they likewise deal in O. K. building paper, (medal brand), wire edge two and three ply ready roofing, tarred papers and dry felts, asphalt, pitch and cold tar, roof coating and paints, etc. Among recent contracts completed by this company may be mentioned the work done on the J. B. Wathen & Bros. distillery, the J. M. Atherton distillery, the Bourbon stock yards, the pavilion at the base ball park, the Rugby Distillery Company's building and many others. Messrs. Bates are natives of the Falls City, and sons of the worthy founder of the house.

ECLIPSE VINEGAR WORKS; Thirtieth Street and Broadway.—Louisville's supremacy as a great producing centre is due to the enterprise and energy of its leading manufacturers, who have concentrated intelligent thought and skill in the production of certain products. Each field of industry has its prominent representatives, and one of the most noted in the production of cider and vinegar, is that known as the Eclipse Vinegar Works, which is managed by Mr. Vincent Davis, who had formerly been for thirty years in the drug business. He purchased these works in 1886, and his trade which is steadily increasing, extends throughout Kentucky, Indiana, Tennessee, Georgia, Alabama, North and South Carolina and Florida. The works have an area of 120x200 feet, connected by switches with the Louisville and Southern Railway, and are fully supplied with the latest improved machinery and appliances operated by a forty horse power engine and boiler. Mr. Davis manufactures sweet and crab apple cider, also orange, cherry and peach cider, while a specialty is made of pure table and pickling vinegar. These goods are recognized standards with the trade, and are unsurpassed for quality, purity and uniform excellence, while they are offered to the trade at extremely moderate prices. Orders are promptly filled and the output of the works is fifty-five barrels of vinegar and large quantities of cider daily. Mr. Davis is a native of Nelson County, Ky., but has resided in the Falls City since 1865. He is highly regarded for his strict integrity, and customers have always the satisfaction of knowing that no inferior cider or vinegar will be sold to them from these works.

THOMAS FERGUSON; Foundry, Machine and Pattern Works; No. 1111 West Main Street.—It is with pleasure that we refer in these pages to the old and reliable foundry of Mr. Thomas Ferguson, that was established in the year 1856 by Mr. Richard Ferguson, the father of the present proprietor. The founder, after conducting affairs alone for some time, admitted first his son, Richard, then Thomas and later Mr. James Nichols, the firm names of Ferguson & Son, Ferguson & Sons and Ferguson & Co., respectively, being adopted, and in 1881 occurred the decease of the founder, after an honorable career. The firm of Ferguson, Melcher & Co., succeeded, then Meyrick & Ferguson, and in 1886 Mr. Thomas Ferguson assumed the sole proprietorship. The foundry and works are spacious, while the equipment is complete, comprising forges, lathes, planers, drills, saws, etc., and only skilled hands are employed. Mr. Ferguson's energies are directed to the making of wood and metal patterns of every description, and of special machinery, while repairs are effected promptly, and machinery, presses, dies, pulleys, and castings in any material are made to order, drawings and specifications are prepared, and great care is exercised in turning out accurate models for inventors and patentees. The house has for years enjoyed a large trade from our leading distillers, etc., all work being executed in a superior manner. Mr. Ferguson is recognized as one of our leading manufacturers, and is a native of this city.

MIKE RAPP, JR.; Grocer; Seventh and Grayson Streets.—Among the many excellent grocery stores and saloons in this section of Louisville, there is probably not one that has secured a more enduring hold on popular favor than the well-known establishment of Mr. Mike Rapp, Jr. This business was established originally in 1848 by Mr. M. Rapp, Sr., who conducted it till in 1882 when he retired in favor of his son Mr. M. Rapp, Jr., who has been thoroughly trained in the business. The premises occupied are spacious, fully supplied with every convenience, rock bottom prices prevail here and purchasers can always rely upon getting full weight and a superior article. The stock is complete, including select teas, coffees and spices, condiments, sauces and table delicacies, dried fruits, provisions, canned goods, etc., also a choice selection of imported and domestic wines, liquors and beer. A specialty is made of the choicest Kentucky bourbon and rye whiskies, and orders are taken and delivered at residences free of charge. Mr. Rapp was born in Louisville, in 1851, and is an energetic and honorable business man. Mr. M. Rapp, Sr., was born in Germany, and came to Louisville in 1844, and by industry and just dealing secured a competency

BOCKEE, GARTH AND SCHRODER; Dealers in Leaf Tobacco; No. 1012 West Main Street.—The representative house of Louisville, actively engaged in the leaf tobacco trade is that of Messrs. Bockee, Garth and Schroder, wholesale dealers, which was established by Mr. J. S. Bockee seventeen years ago, the present co-partnery consisting of J. S. Bockee, C. M. Garth and H. Schroder, being formed in 1883. Large quantities of all grades of leaf tobacco are handled either in original or broken packages, the connections and facilities of the house being such as to enable it to fill the largest orders at lowest market rates. The firm occupies a spacious re-drying, sorting and grading warehouse on Shelby Street, with branch of a similar character at Hopkinsville, this state, equipped with steam power and all the latest improved machinery and devices known to the trade. Forty skilled and experienced hands are employed, an extensive and steadily growing trade being enjoyed with the home and export markets. Mr. Bockee is a native of New York state, and is a director of the

American National Bank of this city, also a member and director of the Board of Trade. Mr. Garth comes from Hannibal, Missouri, has resided here since 1883, and is a director of the Louisville Banking Company. Mr. Schroder is of German nationality and prior to settling here some twelve years ago, resided in New York city.

ADAM BALL; Groceries, Meats and Vegetables; Northeast corner Fifteenth and Walnut Streets. Prominent among the leading houses in its line in this section of Louisville is that of Mr. Adam Ball, who deals not only in staple and fancy groceries, but also in meats and vegetables. Mr. Ball established this business in 1882, and previous to embarking in the grocery trade on his own account, was for several years clerk and salesman to his brother-in-law, Mr. William Brockman of this city. The premises occupied include a well equipped store and residence, and only the best goods, meats, provisions, etc., are handled. The stock includes fresh crop China teas, coffees, spices, canned goods of every description, sugar, syrups, family flour, dried and fresh fruits, vegetables, while a specialty is made of choice meats, fresh butter and eggs. Not only the well-to-do but also the poor patronize this store, as they are always certain of obtaining here the purest and best groceries in the market at lowest market rates. This grocery is noted for its order and cleanliness. Mr. Ball was born in Louisville in 1858. He is an honorable and reliable business man, and well merits the liberal patronage secured in this important industry.

GEORGE HUBER; Brewer of the Celebrated Cream Beer; Nos. 1906 and 1908 Fifteenth Street.—Among the various brewing establishments of Louisville, one of the youngest, but one whose output is already sold and held in high favor, in all parts of the city and surrounding towns, is that of George Huber the popular brewer of the celebrated cream beer. This business was originally established by M. Senn & Bro., coming into the possession of Wegenast and Huber in 1890, who conducted it till 1893, when Mr. G. Huber became sole proprietor. The brewery and malt house are spacious buildings, and the equipment includes the latest and most approved machinery and appliances, operated by steam power, and only the purest and best materials are utilized, and the result is that the beer produced here is unsurpassed for flavor, purity and quality. Old beers that have a reputation of years behind them, are being discarded for it, and if it is kept up to its present standard, Mr. Huber will soon have to enlarge the capacity of his brewery to meet the demand. An idea of the growth of this enterprise is obtained from the fact that already the output amounts to upwards of two thousand five hundred barrels a year, and this is rapidly increasing. Mr. George Huber was born in Louisville, where he is highly esteemed in trade circles for his strict integrity. As a brewer he is a man of wide experience, having been identified with the house of Senn Bros., his predecessors, for upwards of twenty years.

R. S. WITHERSPOON; Manufacturer of Women's and Misses' Shoes; Nos. 231 and 233 Seventh Street.—One of the largest and best managed factories in its line in Louisville is that of Mr. R. S. Witherspoon, manufacturer of women's and misses' shoes exclusively. Mr. Witherspoon was formerly a partner in the firm of Carter, Dunbar & Co., shoe jobbers, Nashville, Tenn. He withdrew from this concern in 1894, and established his present business. The factory is a spacious four-story brick building, supplied with the latest machinery and appliances, and thirty-five skilled hands are employed. A specialty is made of button boots, women's sizes 2 1-2 to 7 and misses' 11 to 2. The capacity of the plant is three hundred pairs daily. The house does a large business throughout Kentucky, Indiana and the southern and middle states, the goods being unrivalled for style, durability and quality. Mr. Witherspoon is a native of Mobile, Ala., and although he has resided in the Falls City only a short time, his integrity and business qualities have already given him a leading place in commercial circles. He is a member of the Commercial Club, and also belongs to the Order of the Knights of Pythias.

FRANK HECK; Grocery and Saloon; No. 709 West Green Street.—One of the most popular establishments in this section of the city, is that conducted by Mr. Frank Heck, grocer and saloon keeper. It is one of the oldest stands here, and under Mr. Heck's management, has prospered to a marked degree. The establishment has the reputation of carrying superior qualities of staple and fancy groceries, brands of wines, liquors, malt beverages and cigars, and as a result it commands the patronage of the best class of people in this locality. Mr. Heck makes a specialty of corn hollow whiskey, which is known as being one of the purest, most reliable and popular liquors in the country. He is of German descent and was born in this city thirty-three years ago. He has hosts of friends and his popularity is well deserved, while he is highly esteemed for his genial disposition and strict probity. His aim has always been to please his patrons and to handle only the best goods, and his business is rapidly increasing as this section of the city grows in wealth and population.

GRAY STREET MARKET; Philipp Ziegler, Proprietor; Corner First and Gray Streets.—The grocery trade has within comparatively recent years developed to immense proportions, and a well-known and reliable firm engaged in it in this city is that of Mr. Philipp Ziegler. This business was founded by the present proprietor about twenty years ago, during which time he has secured a large and paramount patronage. The premises occupied are extensive and a large and carefully assorted stock is carried, including a very fine line of pure teas, coffees and family groceries of every description, also the very best meats, poultry, game, fresh vegetables and all kinds of fish and oysters in season, and the store is fitted up and arranged in the most attractive manner, and four efficient and attentive clerks attend to the wants of customers and nothing is left undone to maintain their establishment at the very highest standard of excellence. Mr. Ziegler, who is a native of Baden, has been a resident of Louisville for the past twenty-five years. He is highly regarded by the community for his business ability and integrity, and justly merits the abundant success in this important enterprise.

F. SCHAICH; Bakery and Confectionery; No. 130 West Market Street.—The baking industry of Louisville is of the greatest importance, and is well represented here by the widely-known bakery and confectionery establishment of Mr. F. Schaich. He is a thoroughly experienced baker and confectioner, who established this business in 1870, and now numbers among his permanent patrons many leading restaurants of this section of the city. His bakery is noted for its neatness and cleanliness, and only the finest grades of flour, sugar and other choice materials are utilized. A heavy and choice stock is constantly carried, embracing plain and fancy bread and cake, biscuits, pastry of every variety, pies and all kinds of confectionery, which are unrivalled for purity and quality, and are offered to customers at very moderate prices. Orders are promptly filled, and a specialty is made of supplying parties, weddings, balls and families. Mr. Schaich was born in Germany in 1841, and came to Louisville in 1866. He is highly esteemed by the community for his integrity, and justly merits the substantial success secured in this useful industry.

GEO. C. KRAFT; Beef, Mutton, Lamb, Veal, Etc.; Corner Fifth and Green Streets.—Prominent among those engaged in supplying the population of Louisville with fresh meats, hams, etc., is Mr. Geo. C. Kraft, who commenced business in 1873. He slaughters his own stock, and his abattoir is at No. 1500 Hamilton Street, and the stands are fully supplied with every convenience, refrigerators, etc., and are models of neatness and cleanliness. He keeps constantly on hand a heavy and choice stock of fresh beef, mutton, lamb, etc., and the prices quoted are always regulated by the market. Mr. Kraft was one of the founders of this market, and helped to build it twenty-two years ago. He was born in the Falls City in 1850, and has made hosts of friends, owing to his sterling integrity and a remarkable fact that argues well for the honorable manner in which he treats customers is that he has many of his first patrons still on his books, and during the whole time he has been in business he has not been absent from his stands a single day since 1873.

MARTIN BECK; Dealer in Pork, Lard and Sausage; Stall No. 9, Second Street Market.—Next to bread, meats are among the most important articles of food, and the enormous demand for these supplies has resulted in the establishment of extensive markets in all large cities. In this connection we desire to refer to Mr. Martin Beck, butcher and dealer in pork, etc., whose stall is recognized as one of the best supplied in the Falls City. Mr. Beck has occupied his present stall for thirty years, and is one of the oldest dealers here, and makes a specialty of handling fresh pork, hams, bacon, pure hog's lard, and all kinds of sausage. He slaughters his hogs at his abattoir, Lexington Avenue, and manufactures all his sausages. His meats and sausages are noted for their quality, and the stall is a model of cleanliness. Mr. Beck was born in Germany, but has resided in Louisville since 1847, where he is highly esteemed in business circles for his strict integrity. He is a director of the Citizens' Market and a member of the Liederkranz Singing Society, and supplies the City Hospital.

H. FRUECHTENICHT & SON; Flour and Feed; Corner First and Green Streets.—Among the leading houses in the Louisville flour and feed trade, is that of Messrs. H. Fruechtenicht & Son, which was established by Messrs. Bevermann & Co., of which firm the present head of the house was a member in 1869, they being succeeded by Mr. Herman Fruechtenicht, he eleven years later admitting his son, Mr. Henry Fruechtenicht, to an interest in the business. The premises occupied comprise a spacious ground floor and basement, each 53x105 feet in area, affording ample accommodation for the storage of stock, the choicest brands of flour, hay, straw, oats, feed, etc., and the prices quoted are always regulated by the market. They have influential connections, and can always offer sub-

LOUISVILLE OF TO-DAY. 177

stantial advantages to patrons. Both members of the firm are natives of this city, the senior Mr. Fruechtenicht being also a stockholder in the German National Bank of Louisville, and a devout member of the German Lutheran Church.

THEODORE GREEN; Manufacturer of Grand, Square and Upright Pianos; No. 545 First Street.—Among the piano manufacturers of Louisville, one of the oldest and best known is Mr. Theo. Green. In 1863 he established this business, and has kept fully abreast of the times, his instruments to-day being up to the very highest standard of excellence, as regards appearance, construction, quality of tone and durability. The factory is thoroughly equipped, and only first-class workmen are employed. All work is done by hand, and the instruments are mostly made to order. The pianos made are in all styles, grand and upright, and in a variety of woods, and are to be found in many of the best homes in the city. Mr. Green superintends all departments of the factory, and is a gentleman whose natural qualifications in this line have been supplemented by years of practical study and observation, which has culminated in the production of the splendid piano that he turns out to-day. He is a native of Luxemberg, Germany, and came to Louisville in 1855 and is prominently identified with the Knights of Honor and the Order of Chosen Friends.

JULIUS STROHMEIER; Baker and Confectioner; No. 645 East Main Street.—One of the leading bakery and confectionery stores in this section of Louisville is that of Julius Strohmeier, which was established by him in 1876, and in 1880 he moved to the present premises, which were built specially by him for the business. Mr. Strohmeier turns out plain and fancy bread, rolls, cakes, pies and confectionery of all kinds and makes a specialty of supplying parties, receptions, weddings, etc., his goods being general favorites wherever introduced, owing to their quality and uniform excellence. The store is well equipped and the prices quoted are as low as the lowest for prime quality. Mr. Strohmeier was born in Germany and came to Louisville in 1865. He is highly regarded for his strict integrity, and numbers among his permanent patrons many of the leading families of this section of the city.

CHARLES CRUSH; Tailor and Clothier; Nos. 500 and 502 East Jefferson Street, corner Jackson Street.—Among those who have been prominent in promoting the standard of elegance in gentlemen's wearing apparel, in Louisville, is Mr. Charles Crush, the popular tailor and clothier. His business was established in 1859 by Messrs. Crush & Fleckenstein at No. 103 East Market Street, who continued together till 1891, when they dissolved partnership and Mr. Charles Crush removed to his present location. He has built up an excellent reputation on the quality and fit of his garments, and the prices quoted are extremely moderate. Mr. Crush also keeps on hand a superior assortment of men's and youths' ready made clothing; the stock being valued at about four thousand dollars. He is highly regarded for his integrity and is well known in church and benevolent work, while he is likewise a member of several aid societies.

LOUISVILLE ELECTRICAL WORKS; No. 148 Fifth Street. Among the new manufacturing enterprises of Louisville, is the Louisville Electrical Works, operating an excellently equipped factory, at the address indicated above, which is the only concern in the South devoted solely to the manufacture of electrical apparatus. This business was established in October 1894 by Mr. Campbell Scott of Louisville, and already their business has grown to such an extent that their products have been introduced into almost every state in the Union, and with the opening of 1895, they expect to see their apparatus introduced into many of the foreign countries. Their attention is devoted solely to the manufacture of apparatus and appliances which are used as accessories to the alternating current system of electric lighting, principal among which is their celebrated Phoenix transformer. Selling agents for their products have been established in all the principal cities, and so rapidly is their business increasing, that it will not be a great while before the Louisville Electrical Works will become one of the representative manufacturing concerns of Louisville.

L. B. BASCOM; House Painter and Decorator; No. 167 Fourth Avenue. —For nearly thirty years Mr. L. B. Bascom has been widely known as one of the most expert artists in Louisville engaged in sign painting and house decoration. He makes a specialty of artistic sign work and lettering on wood, glass, cloth or metal, while he also does all kinds of house painting, giving particular attention to interior decoration, floor painting and polishing, graining and varnishing. His work is to be found in many of the finest residences, stores, etc., in the city, and he is always prepared to furnish original designs for interior decoration, all work being tastefully executed in the most satisfactory manner at the reasonable prices. Estimates are cheerfully furnished. Mr. Bascom is a native of New York, and has resided in Louisville many years. He established this business in 1866, and was succeeded by the firm of Bascom and Reichart, Mr. Reichart retired in 1891, when Mr. Bascom again became sole proprietor. He is a member of the Master Painters' Association and Odd Fellows.

178 — LOUISVILLE OF TO-DAY. —

LAUSBERG & MACKE; Altar Builders; No. 733 Fifth Street.—The wealth and culture of the leading congregations of the Catholic, Protestant, Episcopal and other denominations, render them ardent supporters of the enlightened policy, which endows their church edifices with all the beautiful and artistic furnishings that are fitting attributes of the temples devoted to the purposes of religion. In this connection special reference is made in this volume to the representative and successful firm of Messrs. Lausberg & Macke, the widely-known altar builders and manufacturers of all kinds of church furniture. This industry was established in 1891 by Messrs. Frank H. Lausberg and B. Macke, who have since secured an influential patronage, their work being quite equal to the best imported from Europe. Their workshops are well equipped and they employ constantly twenty-five persons, who are expert sculptors, carvers, fresco painters and cabinet makers. They ship work all over the United States and Canada, and have lately filled large orders in New Orleans, Chicago, the Pacific Coast and eastern cities, their contracts ranging from one hundred to fifteen thousand dollars. They make a specialty of altars, pulpits, baptismal fonts, communion railings, reading desks, etc., and promptly furnish sketches, plans and specifications on application. Their work is unrivalled for elegance of design, finish and quality of materials, while their prices in all cases are noted for their moderation. Messrs. Lausberg and Macke were born in Germany, where they were thoroughly trained in this artistic business, and are highly esteemed for their strict integrity. They are prepared to promptly supply superior woodwork in oak, ash, walnut, etc., for altars, railings, pulpits, etc., also fonts in the purest marble, brass and wrought iron work of exquisite beauty, and in fact everything necessary to the beautification and furnishing of churches and chapels.

C. NALLEY; Livery, Boarding and Sales Stables; Nos. 233 to 239 Second Street, between Main and Market. This business was established several years ago by Mr. Edward Wunch, who conducted it till 1893, when Mr. Nalley, who had previously been engaged in the same line in Springfield, Ky., succeeded to the control. The premises occupied comprise a spacious two-story building, 100x90 feet in dimensions, the stables being well drained and ventilated and having excellent accommodations for about sixty horses. For livery purposes Mr. Nalley has a superior outfit, including new stylish coaches, carriages, buggies, surreys, phaetons, etc., and a well selected stock of fine driving and saddle horses. He has also superior accommodations for the boarding of horses by the week or month, and these stables are also headquarters for the sale or purchase of all kinds of animals. Mr. Nalley was born in Washington County, Ky. He is an honorable, energetic and liberal business man, who is very popular in trade circles, justly meriting the substantial success secured in this useful industry.

BALD BROS.; Harness, Saddles and Fine Turf Goods; No. 515 Third Avenue. This business was established in 1890 by Messrs. Jno. & P. H. Bald, who have since secured a liberal and influential patronage in the city and state. Both partners are thoroughly practical harness makers, who use only carefully selected leather and trimmings and employ first-class workmen, the result being that their harness is not only noted for its elaborate style and finish, but for durability and is warranted to give the best of service. The store is well fitted up and fully stocked with a choice assortment of single and double coach and road harness, saddles and fine turf goods, etc. Only the best goods are handled, and the prices quoted by the firm cannot be discounted in the city. Messrs. Bald Brothers are sole agents in Louisville, for the J. O'Knee California boots, which are general favorites with horse owners wherever introduced. Messrs. Jno. and P. H. Bald are natives of this city, and are highly esteemed for their integrity.

HOTEL VICTORIA; Broadway and Tenth Street. Louisville contains many excellent hotels, and prominent among the number ranks the Hotel Victoria. This hotel was opened twelve years ago, and was formerly known as the Standiford Hotel, the present management, consisting of Messrs. R. L. Cox, H. Cox and M. S. Tracy, assuming the control in 1892, since which period it has been conducted under the existent title. It is a substantial four-storied and basement brick structure, 100x210 feet in area, equipped with all the latest modern conveniences, the rooms numbering one hundred and ten. It is well lighted and ventilated, the sanitary arrangements being unsurpassed, finely furnished and appointed, and is conveniently located to all the lines of travel converging in the city, also to public buildings, business centres, etc. The basement is used for steam heating apparatus and storage, first floor office, writing and reading rooms, cigar and news stand, billiard parlor, barroom, barber shop and dining-room, with seating capacity for one hundred guests, the balance of the building being devoted to sleeping accommodation, rooms being here procurable single or en suite. The cuisine is unsurpassed by that of any similar establishment in the Southwest, while the bar is stocked with all the purest wines and liquors. In short the Victoria is in every respect a model house, affording the comfort of a home, while the rates per day are only from $2.00 to $2.50. That the advantages possessed by this deservedly popular house are appreciated is simply attested by the extensive patronage it enjoys. Messrs. Cox are natives of Kentucky, Mr. Ferrel being a native of Parkesburg, West Virginia. Mr. R. L. Cox formerly conducted hotels at Vincennes, Ind.; Finley, O., Ashland, Ky., and Athbend, Ind.

ROCHE'S PHOTOGRAPHIC STUDIO; No. 542 Market Street, between Third and Fourth.—There is perhaps no establishment in Louisville that shows more plainly the rapid improvement of the methods for producing portraits than that known as Roche's Photographic Studio. This business was established ten years ago by Mr. J. L. Roche, who is fully conversant with every detail of this artistic profession. The studio and gallery are supplied with all improved appliances. A specialty is made of life size portraits in crayon, oil, pastelle and India ink—also of young children and family groups. Four first-class operators are employed, and the patronage of this studio extends throughout the city and state. Mr. Roche is a native of Dayton, Ohio, but has resided in the Falls City since 1887. He has made many friends here owing to his genial disposition, artistic ability and strict probity and is recognized as one of the leading photographers in the state, justly meriting the substantial success achieved in this beautiful art.

WM. MANN; Florist; Nos. 1941-1947 Brook Street.—Among the leading florists of the Falls City is Mr. Wm. Mann, who commenced business eighteen years ago. The premises have an area of an acre, and here are erected seven large green houses, having a floor space of 1,300 square feet, in which flourish the most delicate flowers and shrubs. Mr. Mann has a large patronage from the best class of people, extending all over the city and vicinity. He makes a speciality of artistic floral designs for weddings, funerals, etc., arranged with rare taste and skill. He also furnishes choice cut flowers, and ornamental and bedding plants. Mr. Mann is a native of Louisville, and is one of the most accomplished florists in the state, and has achieved success entirely by his skill and probity. He is a popular member of the Florists' Club.

L. KOELLNER; Practical Plumber, Gas and Steamfitter; No. 510 First Street.—A house noted for its thoroughness in everything appertaining to sanitary plumbing in Louisville is that of Mr. L. Koellner. This house was founded in 1891 by the present proprietor, and it presents a striking instance of what may be accomplished by a steady application to business and a just and honorable course of dealing. The premises occupied are commodious and fitted up with every appliance and facility for the prosecution of the business. None but skilled workmen are employed and the utmost satisfaction is guaranteed in every instance. Contracts of all kinds are entered into and the complete fitting up of buildings is satisfactorily performed, while particular attention is paid to all kinds of repairing. Mr. Koellner, who is a native of New Albany, Indiana, is a man of marked ability in his calling. He is a member of the Louisville Master Plumbers' Association, and is held in high esteem in commercial circles as a reliable business man, and those forming business relations with him will derive every advantage from the connection.

THE CRUTCHER BROTHERS COMPANY, (Incorporated); Dealers in Coal; Office, 208 West Main Street.—The Crutcher Brothers Company is known as one of the largest dealers in the best quality of Pittsburg and other coals in Louisville and its vicinity. The concern was organized two years ago as Crutcher Brothers & Company, and was incorporated in August, 1896, under the laws of Kentucky, with a capital of $8,000. From the start a large business has been handled which is being steadily extended. The company has no yards but buys on order and its facilities are such that it is enabled to handle coal in any quantities at the smallest margin of expense, and can thus offer to patrons the most liberal terms. It buys on order any kind of coal, and delivers in quantities to suit, either by the ton or car lot. Fifteen men and teams are employed in the delivery of orders. The offices have telephone connection, the calls being Nos. 1446 and 2289, and orders sent direct in this way receive prompt attention. The executive officers are as follows: James L. Gardner, president; Thos. B. Crutcher, secretary and treasurer, and P. S. Crutcher, manager. Mr. Gardner is a native of Louisville, and is secretary and treasurer of the Union Warehouse Company. The Messrs. Crutcher are also natives of Louisville. Mr. Thomas B. Crutcher was formerly a bookkeeper for the Gaytor Electric Company, and Mr. P. S. Crutcher was with McDonald Brothers & Company, brick manufacturers, before starting in business for himself. They also handle all kinds of freight and do a general transfer business to and from all depots.

180 — — LOUISVILLE OF TO-DAY. — —

DREW BROTHERS; Groceries, Wines and Liquors; No. 601 East Main Street.—Louisville is the centre of a growing trade in groceries, wines and liquors, and one of the most reliable houses in this line, is that of Messrs. Drew Brothers. This business was established in 1875 by Mr. Chas. Drew, who conducted it till 1893, when he was succeeded by his sons Messrs. Gus and Henry Drew, the present proprietors. They handle only choice goods and customers have always the satisfaction of knowing that nothing inferior or adulterated will be sold to them. The store is spacious and finely appointed, containing a full assortment of fresh crop teas, coffees, spices, canned goods, dried fruits, sugars, flour, table delicacies, butter, bakers' and laundry supplies, etc., also an excellent selection of pure wines and liquors, suitable for a superior class of trade. Lowest prices prevail, order, and cleanliness are observable on all sides, while orders are taken and delivered at residences free of charge. Messrs. Drew Brothers number among their permanent customers many leading hotels, restaurants and private families of this section of the city. They are honorable business men, and their establishment is an important adjunct to the grocery trade of the city. They also own and operate a well equipped saloon at the northwest corner of Hancock and Market Streets, where they cater to a first-class trade.

W. A. THOMSON & CO.; Receivers and Shippers of Grain; No. 251 West Main Street.—The enormous amount of capital invested in the grain business in the United States and the general interests involved, impart to this branch of industry an importance that does not attach to many of the other leading lines of commerce. One of the leading houses engaged in the handling and shipping of grain in Louisville is that of Messrs. W. A. Thomson and Co. Mr. W. A. Thomson the present proprietor although but recently established on his own individual account, was formerly a partner in the firm of Messrs. Bullitt and Co., and has been for many years identified with this important trade. He carries grain on consignments in public warehouses and disposes of the same to the local distillers and others throughout the South. Rye, oats and barley are the grains mostly handled which are sold in car lots. Mr. Thomson handles these products on commission and guarantees quick sales and prompt returns. Liberal advances are made on consignments and the facilities enjoyed by this responsible house enable it to further in the highest degree the interests of both producer and buyer. Mr. Thomson was born in Ireland but has resided here many years. He is very popular and respected in business circles and is a thorough-going exponent of the great cardinal principles of equity and probity, which form the only basis of enduring prosperity in mercantile life.

THE KLEE, COLEMAN & CO.; Mineral Waters, Etc.; No. 719 Second Street.—Aërated mineral waters, are now largely consumed during warm weather, and one of the leading houses in Louisville engaged in their manufacture is that of The Klee, Coleman & Company. This concern was established some ten years ago, and became a corporate organization under the laws of the state of Ohio in 1892. The company has an ample capitalization, the management of its affairs being vested in the following capable hands: J. Klee, also engaged in the same business as senior partner in the firms of Klee and Coleman at Indianapolis, and J. Klee & Son at Dayton; H. Coleman, the well-known carriage manufacturer of Dayton; and S. Leidigh, the resident manager here, and a prominent member of the Louisville Commercial, and Fish and Game Clubs. The premises occupied comprise a substantial two-storied brick structure, 40x100 feet in dimensions, equipped with the latest improved carbonating, distilling, bottling, filtering and kindred apparatus operated by adequate steam power. Here twenty skilled hands are employed, the range of production embracing all varieties of mineral waters, saline and sulphurated, southern choice ginger ale, champagne, orange cider, and seltzer water—a special feature being made of the rental of fountains and the charging of portable fountains. As purity plays an important part in the production of this class of liquid beverages, we do not deem it out of place to state here that the water alone made use of by this company is subjected to several distinct processes of exact filtration before it is deemed fit for public use. Orders are filled with care and dispatch, and the trade of the house extends not only throughout Kentucky, etc., but also as far as Florida and Texas.

KENTUCKY WALL PLASTER COMPANY, (Incorporated); Water Street, between First and Brook.—An industry of great utility in Louisville is that of the Kentucky Wall Plaster Company, manufacturers of the celebrated Diamond Brand wall plaster. Four years ago, under the style of B. J. Campbell & Sons, the house was established, the present company having been incorporated in 1892, under Kentucky laws, the officers being: president and treasurer, B. J. Campbell; secretary, J. B. Campbell, and manager, B. J. Campbell, Jr. The factory is a two-story structure, 100x160 feet in area, fully supplied with modern appliances operated by electric power, and the output finds ready sale in this and the neighboring states. The Diamond wall plaster is admitted to be unsurpassed by its particular line. The old-fashioned plasters are always requiring repairing, and when a portion of the plastering falls from a wall or ceiling, great annoyance is always experienced, the "Diamond" contains all the necessary ingredients, except water, in their proper proportions, thoroughly mixed by machinery, and when applied clings to the wall with adamantine firmness. The capacity of the works is five hundred and fifty sacks daily. This plaster has been used successfully in many of the principal buildings of this and other cities. Mr. B. J. Campbell was born in Ireland, but has lived here almost all his life, and ranks high in the esteem of our citizens. Messrs. J. B. and B. J. Campbell are young, honorable business men and are natives of Louisville.

ED. STOKER; Tin Roofing, Guttering, Spouting and All Kinds of Job Work, Etc.; No. 639 East Main Street.—A prominent house in its line in the Falls City is that of Mr. Ed. Stoker, roofer and dealer in stoves, etc. This business was established in 1852 by Mr. Stoker, who is a thoroughly practical roofer, using only the best materials and employing first-class workmen. He occupies a spacious three-story brick building, 16x102 feet in area, fitted up with every convenience. Here is kept a heavy and choice stock of stoves, ranges and heaters, tinware and kitchen utensils, which are unrivalled for reliability and efficiency. Moderate prices prevail for all goods, and a specialty is made of guttering, spouting and all kinds of job work. The roofs constructed by Mr. Stoker have met with the hearty approval of architects, builders, etc., and are finished at prices which compare favorably with those charged for inferior work elsewhere. Mr. Stoker has roofed some of the finest buildings in the city and its vicinity, and has lately finished the Melwood Distillery. He was born in Louisville and his house is the oldest of the kind in the city. Mr. Stoker is highly esteemed for his skill and strict probity, and is a member of the I. O. O. F.

WM. H. FISHER; Hardware and Butcher Supplies; Southwest corner Hancock and Market Streets.—Among the leading houses engaged in this industry in Louisville that have gained a wide reputation for excellent goods and just dealing and worthy of special mention in this volume is that of Mr. Wm. H. Fisher. This is the oldest established hardware house in the Falls City and was founded in 1848 by Henry Flagner, who was succeeded by Mr. Wm. Berkley, afterwards in 1854 by Mr. J. G. Woerner, and eventually in 1887 by Messrs. Schlueter and Fisher. They dissolved partnership in 1888, when Mr. W. H. Fisher became sole proprietor. The premises occupied are spacious and well equipped and are fully stocked with everything found in a first-class hardware store. A specialty is made by Mr. Fisher of handling butchers' supplies, and he is agent in Louisville for Messrs. Smith & Son, manufacturers of the famous Buffalo double crank choppers, self-mixers and other butcher specialties, and in this line carries the largest and best stock in the city, and the trade of the house extends throughout all sections of the city and state. Mr. Fisher is a native of this city, and is a member of the Builders' and Traders' Exchange.

THE NORMAN LUMBER CO., (Incorporated); Columbia Building.— Among the leading houses in Louisville that have obtained prominence in the wholesale hardwood trade should be mentioned the name of The Norman Lumber Company. This concern was originally founded by Mr. Henry S. Cooling in 1868, who conducted the business till 1890, when it was incorporated under the laws of Kentucky with a capital of $50,000, as the Henry S. Cooling Lumber Company, the executive officers being Henry S. Cooling, president and secretary, and A. E. Norman treasurer and manager. In June 1894 the business was reorganized and the present concern formed of which Mr. A. E. Norman is president and treasurer, and Miss E. Connolly secretary. In their large yards, which are 200x300 feet in area an immense stock of thoroughly seasoned ash, oak, cherry, walnut, hickory and particularly yellow poplar is carried. These woods are received direct from Kentucky, Tennessee and Indiana, and are sold chiefly to furniture manufacturers in the North and East, and also export to Canada and England. Being situated on the main line of the Louisville and Nashville Railroad the facilities for receiving and shipping lumber are unsurpassed, and its influential connection enables the company to offer special advantages in prices to customers, and to fill all orders in a prompt and satisfactory manner. Mr. Norman, the president, is highly regarded for his strict integrity and under his careful guidance the future prospects of the Norman Lumber Company are of the most favorable character.

LOUISVILLE ELECTRO-PLATING COMPANY; No. 218 First Street, between Main and Market.—For first-class workmanship and elegantly finished goods, it is conceded that no concern in the Falls City stands higher than the Louisville Electro-Plating Company, of which Messrs. Andrew Vogt and Fred. Bartels are the enterprising and popular proprietors. They established this artistic industry in 1890, and have since secured a liberal and influential patronage in the city and state. Both partners are thoroughly expert and experienced electro-platers and formerly were engaged for several years in the Williamson Art Metal Works of this city. They are artistic electro-platers in gold, silver, nickel, copper and brass, and execute also antique, oxidized and plain finishing on all metals, including lacquering and bronzing. Messrs. Vogt and Bartels also manufacture promptly to order office, bank and bar railings, brass store fixtures, window fixtures, guards, brackets, etc. The premises are fully equipped with the latest improved appliances operated by steam power, and only first-class workmen are employed. Mr. Vogt, who is a prominent Freemason, was born in Nashville, Tenn., while Mr. Bartels is a native of Louisville. They are highly regarded in trade circles for their skill and integrity.

WILLIAM JACKE; Grocery and Saloon; Corner Eighth and Jefferson Streets.—Among the leading business men of Louisville, prominent mention should be made of Mr. William Jacke, whose career furnishes us with an excellent example of what perseverance and integrity can accomplish. Mr. Jacke was born near Hanover, Germany, and came to Louisville fourteen years ago. He obtained employment with Funk, the Eighth Street grocer, where he remained five years, after which he worked with Mr. Gottbrath, Eighth and Market Streets, leaving that position to embark upon his present venture. From the outset he was successful, and has built up a liberal and influential patronage. The building occupied is a spacious and well-appointed structure, 22x75 feet in area, and is one of the neatest and most inviting business houses in the city. Electric fans, electric lights, large show windows, handsome fixtures, all combine in bringing about an excellent result, and it is a pleasure for patrons to visit this store, where the choice stock is so temptingly displayed. Groceries of all kinds, from the choicest delicacies, down to staple goods, wines and liquors and cigars, are carried, these coming direct from the best sources. A well-managed sample room, this having a separate entrance from Eighth Street is conducted and here are found the choicest foreign and domestic wines, brandies, whiskies, also beers, etc., specialties being made of old prentice sour-mash, Kentucky whiskey, Oscar Pepper, sour-mash, etc. There is no grocer in the city held in higher esteem than Mr. Jacke in society circles. He is very prominent, being a member of the K. of P., the I. O. O. F., the Mutual Benefit Association and a Royal Arch Mason, and is one of the leading spirits in Masonry here, and is largely contributing to the success of the order in this city.

WILLIAM JACKE.

H. A. KRAFT; Wholesale and Retail Dealer in Meats; Corner Fifth and Green Streets.—Among the leading establishments in its line in Louisville, ranks that of Mr. H. A. Kraft, the widely-known wholesale and retail dealer in beef, mutton, lamb, etc. Mr. Kraft established this business in 1873, and was one of the founders of the Kentucky Market, and now numbers among his permanent customers many leading hotels, restaurants and families of the city and its vicinity. His stall is noted for its cleanliness and neatness, and is supplied with all modern conveniences, refrigerators, etc. Mr. Kraft spares no expense to provide the choicest meats, and his facilities for doing this are not surpassed by those of any competitor. He slaughters all his own stock, and runs a well appointed abattoir at No. 1304 Hamilton Avenue, and keeps constantly on hand full supplies of prime beef, mutton, lamb, veal, pork, dried tongues, corned, dried and spiced beef. Orders are promptly filled and delivered at residences, etc., and his prices in all cases are as low as the lowest for first-class quality. From the commencement of his business, Mr. Kraft determined to keep only the primest meats, and has never wavered from that policy. Mr Kraft was born in Germany and came to Louisville in 1859 when only eighteen years old. He is highly esteemed for his strict probity, and justly merits his liberal patronage.

J. T. BARNETT; Livery, Boarding and Sale Stables; Nos. 221, 224, 226 and 228 West Green Street.—For variety and elegance of turnouts, the livery, boarding and sales stables of Mr. J. T. Barnett, are unrivalled in the city of Louisville. These stables are in every respect ably managed and well equipped and receive a very influential patronage. Mr. Barnett commenced business in 1884, at No. 713 Green Street, and eventually in 1887 erected his present establishment. It is a spacious two-story brick structure 75x190 feet in area, fully equipped with all modern appliances. These are the best ventilated and drained stables in the city, and have excellent accommodations for fifty-four horses. Here are nine box stalls each 12x12 feet, while the oval stalls are 6x10 feet each. Mr. Barnett has some of the finest and most stylish equipages to be found here, and a stock of superior horses, which can be hired for business or pleasure, night or day, on moderate terms. He also carefully boards horses, and his stables are headquarters for the sale and purchase of animals, and experienced grooms are always in attendance. Mr. Barnett was born in Estill County, Kentucky, and during the Civil War served in the Eighth Kentucky Infantry, three years and three months. He was noted for his gallant conduct and devotion to the cause of the Union, and eventually retired from the service. Mr. Barnett is highly esteemed by the community for his strict integrity, and is an active member of the I. O. O. F.

LOUISVILLE OF TO-DAY. 183

BRADLEY CARRIAGE COMPANY; J. J. Burkholder, Proprietor; No. 128 West Main Street.—Among those engaged in the manufacture of first-class vehicles enjoying a wide reputation for superior work in Louisville ranks Mr. J. J. Burkholder, proprietor of the old established Bradley Carriage Company. This time honored house was founded by Messrs. Stine and Bradley in 1839, to whom succeeded Mr. C. Bradley in 1845, the business for some period subsequently being conducted under the style of C. Bradley & Son. In 1884 Mr. J. J. Burkholder acquired control of the business, and wisely retained the existent trading title. The premises occupied comprise a substantial four-storied brick building, 35x90 feet in dimensions, the first floor being devoted to office and showroom in front portion, with well appointed factory and workshop in rear, second, third and fourth floors, painting, trimming and general stock storage departments. Here a force of fifteen skilled hands is employed, the range of production being devoted to the building of fine carriages, buggies, surries, etc., as also light-weight business wagons. These are all constructed of the soundest and best seasoned woods,—steel, iron and other materials,—and are light running, durable and convenient for city or road purposes, while every care, at a moderate scale of charge, is given to all kinds of repairing in this line. Mr. Burkholder is of German nationality, a prominent member of the Catholic Knights of Labor, and has been a highly respected resident of Louisville for the greater portion of his lifetime.

EDW. B. SCHIEMAN; Pharmacist; Nos. 101 and 103 West Walnut Street, corner First.—Among the leading and most reliable members of the pharmaceutical profession in this section of Louisville may be named Mr. Edw. B. Schieman, who is a thoroughly practical and able chemist and a member of the Louisville College of Pharmacy, while he is also an active member of the Botanical Club, State Board of Pharmacy and American Pharmaceutical Association. He established this business September, 1879, and has since secured a liberal and influential patronage. The store is handsomely fitted up, and supplied with every convenience. The stock embraces full lines of pure fresh drugs and chemicals, pharmaceutical preparations, patent medicines, druggists' sundries, etc. A prominent specialty is made of the prescription department, physicians formulæ and family recipes being compounded at any hour of the day or night. Mr. Schieman also keeps on hand several preparations of his own compounding, which are highly recommended by leading members of the faculty for their efficacy and reliability, such as Benzo-Almond, a toilet preparation, Concho-Quinine for the hair and White Pine Cough Syrup. Mr. Schieman is a native of this city. He is highly esteemed for his courteous manners and strict integrity.

ROBERT ROWELL; Printers' Warehouse, Electrotyping, Etc.; Corner Third Avenue and Market Street.—Louisville has long been the recognized centre for the southern states, for the trade in presses, type, etc., and a representative house in this line is that of Mr. Robert Rowell, the widely-known dealer. This business was established in 1865 by Messrs. Rowell and Cullin, who soon

dissolved partnership, Mr. Robert Rowell continuing on his own account. He brings great practical experience to bear, while his facilities are perfect and his connections with the most noted manufacturers of a most influential character. The premises occupied are spacious and the workshops are fully supplied with special appliances and machinery, and a full staff of skilled workmen is constantly employed. Mr. Rowell keeps constantly on hand a well selected and choice stock of presses, type, rules, cuts, printing machinery, also dating stamps, dies, and dating ribbons, which are offered to customers at very moderate prices. He also conducts a general electrotype business, making superior plates for all printing purposes on wood or metal bases. Half tone work is a special feature of this house and stamps are furnished for bookbinders for embossing, etc., and the trade of the house now extends throughout Kentucky and the southern states. Mr. Rowell is the pioneer in this line of business in Louisville, and is highly esteemed in trade circles for his mechanical skill and strict integrity. He was born in Cincinnati and came to Louisville in 1865.

FALLS CITY WIRE WORKS; Nos. 227 and 229 Third Street.—Prominent among the reliable houses in its line in the state is that of Mr. H. W. Fuchmann, sole proprietor of the Falls City Wire Works, located at Nos. 227 and 229 Third Street. This is the only business of its kind in Louisville, and was founded by Mr. Fuchmann seven years ago, since which time he has succeeded in building up a large trade, extending throughout this and neighboring states. The works are fitted throughout with the latest improved machinery and appliances, while Mr. Fachmann makes a specialty of wire frames for florists' pieces for funeral and wedding decorations. His superior skill and taste have been abundantly demonstrated and he has received a diploma of honorable mention at the Columbian Exhibition for the originality and beauty of his designs. Mr. Fachmann, who is a German by birth, is universally respected, and brings not only ample resources to bear on his business, but likewise that trained and intelligent apprehension of the beautiful in design that makes his work so highly appreciated by florists and a critical public.

ED. STARKE; Baker; No. 1327 Portland Avenue.—The leading bakery of Louisville is that conducted by Mr. Ed. Starke, who is one of the oldest in this line of trade in the city. The business was started in 1858, under the style of Starke and Miller, and has been conducted under the present style for thirty-two years. The premises occupied are especially adapted to the business and are commodious and very conveniently arranged. The front portion of the store is utilized for the retail salesroom where a full line of bread, cakes and pastry is always displayed most attractively, and the bakery in the rear has the most improved facilities including a cake oven. A force of competent journeymen is employed and by the use of the best materials, the highest quality of product is maintained. Having been located on its present site for the last twenty-two years, this bakery is one of the land marks of the city and is the best known in Louisville. Mr. Starke is a native of Germany and came to the United States in 1854, locating in Louisville. He early identified himself with the best interests of the city and during the war served with credit in the famous Fifth Kentucky Infantry for three years and three months. He is a Royal Arch Mason and a member of Post No. 327 G. A. R.

GUS. C. RIETZE; The Hatter; No. 340 East Market Street.—It is a well-known fact that "Rietze the Hatter" is the leader in fashions and styles of men's headwear in this section of the city of Louisville. This business was established in 1869 by Mr. H. E. Rietze, who conducted it till 1892, when Mr. G. C. Rietze succeeded to the control. He occupies a spacious three-story building, the store being elegantly equipped, and he numbers among his permanent customers many of our leading citizens. The stock carried includes a full line of hats and caps suitable for all seasons of the year, including the latest styles in silk hats, derbies, also soft felt hats, and fur hats. Straw goods of all kinds are on hand during the season and all the new styles made popular by the decrees of fashion are to be found in this establishment as soon as brought out. Here likewise can be obtained, superior gloves, umbrellas, canes, etc., while his prices are noted for their moderation, and his goods are unrivalled for elegance of style and uniform excellence. Mr. Rietze is an active Freemason and is highly esteemed by the community for his enterprise and strict probity, and is always the first in the city to offer for sale the newest, most stylish, seasonable and fashionable hats, and his success is as substantial as it is well deserved. The stock is valued at about $20,000. He is also a partner in the firm of Rietze and Spies, dealers in gents' furnishing goods. Mr. Spies having been admitted into partnership in 1892, when Mr. Henry E. Rietze his brother died. Both the hat and furnishing goods business are conducted in the same building.

WM. F. KELLER; Groceries; Southwest corner First and Walnut Streets—A business enterprise in Louisville of comparatively recent growth is that which is so successfully conducted by Mr. Wm. F. Keller, dealer in staple and fancy groceries. This establishment which now has a very large share of the best family retail trade in Louisville is less than two years old, having been founded by the present proprietor in 1891, and the comparatively short period in which an extensive and influential patronage has been built up in competition with older dealers not only shows the ability and energy of the proprietor but affords an illustration of the business opportunities offered in this city to capable men who have the essential requisites for success. Mr. Keller was born and raised in Louisville and is a young man of the highest standing in the community and a business man of proved capacity. The store, which is most favorably located on an important corner, occupies the first floor, 30x100 feet in area, in a three-story brick building and is finely appointed with all modern conveniences for the conduct of a first-class trade.

HEDDEN DRY GOODS COMPANY; Dry Goods and Notions; Corner State and Market Streets.—This business was founded many years ago by David Hedden who first began his business career as a clerk for Elias Ayers and eventually was taken into partnership in 1829. In 1836 Mr. Silas Day also became a partner, and after the death of Mr. Ayers, the firm of Hedden, Day & Co., succeeded to the control. This continued till 1878 when the firm of Hedden, Phelps & Co., was organized, Mr. W. A. Hedden being the senior partner, and took charge of the business. On March 1st, 1892 the enterprise was incorporated under the laws of Indiana with a paid-up capital of $25,000, Mr. W. A. Hedden being the president, and Mr. W. A. Beach, manager. This is the oldest house of business in New Albany, and is larger than all the other dry goods stores combined. Mr. Hedden was born in this city and has been engaged in business since 1862, while he is also largely interested in real estate and other enterprises. Mr.

W. A. Beach is an able and enterprising dry goods merchant who carefully supervises the store. He is a native of Washington County, Ind., and was previously engaged for ten years with the old firm of Hedden, Phelps & Co. The premises occupied comprise a commodious three-story brick building 38x65 feet in area with an ell 38x65 feet in size. The different departments are finely fitted up and twenty competent clerks, salesladies and assistants are employed. The stock is not only the finest and largest here, but is equal to any in Indiana or Kentucky.

H ILTON COLLINS; Manufacturer of Single and Double-trees, Neckyokes, Etc.; No. 2200 Twelfth Street.—An enterprise of prominence in Louisville is that of Mr. Hilton Collins, manufacturer of single and double-trees, neckyokes, etc. This business was established eighteen years ago, by Mr. H. Collins, who has since secured an extensive and permanent patronage. The premises cover an area 30x180 feet and the factory is a twostory building, 30x80 feet in area. **The equipment includes all** the latest and most approved machinery **and appliances operated by a forty horse power steam engine. The tracks of the Louisville Southern** Ry., passing along side the works, afford exceptionally advantageous receiving and shipping **facilities.** The single and double-trees, etc., manufactured by Mr. Collins are unrivalled for utility and efficiency, and have no superiors in this country or abroad and are now sold largely in all parts of the United States, Canada and Mexico, the capacity of the factory being twenty-two thousand dozen. Mr. Collins is a native of Louisville and is one of her most progressive and esteemed citizens. He devotes all his time to the management of this fast developing business and in business circles is highly regarded for his persevering, energetic and reliable characteristics. We bespeak a future of the brightest order for this **important enterprise.**

H ENRY MESTEMACHER; Locksmith and Bell Hanger; Electric Bell Work a Specialty; No. 1012, corner West and Green Streets.—One of the most essential of the mechanical industries of all cities is that of the locksmith and bell hanger, and to be successful in these modern days necessitates a knowledge of electricity. Prominent in Louisville actively engaged in this line of business is Mr. Henry Mestemacher, whose business was established forty years ago by Mr. Frank Mestemacher. He conducted it till 1889, when he died, and was succeeded by his son, Mr. Henry Mestemacher, the present proprietor. Mr. Mestemacher is a practical locksmith and bell hanger, who makes a specialty of electric bell work, speaking tubes, etc. He also attends carefully to key fitting, lock repairing, the adjustment of night latches and the fixing of burglar alarms, annunciators, etc., and has done a large amount of work for some of the finest buildings in the city. Estimates are promptly furnished and contracts completed, charges being invariably placed on a scale of moderation. Mr. Mestemacher is highly regarded in trade circles for his mechanical skill and strict probity, justly meriting the liberal patronage secured in this useful industry. He was born in this city, and we can safely recommend this house, being confident that all work entrusted to it will be completed in a first-class manner.

J. C. LEISMAN; Dealer in Groceries, Provisions, Flour, Notions, Wines, Liquors, Etc.; Nos. 104 and 106 West Jefferson Street.—It is always a matter of great convenience to any community to have located in its midst such a reliable house as that of Mr. J. C. Leisman, dealer in groceries, provisions, flour, etc. The business was established in 1870 by Messrs. J. C. & Frank Leisman, who conducted it till 1874, when Mr. Frank Leisman died and Mr. J. C. Leisman became sole proprietor. Mr. Leisman has had long experience in the grocery trade, and possesses an accurate knowledge of the needs of critical patrons. The store is spacious and contains a heavy and choice stock of groceries, country produce, provisions, flour, also fresh crop teas, coffees, spices, sugars, dried fruits, canned goods, etc., while a specialty is made of first-class imported and domestic wines and liquors. Only the purest and best goods are handled, while orders are carefully filled at lowest figures, and the trade of the house extends throughout the city and its vicinity. Mr. Leisman was born in Germany in 1847, and came to the Falls City in 1866. He is an honorable business man, who is very popular with the community, and has won by sheer merit his present prominent position in the grocery trade of this section of the city.

R ECTANUS & SCHILLING; Druggists; Corner Shelby and Jefferson Streets.—Prominent among the leading Louisville pharmacies is that of Messrs. Rectanus & Schilling, which was opened many years ago by Mr. Zausinger, who was succeeded by Mr. Bell and by Mr. Fred'k Bender, the last named gentleman conducting till 1886, when Mr. Theodore Rectanus became the proprietor, Mr. Schilling becoming a partner in 1889. Both partners are active members of the Pharmaceutical Society of Kentucky and Botanical Club of Louisville. The store is elegantly fitted up and supplied with every convenience, and the stock includes pure, fresh drugs, chemicals and pharmaceutical preparations, mineral waters, proprietary medicines, etc. A specialty is made of compounding physicians' prescriptions and family recipes with accuracy and precision at moderate rates. Physicians and the public have long recognized the fact that what they obtain at this pharmacy is not only good but of the best quality. Both partners are honorable business men, whose future prosperity in the drug trade of the city seems well assured.

CHAS. A. ROGERS; Importer and Dealer in Catholic Books and Church Goods; No. 232 West Market Street.—The largest and most complete stock of Catholic books and church goods in the Southwest is that carried by Mr. Chas. A. Rogers who ranks as one of the leading merchants of the city. Mr. Rogers has been engaged in this business since 1871, and has a well established local trade and all through the South. He carries a full line of Catholic school and miscellaneous books, religious works, lithographies and stories and also handles a general line of Catholic goods, such as beads, pictures, crucifixes, etc. He imports standard works from Europe. He also carries a general line of high-class literature and can supply at short notice any work published at home or abroad. A specialty is made of picture framing in any style and mats and mouldings for frames are carried in stock. Mr. Rogers was born in Bardstown, Ky., and has long resided in Louisville where he is well-known and highly esteemed. He is also well-known all through the South where he has many permanent patrons of long standing and he has a large trade both among clergy and laity.

JOHN JUSTI; Wall Paper and Window Shades; Nos. 331 and 333 Jefferson Street, between Third and Fourth.—The largest and finest assortment in Louisville of wall and ceiling papers in a wide variety of artistic patterns, including all the latest designs from the leading manufacturers, window shadings in all widths and colors and stained glass substitute suitable for dwellings and public buildings, in fact everything requisite to the most artistic finish of walls, ceiling and windows in any room, all at the very lowest prices for the quality are found at the store of Mr. John Justi. The proprietor employs five trained assistants, and has a large share of the best local trade as patrons are always assured of obtaining prompt and courteous attention and receiving the best value for their money. For the further convenience of customers the office has telephone connection the call being 1163-2. The business was established on Market Street in 1869 by Mittler and Justi. Mr. Mittler retired in 1877 since which time Mr. Justi has been the sole proprietor and has occupied his present store for the last eight years. He is a native of Louisville and was before engaging in the present business a member of the well-known firm of John Sinn & Co., manufacturers of furniture. He is personally popular and is a member of the Knights of Honor, Royal Arcanum and Ancient Order of United Workmen.

E. SCHEFFER; Chemist; Office and Laboratory, No. 173 Shelby Street, north of Franklin.—One of the leading chemists in this section of Louisville is Mr. E. Scheffer. Mr. Scheffer, who is an expert chemist established this business in 1873, since which period he has secured a liberal patronage, his trade extending throughout the entire United States. The laboratory is equipped with modern appliances and several skilled hands are employed. Mr. Scheffer makes a specialty of manufacturing dry pepsin, also concentrated saccharated and liquid pepsin. These pepsin preparations are recognized standards with the trade and possess all the qualities claimed for them by Mr. Scheffer, who is highly esteemed in trade circles for his professional ability and strict probity. These pepsin preparations were awarded medals at the Centennial, Philadelphia, 1876, Vienna Exposition, 1873, and also at the Southern Exposition, Louisville. He is one of the founders and ex-president of the Louisville College of Pharmacy and is likewise a popular member of the State Board of Pharmacy.

FINK & FELDHAUS; Wholesale Saddlery; No. 512 West Main Street.—In no branch of the manufacturing interests of the country is it more important to have good workmanship and first-class materials, than in the saddlery and harness trade. We refer in this connection to the representative firm of Messrs. Fink & Feldhaus, who are thoroughly practical and expert saddlers and harness makers. They commenced business here in 1877, and their patronage, which is steadily increasing, now extends throughout the entire United States. The premises occupied comprise a spacious three-story and basement building, 20x125 feet in area, the first floor being devoted to offices, showrooms, etc., and the other floors to manufacturing and stock, and they keep constantly on hand a heavy and choice stock of fine handmade coach and road harness, saddles, bridles, collars, whips, blankets, etc. Only the finest leather, trimmings, etc., and superior workmen are employed, and the saddles and harness produced are noted not only for their elaborate finish, but also for lasting durability. Eighteen skilled hands and several traveling salesmen are employed, and all goods are strictly handmade. They are patentees and owners of Fink's Leather Tree Saddle, which was patented May 26th, 1885, May 15th, 1888, and April 23rd, 1889. Orders are filled at moderate prices, and complete satisfaction is guaranteed patrons. Mr. Fink was born in Germany, but was raised in Louisville, while Mr. Feldhaus is a native of the Falls City. They are highly esteemed for their skill and strict probity, and are popular members of the Board of Trade, and from 1892 to 1894 Mr. Feldhaus represented the Third ward in the City Council.

KREMELBERG & CO.; Buyers of Leaf Tobacco; No. 1004 West Market Street.—One of the leading houses in its line in Louisville is that of Messrs. Kremelberg & Co., buyers of leaf tobacco on commission. This prosperous house is a branch of the New York city firm of the same name, and was established as such March 1st, 1875. The individual members of the firm are Messrs. George Kremelberg, resident in New York, Adolph Engler, also of New York, Chas. A. Martin, representing the Baltimore interests of the house and F. W. H. Hahn, conducting the business interests of the concern from this point. The operations of the house are chiefly confined to the buying of leaf tobacco on commission. The trade here controlled, has augmented from year to year under Mr. Hahn's able guidance and gives assurance of still further increase in the future. He is a native of Staten Island, New York, and has been identified with the house since 1872. He is treasurer, and on the executive committee of the Louisville Leaf Tobacco Exchange.

WILLIAM JACKE; Grocery and Saloon; Corner Eighth and Jefferson Streets.—Among the leading business men of Louisville, prominent mention should be made of Mr. William Jacke, whose career furnishes us with an excellent example of what perseverance and integrity can accomplish. Mr. Jacke was born near Hanover, Germany, and came to Louisville fourteen years ago. He obtained employment with Funk, the Eighth Street grocer, where he remained five years, after which he worked with Mr. Gottbrath, Eighth and Market Streets, leaving that position to embark upon his present venture. From the outset he was successful, and has built up a liberal and influential patronage. The building occupied is a spacious and well-appointed structure, 22x75 feet in area, and is one of the neatest and most inviting business houses in the city. Electric fans, electric lights, large show windows, handsome fixtures, all combine in bringing about an excellent result, and it is a pleasure for patrons to visit this store, where the choice stock is so temptingly displayed. Groceries of all kinds, from the choicest delicacies, down to staple goods, wines and liquors and cigars, are carried, these coming direct from the best sources. A well-managed sample room, this having a separate entrance from Eighth Street is conducted and here are found the choicest foreign and domestic wines, brandies, whiskies, also beers, etc., specialties being made of old prentice sour-mash, Kentucky whiskey, Oscar Pepper, sour-mash, etc. There is no grocer in the city held in higher esteem than Mr. Jacke in society circles. He is very prominent, being a member of the K. of P., the I. O. O. F., the Mutual Benefit Association and a Royal Arch Mason, **and is one of the leading spirits in Masonry here.**

UNION MILLS; Flour and Mill Feed; Corner Seventeenth and Main Streets.—The milling interests in Louisville are well represented by the Union Mills, of which Mr. John B. Graves is the proprietor and manager. The mills are located at Jasper, Indiana, but the distributing point is here, where a large stock of all brands is always carried. The business was established seven years ago by Messrs. Graves and Alvots; at the end of six years, however, Mr. Graves became the sole owner. The office and storage rooms occupy a substantial three-story brick building, fitted with an elevator, etc. The Union Mills manufacture all kinds of flour and mill feed, making specialties of rye, graham, spring and buckwheat flour, and some other well-known brands are Angel Food, Gilt Edge, Chieftain, Prince, Kitchen Queen and Old Times. The building has a storage capacity of one thousand barrels, the brands being favorites with bakers, confectioners and consumers generally. Mr. John B. Graves is a native of Louisville. He is enterprising and honorable, **and a** representative of Louisville's business men.

MACFARLANE & CO.; Iron and Coke; No. 508 Columbia Building.—One of the leading houses actively engaged in the fuel business in Louisville, is that of Messrs. Macfarlane & Co., wholesale dealers in coal, iron and coke, and miners and shippers of Kentucky cannel coal. This business was established in 1888 by Messrs. Graham Macfarlane and Thomas N. Mordue, as an incorporated company, with a paid-up capital of $50,000, and was continued till 1894, when on the retirement of Mr. Mordue, Mr. Macfarlane became sole proprietor. Mr. Macfarlane is an able and honorable business man, and is the representative of two superior cannel mines, one, the "Bear Creek," Pineville, southeastern Kentucky, connected by switches with the tracks of the L. & N. Railroad; the other, "Chattard," in eastern Kentucky with C. & O. R. R. connections. He deals extensively in coal, iron and coke, and also exports cannel coal to Europe, while he is likewise agent in Louisville for the Mt. Carbon Co., Ltd., foundry coke, Woodward Iron Co., of Alabama; Lehigh Valley Coal Co., P. & R. C. and I. Co.'s, anthracite coal, and the Fire Creek Smithing Coal. The business is strictly wholesale, and orders for a cargo or car lot of coal, cannel or coke are promptly filled at lowest market rates, and the trade of the house now extends throughout the entire United States, while the coal, cannel and coke handled have no superiors in this country. The sales of this house last year amounted to over one hundred thousand tons of coal, coke, etc., and the trade for the current year will be considerably greater. Mr. Macfarlane **was** born in Pennsylvania, but has resided in Louisville for the past seven years, and is an active member of the Kenton Club, and handles more coke here than any other house in the business.

— LOUISVILLE OF TO-DAY. —

KILLGORE & STILTZ; Manufacturers of Platform, Elliptic and Side Spring Wagons; Nos. 217 to 223 First Street.—One of the most noted in its line in Louisville is that of Messrs. Killgore and Stiltz, the well-known manufacturers of platform, elliptic and side spring wagons, hose reels and hook and ladder trucks, etc. This concern was established by Messrs. R. M. Killgore and J. D. Stiltz in 1875, who by strict attention to business, coupled with a thoroughly practical knowledge of its every detail, have deservedly succeeded in rearing an extensive trade, which is broadly distributed throughout Kentucky, Indiana and Tennessee. The partners have had long experience, and are fully prepared to execute in a superior manner, all work entrusted to them, using nothing but the best materials, and employing only the most skilful workmen. This house turns out a class of spring wagons which will bear favorable comparison for durability, ease of draught and finished workmanship with the output of any similar establishment in the country. They satisfactorily filled the supply contract for hose reels for the city, also wagons for the Standard Oil Company, the Adams Express Company, and other representative corporations.

H. W. NEWMAN; Plumber, Gas and Steam Fitter; No. 320 West Green Street, between Third and Fourth Streets. — Louisville is fortunate in possessing a number of superior sanitary plumbers, and prominent among these is Mr. H. W. Newman. This business was established in 1876, by Messrs. Strouse & Newman, who conducted it till 1880, when Mr. Strouse retired and Mr. H. W. Newman became the proprietor. Mr. Newman is an expert sanitary plumber, who enjoys a widespread reputation for the excellence of his work. He occupies a spacious three-story brick building 20x185 feet in dimensions, the first floor being devoted to offices and show rooms with workshops in the rear, while the other floors are utilized for stock. Here is kept a heavy stock of bath tubs, water closets, hydrants, boilers, sinks, artistic gas fixtures, chandeliers, etc., which are offered to customers at extremely low prices. Mr. Newman is agent for the Dunning boilers, McConnell's germ proof filters, and makes a specialty of bath room ventilation and natural gas fitting. He has done a large amount of work on many of the finest buildings in the city, among which may be mentioned Harris' Theater, Fourth Avenue; Central College, Danville, Ky.; Potter College, Bowling Green, Ky.; Masonic Temple, Fourth and Green Streets, this city, etc. Twenty first-class workmen are employed, and all work is accomplished in a superior manner. Mr. Newman is highly regarded for his mechanical skill and integrity, and is a popular member of the Builders' and Traders', and also of the Master Plumbers' Association.

PETE BROWNING; Proprietor The "Gladiator's" Place; No. 1235 West Market Street.—One of the most popular resorts in the city is that known as the "Gladiator's" Place. The proprietor, Mr. Pete Browning is a gentleman widely known in this community. He was born in Louisville in 1861, and has since resided in this city. For many years he has been closely identified with baseball interests, and is an enthusiastic player himself, and as such is well-known throughout this section of the country, having been identified with the Louisville, Cincinnati, Pittsburg and Cleveland clubs. As an authority on baseball matters he is recognized as having no equal in Louisville. His saloon has become the favorite headquarters for the baseball players of the country, and his patronage is drawn from the best class of business men. Mr. Browning handles only the finest Kentucky whiskies as well as the choicest liquors of all kinds. He also has always on tap or in bottles the products of the famous Pabst Brewing Company. In fact there is no more popular saloon in this section of the city, than the "Gladiator's" Place, and Mr. Browning is one of the most popular and successful business men in this line of business in Louisville. Every one is sure of a cordial welcome, and his customers have learned to esteem him as a whole-souled liberal fellow in every sense of the word.

THE BERGEN & MEEHAN COMPANY; Manufacturers and Dealers in Staves, Headings, and Cooperage for Export; Corner Shipp Avenue and Brook Street.—The extraordinary increase in the shipment of merchandise of all kinds, and in the consumption of liquors, has imparted to the cooperage industry an interest and importance almost entirely unknown some thirty or forty years ago. One of the best known concerns in Louisville engaged in this line is that of The Bergen and Meehan Company, manufacturers of staves, headings, etc. This prosperous concern was founded in Central City, Kentucky, under the firm style of Thomas H. Meehan & Co., removal being made to Louisville in 1887, state corporate charter under the existent trading title being secured in 1891. The company has an ample cash capital, the executive officers being Z. Bergen, president; M. Meehan, vice-president; and T. H. Meehan, treasurer and general manager. The premises occupied cover six and a half acres, several large shops being included therein, the machinery equipment being of the latest improved pattern, stave mills being likewise operated at Alexander, Kentucky, and at Brinkley, Arkansas. Employment is provided for a force of from forty to seventy hands, according to the season of the year, the range of production embracing A1 rived listed staves, dressed heading and circle heads, also cooperage for export. The company ships largely sugar, molasses and rum shocks whiskey barrels, etc., to all parts of the United States, also abroad. President Bergen resides in Brooklyn, New York, and is prominently identified with several other business interests in New York city. Messrs. Meehan are brothers, thoroughly practical coopers and natives of Portland, Maine. Orders are filled with dispatch at extremely moderate figures, and entire satisfaction is guaranteed patrons.

W. D. KEMPER; Grocer; No. 2000 West Main Street.—This store was opened two years ago by George Tepe and was purchased by Mr. Kemper, June 22d, 1895. Mr. Kemper, who is a painter by trade, was formerly, before purchasing this store, in the employ of David & Echsner. The business as purchased by Mr. Kemper was already well established with a valuable good will and an extensive patronage which has steadily increased under his judicious management. He handles all the leading brands of Kentucky whiskies, including the famous Mayflower brand and the Ackerman beer which has gained such a wide favor among discriminating drinkers of beer as a beverage. Employing thoroughly trained assistants Mr. Kemper has succeeded in most satisfactorily filling the wants of his numerous customers and through courteous and careful attention and the prompt and accurate filling of orders he is steadily extending his already large connection. He is a native of Louisville, where he is well known and esteemed and deservedly popular, and he is a member of the Young Men's Institute.

GEO. BICKEL; Groceries, Produce, Feed, Etc.; Corner Ohio and Van Buren Streets.—One of the most reliable grocery establishments in this section of Louisville is that of Mr. George Bickel, which was established many years ago by Mr. Berdelle, who conducted it till 1856, when Mr. Geo. Bickel became the proprietor. Mr. Bickel has always made it a rule to handle only the purest, freshest and best groceries and produce in the market. The store and premises are spacious and are well fitted up with every convenience. Here is kept a heavy and choice stock of staple and fancy groceries, teas, coffees, spices, canned goods of every description, sugar, butter, cheese, produce, feed, etc., and customers can always implicitly rely that nothing inferior will be sold to them. This grocery is noted for its cleanliness and several assistants are employed. Mr. Bickel was born in Germany in 1836, but has resided in Louisville since 1848. He is an able and honorable business man, and has gained the entire confidence of his numerous customers in all parts of the city and its vicinity.

R. MOOSMANN; Merchant Tailor; Nos. 1425 and 1427 West Market Street.—Prominent among the leading merchant tailors of Louisville is Mr. R. Moosman who has achieved an excellent reputation for the superiority of all his garments. Mr. Moosmann, who is an expert cutter and merchant tailor, established this business in 1874, and has since built up an influential patronage. He first started on Market Street, between Fifteenth and Sixteenth Streets, and eventually in 1880 built his present substantial building. The store is fully stocked with the choicest imported and domestic woolens, broadcloths, suitings, etc., and all garments made here are recognized by a critical public as perfect in style, fit, and workmanship, while the prices quoted are extremely moderate. Mr. Moosmann was born in Germany in 1843, but has resided in Louisville since 1868, where he is highly esteemed for his strict integrity. He is an active member of the I. O. O. F. and Knights of Honor, and is now ably assisted by his sons in the business, who are young men of great promise. Among his constant customers are many of our best dressed citizens, who find in this store not only the best goods, but a place where the style and fitting of a garment are matters of careful study.

HOME LAUNDRY COMPANY; No. 315 Sixth Street.—No concern in the city has achieved a higher reputation for first-class work, than the Home Laundry Company. This business was established in 1884 and has been duly incorporated under the laws of Kentucky with ample capital, Mr. Owen Sullivan being the president and manager. Mr. Sullivan was born in the Falls City, in 1857. When he began business, there were only five laundries here, now there are thirty, and any one of these does more work than the whole of the previous five. The laundries of Louisville now expend over $6,000 weekly in wages only to help, and their paid-up capital amounts to nearly $200,000. Mr. Sullivan owns the Home Laundry, which was built specially for the business in 1895, and is fully equipped with the latest improved appliances, operated by steam power, and from twenty-five to thirty skilled hands are employed. Much of the machinery utilized was invented by Mr. Sullivan, who is highly esteemed for his skill and strict integrity. All work is executed in a superior manner without injury to garments, while several delivery wagons are in constant service. Lace curtains, fine shirts, chemises, collars and cuffs, embroidered articles, etc., are laundried in a skilful manner, and the annoyance of having articles changed for those of others is carefully guarded against. Orders by mail or telephone are immediately attended to, and despite the superiority of the work, very moderate prices are charged. Mr. Sullivan is an honorable business man, and has achieved success by his careful attention to the wants of customers.

GEO. L. SMITH MANTEL COMPANY; Nos 106-108 East Green Street.—One of the most gratifying features of the present age is the development of the fine arts, as applied to the general outfit and fitting up of offices, stores, etc. In this connection reference is made to the representative Geo. L. Smith Mantel Company, designers and contractors for all kinds of art tile work, etc. This company was organized in 1893, under its present title, with ample capital, Messrs. Geo. L. Smith and Alfred Greenaway being the proprietors, the latter of whom is a thoroughly practical tile setter, and has been constantly in the employ of some one of the mantel firms in this city for the past thirty years. He is the inventor of several patent grates, fenders, dampers, heaters, tile holders, etc., which are manufactured and sold by this house. They occupy a spacious first floor, the workshops and storeroom being in the rear. Mr. Smith owns the building, and uses the other floors for galvanized iron and sheet metal works. In their salesrooms they keep constantly on hand all kinds of wood and iron mantels, brass, iron and plated frames, summer front and fenders, and make a specialty of Al. Greenaway's patent recess grates and heaters. They also carry in stock hearths, facings, floors, wainscoting, fireplace linings and art tile work in general, while careful attention is given to the setting and resetting of grates and curing defective flues, etc. Their work is highly endorsed by leading architects, builders, etc., owing to its elegance and durability, while the prices quoted by the house are extremely moderate. The partners are Kentuckians, and are highly esteemed by the community for their strict integrity. Mr. Smith is an active Freemason, and a popular member of the Builders' and Traders' Exchange, I. O. O. F., and Knights of Pythias, while Mr. Greenaway is also a member of the Knights of Pythias and likewise of the Knights and Ladies of Honor.

CHAS. HEGEWALD COMPANY; Founders and Machinists; Water Street, from State to Lower First, New Albany, Ind.—This extensive business was established in 1880 by Mr. Chas. Hegewald, who had previously been identified with the widely-known house of Chas. Hegewald & Co. On January 1st, 1894, the enterprise was incorporated under the laws of Indiana with a paid-up capital of $30,000 as the Chas. Hegewald Company, the executive officers being Mr. Chas. Hegewald, president, Mr. E. J. Hewitt, secretary, and Mr. A. F. Hegewald, superintendent. Mr. Chas. Hegewald was born in Saxony, Germany, where he learned the trade of a machinist and mechanical engineer. He came to the United States in 1853 and worked for several years in a New Albany machine shop. During the Civil War he was foreman of the American Foundry and is recognized as one of the ablest mechanical engineers in the state. Mr. A. F. Hegewald is a native of this city and a son of Mr. Chas. Hegewald, while Mr. Hewitt was born also in New Albany and has been office man with Mr. C. Hegewald since 1876. The premises occupied comprise a spacious brick building extending from State to Lower First Street, and the equipment includes two cupolas having a capacity of twenty-five tons of metal daily, a brass foundry, also a complete boiler and machine shop, etc., the machinery being operated by steam power. One hundred and twenty-five skilled hands are employed and they make a specialty of steamboat engines, boilers, machinery, and have fitted up more than two hundred steamboats, seven of them being for the Low and Evansville Mail Line, for which they are now building the "Rose Hite." This company possesses every facility for building machinery of every description, and turns out first-class work at extremely moderate figures. The officers are highly esteemed in trade circles for their strict integrity and ability, and are thoroughly identified with the growth and prosperity of New Albany, which they have greatly advanced by the establishment and maintenance of this useful and important industry.

JOSEPH E. MARRET; Florist; No. 1314 East Broadway.—Louisville is noted for the beauty and extent of her greenhouses, and among the largest of which, those of Mr. Joseph E. Marret are prominent. Mr. Charles Rompers established this business twenty years ago, and after conducting it for some time, admitted Mr. Joseph E. Marret into partnership in 1880. A few months later Mr. Rompers retired and since then it has been carried on by the present proprietor. The greenhouses and grounds are spacious and well arranged. Every modern appliance for the successful development of flowers is provided, while the facilities are such that the largest orders can always be promptly filled. Plants of all kinds, from the sturdy geranium down to the most delicate tropical and foreign productions, are found here in profusion, and the rosery is especially noticeable for the beauty and variety of its blooms. Several careful assistants are employed and a large city and Cave Hill Cemetery trade is done. A specialty is made of promptly filling orders for weddings, parties, etc., and the bulk of the fashionable trade falls to the lot of Mr. Marret. There are few professions requiring more artistic taste than that of the florist, and this quality Mr. Marret possesses in a marked degree. Mr. Marret was born in

Louisville, and is the son of the late Peter Murret, one of Louisville's highly respected citizens. He is a young man of energy and integrity, and his success is but the merited reward of strenuous effort and liberal dealing.

SEELBACH'S EUROPEAN HOTEL AND RESTAURANT: Corner Sixth and Main Streets.—A perfect exponent of the science of hotel keeping in Louisville, is Seelbach's European Hotel and Restaurant. This hotel was opened fifteen years ago by Mr. Louis Seelbach, who has since secured a liberal patronage, and guests who have once stopped here are sure to return when again visiting the Falls City. The hotel is a substantial five-story brick building 40x125 feet in dimensions, the first floor being devoted to offices, bar, café, cigar and news stand, the second, to reading and dining-rooms, while the other floors are utilized for bed chambers. It is provided with all modern improvements, electric lights, fans and bells, elevator, etc., while the sanitary arrangements and means of escape in case of fire are perfect. The rooms are well ventilated and comfortable, and the hotel is a model of neatness and cleanliness. The table is amply supplied with all the delicacies in season, and the best in the market, properly cooked, and the attendance upon guests is all that can be desired. The hotel is conducted on the European plan, rates being only $1 per day and upwards, according to size of room and location. The café comfortably seats sixty, and the ladies' dining-room twenty guests, while the bar is fully supplied with the choicest wines, liquors, ales, beer, cigars, etc. Mr. Seelbach was born in Germany, but has resided in the Falls City for the last twenty-six years, where he has made hosts of friends, owing to his genial disposition and strict probity. He was formerly in the employment of the Galt House, and is a director of the Commercial Club, Commercial Land Company, while he is likewise a popular member of the I. O. O. F.

N. A. FRANKEL & CO.: Commission Merchants and Wholesale Liquor Dealers; No. 123 West Main Street.—This firm are brokers and dealers in Kentucky whiskies, also controllers of the well-known Murphy, Barber & Co.'s Cane Spring. Mr. Frankel came to this city in 1872 with hardly any capital at all, reliant solely upon indomitable perseverance, backed by competent knowledge of the business, gained by practical experience. In 1880 he associated himself with Mr. N. F. Block, under the style of Frankel & Block, which firm was dissolved seven years later, Mr. F. continuing as N. A. Frankel & Co. his present enterprise. He understands the liquor business in all its modern details and has long since taken his place among the active, stirring, shrewd, liberal men of the day, winning a name for integrity that time only strengthens. The labor, enterprise and energy he displayed at the outset, was but the prelude to the prosperous business of to-day, whose foundations he was instrumental in laying, and he is now in the enjoyment of the ripened fruits of his efforts. Several salesmen are employed, and kept constantly on the move visiting the trade. Mr. Frankel is widely known and influential. He is a prominent member of the Board of Trade, the Commercial Club, the Standard Club, and other leading organizations.

KICE & COMPANY: Real Estate; No. 429 West Jefferson Street.—This business was established ten years ago by Mr. M. S. Kice, who is sole proprietor. He has developed a widespread connection of a superior character including among his permanent patrons many leading capitalists and operators in realty, while he is also a recognized accurate authority on the present and prospective values of realty in all sections of the city and its vicinity, so that the utmost reliance can be placed upon his judgment and advice by intending investors. Mr. Kice, with a force of eight of the best real estate men in the city, transacts a general real estate business, buying, selling, exchanging and renting, and has carried through to a successful issue many important transactions. He also negotiates loans promptly on bond and mortgage, collects rents, takes entire management of estates, makes a speciality of handling non-resident property, being the introducer of the monthly payment plan in selling homes. He was born in this city, and

is familiar with every suburb street and alley, and is an active member of the Commercial Club. If you are thinking of making an investment of any nature in real estate, or have real estate to sell, exchange or rent, you will find it greatly to your interest to call on Kice & Company.

EDWARD KLAUBER; Photographer and Art Dealer; No. 332 Fourth Avenue.—Among the reliable and widely known photographers of the city of Louisville is Mr. Edward Klauber, who commenced the practice of his art in 1855, and has since secured a liberal patronage with the best classes of society in the city and state. He has always been a close student of his art and his work is pronounced by experts as fully equal to that of the best artists in the country. The parlors are elegantly furnished, and the gallery is fully supplied with the latest improved apparatus and appliances necessary for the successful prosecution of this artistic industry. Mr. Klauber executes all kinds of work, from the carte de-visite to the imperial cabinet, and makes a specialty of life size portraits in crayon, oil, pastelle and India ink, and his water color miniatures are the finest that can be seen. Pictures are taken by the instantaneous process, and thus patrons are enabled to obtain accurate and perfect photographs of themselves, groups and children. Mr. Klauber also deals in and keeps on hand a choice stock of art goods, pictures, engravings, etchings, picture frames, artists' materials, etc. He has become famous for securing to sitters before the camera a graceful and natural pose and lifelike and pleasing expression, and in all his work is to be seen the master hand of the talented artist. Pictures and photos are promptly framed to order, and popular **prices** prevail. Mr. Klauber was born in Austria in 1835, and came to Louisville in 1855. He is highly regarded for his strict probity and no more successful and able photographer can be found in the ranks of the profession.

J. W. HENNING'S SONS; Real Estate and Fire Insurance; No. 226 Fifth Street.—The steady development of the real estate market of Louisville is one of the most positive indications of its solid prosperity, as its realty is being more than ever sought after, as first-class remunerative investments. The facilities for acquiring property here were never better than at the present time, and in this connection prominent reference is made to the old established and reliable house of J. W. Henning's Sons, the popular real estate and fire insurance agents. This business was established in 1846 by J. W. Henning and Josiah S. Speed, under the firm name of "Henning & Speed," who were succeeded by J. W. Henning & Son. Mr. J. W. Henning died in 1887, when the present firm assumed control under the title of J. W. Henning's Sons, the partners being Messrs. S. C. Henning and P. M. O'Reilly. Mr. O'Reilly, who is the active manager, possesses an accurate knowledge of the present and prospective values of all kinds of realty in the Falls City and its vicinity, and has developed an influential patronage, numbering among his permanent patrons many wealthy investors and property owners. He buys, sells, exchanges and lets all descriptions of city and suburban property, takes entire management of estates, pays taxes, effects repairs and makes a specialty of the negotiation of loans on bond and first mortgage. Mr. O'Reilly also promptly effects insurance at lowest rates and represents the following first-class companies, viz: Reading Insurance Company, Reading, Pa.; Prussian National Insurance Company, Germany; Merchants Insurance Company, Newark, N. J.; North Western National Insurance Company, Milwaukee, Wis., etc. The offices are the finest of the kind in the city, and all commissions are faithfully attended to. Mr. O'Reilly is an energetic, honorable and popular gentleman, highly esteemed in social and financial circles and a most public spirited citizen. He is an active member of the Board of Trade and Board of Aldermen and has even given a cordial support to all measures conducive to the benefit and welfare of the entire community.

THE F. WUNDERLICH COMPANY; Wholesale Liquor Dealers: No. 106 State Street, New Albany.—This business was established in 1866 by Mr. Fred Wunderlich, who conducted it till 1885, when he admitted his son-in-law, Mr. Louis Michel, into partnership, the firm being known as Wunderlich & Michel. Mr. Michel died February, 1889, and the business was eventually incorporated under the laws of Indiana, May, 1889, with a paid-up capital of $25,000, Mr. Fred. Wunderlich being the president and manager. This business was formerly conducted in the Masonic Building, corner Pearl and Spring Streets, but in November, 1894, was removed to the present location. The premises occupied comprise a spacious store and cellar each 18x100 feet in area, fully equipped with every convenience. Here is kept always a heavy and choice stock of the most noted whiskies, brandies, gin, rum, cordials, imported and domestic wines, **etc.**, while a specialty is made of the "Stylus Club" whiskey **and** Wunderlich's world-renowned aromatic stomach bitters. Only the purest and finest wines and liquors are handled, and the trade of the house extends throughout Indiana and the adjacent states. Mr. Wunderlich was born in Germany, and first commenced business in the United States as a shoemaker in Portland, Ky., in 1851. He afterwards purchased the largest shoe store in southern Indiana, and then conducted a shoe store on State Street, New Albany. In 1884, Mr. Wunderlich retired from the shoe business and was some time in the wholesale grocery trade, and after that in the wholesale liquor business. He is highly esteemed in trade circles for his strict integrity, and justly merits the liberal and influential patronage secured in this important business. Mr. Wunderlich is a prominent Mystic Shrine and Scottish Rite Mason, and treasurer of the Glenivin Park R. R. Co., and also served three terms in the city council. He was one of the organizers of the Pythagoras Lodge No. 355, which was the first German one in New Albany, and has been treasurer of it since 1875, and joined the Masonic Order in Portland, Ky., forty years ago.

GEO. P. BOHN; Tin, Copper and Sheet Iron Ware; No. 211 East Jefferson Street.—A reliable roofing establishment in Louisville is that of Mr. George P. Bohn, roofer and manufacturer of tin, copper and sheet iron ware. This business was established many years ago by Mr. John Sell, who conducted it till January, 1865, when Messrs. Brant & Bohn purchased his interest. In 1866 they sold out, and Mr. Bohn became a partner with Mr. J. H. Cowen on Fifth Street. They purchased the business formerly conducted by Jones & Somerville, and after three years Mr. Cowen sold out to Mr. George Gans. Messrs. Bohn & Gans continued together till 1882, when Mr. Bohn retired and started for himself on Market Street, between Fourth and Fifth Streets, and eventually in July, 1892, removed to his present location. The premises occupied are spacious and every facility is at hand for the successful conduct of the business. A well selected and choice stock of stoves, ranges, heaters, tin and iron ware, gas stoves and house furnishing goods is always on hand, and the prices quoted for them cannot be discounted in the city or elsewhere. Estimates are promptly furnished for all kinds of roofing, repairing and out-door work, and only first-class workmen are employed. Mr. Bohn has roofed some of the finest buildings in the city and its vicinity, his work being highly endorsed by architects, builders and owners, and while of such strength and workmanship his roofs are constructed at prices lower than those charged for inferior work elsewhere. Orders are promptly executed, and complete satisfaction is guaranteed patrons. Mr. Geo. P. Bohn was born in Germany in 1839, and came to Louisville in 1854. He is highly regarded for his skill and strict probity, and has won by sheer merit his present prominent position in this useful industry. During the civil war he joined the Union army, and in the action of Liberty Gap was severely wounded, the bullet still remaining in his body. He is a popular member of the G. A. R.

GEO. E. ADAMS EXCHANGE; Groceries and Liquors; Southwest corner Eighteenth and Walnut Streets.—The establishment of Mr. George E. Adams is one of the most complete of its kind to be found in Louisville, and is deservedly popular with the public. The enterprise was inaugurated in 1880 by its present proprietor and from the outset has prospered. The building is a substantial two story brick structure, 25x80 feet in area, and is in its appointments a thoroughly up-to-date business house. On the ground floor is the store, and here is found a comprehensive stock of staple and fancy groceries, choice teas and coffees, sugars, canned goods, condiments, dried fruits, vegetables and fruits in season, etc., also wines and liquors of the most celebrated brands. In the rear of the store is a superior saloon, catering to the best patronage. Among the liquors carried are the finest Kentucky whiskies and Ackerman draught beer, Nadorf Brewing Company's draught beer, Pabst Milwaukee beer, etc. On the second floor is a spacious billiard hall, containing several tables and managed in the very best manner. Mr. Adams guarantees every article he sells, and is honorable in all his business methods. As a consequence his establishment is a very popular one and cannot be too highly recommended. Mr. Adams was born in Shelbyville, Ky., and came to Louisville in 1880. He has made hosts of friends here and is highly esteemed in both business and social circles, and is a member of the Knights of Honor and of the Knights and Ladies of Honor, and likewise of the Kentucky Commandery, No. 40.

J. N. PFEIFFER & CO.; Hatters and Clothiers; Seventh and Market Streets.—This business was originally established by Mr. Rosenfield in 1870, Mr. Pfeiffer succeeding in 1883, and three years later admitting Mr. Philip C. Klapper to partnership under the present firm name, assuming sole control again in January 1895. This establishment is famed for the style and high-quality of its hats, every kind being kept in stock for men, youths and boys, together with caps, helmets, straw hats, gloves, umbrellas and canes, this being unquestionably the best place in the city in which to make purchases; the stock also includes a very fine array of imported and domestic cloths, suitings, vestings, and overcoatings, in all the latest shades and patterns. The firm has in its employ a first-class cutter, and an accomplished master of the tailors' art, and, as they employ only skilful hands, and utilize only the best of trimmings, materials, etc., to be clothed by them is to be perfectly dressed, and in the height of the fashion. Mr. Pfeiffer is a native of Louisville, and has always lived here, making hosts of permanent friends, by his honorable dealing, in all ranks of life. We would suggest to our visiting friends that they take advantage of the opportunity to make fall and even winter purchases of hats, suits, overcoats etc., as they can select here from a really splendid stock, carefully augmented from the best sources of supply for the occasion, and they may rely upon prices being the same as on an ordinary occasion, which is surprisingly reasonable.

LOUISVILLE OF TO-DAY.

SAMUEL M. BAUER: Jobber of Drugs, Chemicals, Pharmaceuticals and Sundries; No. 228 West Main Street.—The importance of Louisville as a wholesale purchasing point, is unquestionably the result, apart from geographical advantages, of the distinguished enterprise and progressiveness of the proprietors of her leading business houses. They are the first always to afford buyers the benefits of the fluctuations of the market, also full assorted stocks, including many specialties. The above facts are especially noticeable in the wholesale jobbing trade in drugs and chemicals, as represented by the reliable house of Mr. Samuel M. Bauer. Founded but a brief six years ago, this house has, during the comparatively brief intervening period to the present, risen to a position in the front rank of the trade, Mr. Bauer's business operations to-day, exceeding those of any similar concern in the South. He originally engaged in business on the attainment of his majority in 1889, on a modest borrowed capital, his first quarters consisting of a second-story room, 12x12 feet in dimensions; as year followed year the steady increase of the business demanded larger

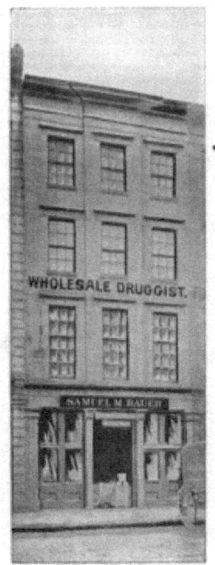

premises, and in 1891 he secured his present commodious establishment. It consists of a substantial four-storied and basement brick building, 20x100 feet in dimensions on the lower portions, the second, third and fourth floors having a lineal frontage and depth of 20x60 feet. As an importer and jobber, Mr. Bauer keeps constantly on hand a fresh stock of drugs, chemicals, pharmaceuticals and sundries. His list of drugs is complete, including many little known medicinal roots, herbs, leaves, gums, etc., the particularization of which could not be attempted in this brief sketch. Extracts, tinctures, powders, acids and fine chemicals are always found here of the best quality. The chemical department contains all the finest preparations from the most celebrated manufacturing chemists in the world. The selection of druggists' sundries, perfumery, soap and toilet requisites, comprise the most approved manufacturers, both foreign and domestic. The connections of the house are of a superior character, Mr. Bauer's facilities of supply being such that he is enabled to quote figures to the trade, which few if any of his business competitors in this section can profitably afford to duplicate. He is a native of this city, and for some six years prior to engaging in business on his own account, was favorably identified in a subordinate capacity with one of our leading wholesale drug houses. He is a prominent member of the Botanical Club, and a graduate of the Louisville College of Pharmacy.

DRACH, THOMAS & BOHNE; Architects; Fifth and Main Streets.—Among the leading architects of Louisville the firm of Drach, Thomas and Bohne must be given a prominent place. Under the style of Drach and Thomas the business was founded six years ago and was thus conducted until April, 1894, when Mr. F. W. Bohne was admitted into partnership and the present style adopted. They furnish plans and specifications for edifices of all kinds, and among some of the leading buildings they have designed may be mentioned, the I. O. O. F. Building, the office of the Cave Hill Cemetery, and two schoolhouses at Owensboro, Ky.; Hodge Tobacco Works, Henderson, Ky.; Catholic church, Hardingsburg, Ky.; Louisville Electric Light Company's plant; Danville Gymnasium for Centre College, Danville, Ky.; German Baptist Church, Louisville, Ky., and many others. The members of the firm are Max Drach, John H. Thomas and F. W. Bohne, all of whom are architects of wide experience and exceptional ability. Messrs. Drach and Thomas were formerly draughtsmen for McDonald Brothers, architects of this city, and are active members of the Engineers' and Architects' Club. Mr. Bohne was formerly a draughtsman for the firm before becoming a partner and previous to that was with Mabry and Bohne, architects.

LOUISVILLE OF TO-DAY.

BESTEN & LANGEN; Wholesale and Retail Cloaks, Furs and Suits, Wrappers, Waists, Etc.; No. 528 Fourth Avenue.—In 1891 this flourishing house was established, and though one of the youngest commercial enterprises of Louisville, it already occupies a prominent place among the large and influential establishments. Messrs. H. Besten and E. O. Langen are the proprietors, and nothing has been neglected that could

add to the attractiveness and convenience of the house or facilitate operations, while the stock carried embraces everything in the line of cloaks, furs, suits, wrappers, waists, and in short everything in the line of ladies' ready made garments, all purchased direct from the leading foreign and domestic sources of supply, with whom the firm enjoys exceptionally advantageous relations, and the extent of their operations enables them to offer inducements which smaller houses cannot think of duplicating. Several assistants are employed in the various departments, and the trade which is both wholesale and retail, comes from all parts of the city and vicinity. This is the only house in this city, dealing exclusively in cloaks and ready made goods for ladies. Each year shows a decided increase in the extent and volume of their sales, and as earnestly have they striven to deal liberally and honorably with all customers, that to-day the name of the house is a synonym to the trade of reliability and liberality, and from their unselfish efforts to advance the interests of patrons, has sprung their own advancement. Messrs. Besten and Langen are young men of wide experience in this line. Mr. Besten came to Louisville from Detroit, Michigan, and Mr. Langen from Terre Haute, Ind. They are young men of energy, integrity and exceptional business qualifications, and as well as winning for themselves a foremost place among the business men of the city, they have gained the esteem and respect of all with whom they come in contact.

STRENG & THALHEIMER; Jobbers and Manufacturers of Boots and Shoes; No. 635 West Main Street; Boston No. 130 Summer Street.— The wholesale boot and shoe trade of Louisville has grown to enormous proportions, as besides supplying the needs of an immense urban and suburban population, this is the principal distributing point for the immense territory south of the Ohio River and extending from the Falls to the Gulf of Mexico. There are several important and influential jobbing houses here engaged in this branch of commerce, in addition to quite a number of factories, and many Eastern manufacturers have their special representatives in this market. Competition is brisk, extremely so, but not to a dishonorable or suicidal extent, and the trade in general is in a healthy condition. In this active and honorable competition, the most prominent part has been borne by Messrs. Streng & Thalheimer, jobbers of boots, shoes and rubbers, at No. 635 West Main Street. This prosperous house was established some fourteen years ago and immediately went to the front rank and did, and are doing the largest and leading boot and shoe business in our city and to-day have a commercial reputation for fair and honest dealing second to none in this country. Manuel J. Streng and William Thalheimer compose the firm. They occupy the entire premises No. 635 West Main Street, a substantial four-storied and basement building, 25x210 feet in dimensions, giving them ample accommodation for the manipulation and storage of the large and valuable stock they carry at all times and the general advantageous prosecution of their business. The firm handles the largest stock of boots and shoes and rubbers carried in the city of Louisville and sell exclusively to the trade at wholesale. Their stock consists of every variety and grade of men's, women's, misses' and children's shoes, from the cheapest to the best and we doubt if there is another house in the country whose assortment is as complete and so far as their prices are concerned, their uninterrupted success and reputation, for nearly fifteen years speaks for itself. Likewise, they carry a full line of Imperial, Connecticut and Wales Goodyear Rubber Company's goods, in staples, medium and the celebrated specialties in all toes and styles and are justly styled the "Southern Rubber Agency." These goods are the output of the most noted manufacturers in the country. Twenty assistants in various capacities are provided with employment in the home establishment and the interests of the house on the road are ably represented by a corps of twelve travelling salesmen, controlling a large, lucrative and steadily growing trade, which is broadly distributed throughout Kentucky, Indiana, Mississippi and Tennessee. Mr. Streng is a Kentuckian by birth and formerly resided at Henderson, this state. Mr. Thalheimer is a native of Rochester, N. Y., and has now resided in Louisville for the past fifteen years. He is a director of the Board of Trade and both gentlemen are members of the Standard and Commercial Clubs and the order of Free and Accepted Masons and are thoroughly identified with the interests of our city and the shoe trade in particular.

LOUISVILLE TRANSFER COMPANY; Corner of Ninth and Green Streets. One of the most important and necessary requirements of a large city is a first-class transfer line, which will afford prompt and reliable service to the business and traveling public. Louisville is admirably supplied in this particular by the Louisville Transfer Company, which is one of the finest equipped and best managed institutions of its kind in the country. The company was established in 1867, and has from the time of its organization, met with the liberal patronage of the best people in the city. The late Colonel Horace Scott, was its first president and most active organizer; the executive ability displayed by him in its management caused the business to rapidly increase, necessitating continual enlargement of the company's facilities and equipments. At the decease of Colonel Scott in January, 1895, he was succeeded in the presidency by his nephew, Col. Albert Scott, president of the Kentucky Trust Company, Ex-United States revenue collector, and one of the most prominent and highly respected citizens of the state. A deal was recently completed whereby an entire change took place in the management of the company. Col. Scott was succeeded in the presidency by Mr. J. E. Morand, formerly general manager of the Indianapolis Transfer Company, and having an experience in the business of fifteen years, Mr. Morand is placed in entire charge of the business and his long experience and ability are already manifesting themselves in numerous changes and improvements which greatly increase and facilitate the transaction of business. Associated with him in office are Mr. P. F. Ingoe, secretary and treasurer; P. J. McGuire, assistant secretary and treasurer; and A. Polin, superintendent. The company's office and stables occupy a substantial two-and-a-half story brick building, 105x 200 feet in area. The building was designed and constructed especially for this company, and is admirably planned and perfectly arranged. The stables are large, well ventilated and remarkably clean, an entire floor is used for the storage of carriages, coupes and wagons of all descriptions. In the front of the building are located the offices, which are continually open day and night, carriages can be sent to any address or baggage transfers arranged for on short notice. The company owns one hundred fine horses and over one hundred vehicles of all kinds, including carriages, coupes, transfer and baggage wagons, omnibuses, picnic and band wagons. Their carriages are elegantly furnished and upholstered, kept in perfect order, and their employees are noted for their efficiency and sobriety, guaranteeing perfect satisfaction. An important and valuable feature of the fine service given by this company is their system of checking baggage and luggage of all kinds, which can be checked at the residences, hotel, or place of business through to all railroad points, prompt transfers are made to and from depots, and the patrons of the company are thus saved all the worry and trouble of attending personally to their trunks. The Louisville Transfer Company does practically all of the baggage and passenger business of Louisville and the vicinity, a staff of one hundred men are kept on its pay roll, and they have invested in the business a cash capital of over $150,000. The company is in every respect a model business concern, having an able management, complete equipment, prompt service and only charging moderate rates. Only a few remarks are necessary regarding the personnel of the company. Mr. J. E. Morand, the newly appointed president, bringing a long and practical experience of the business to his position has already shown that he fully merits the trust and confidence placed in him by the directors of the company. Mr. Morand intends to do business on a metropolitan scale, and will introduce many improved vehicles of the latest patterns, many with rubber-tired wheels, giving Louisville a transfer line, equal to any in New York and the large Eastern cities. Mr. P. F. Ingoe, the secretary and treasurer of the company, and likewise a member of the board of directors, is a resident of Indianapolis, where he is connected with various interests. Mr. McGuire, the assistant secretary and treasurer, has been connected with the company for a number of years, his superior business ability and personal popularity have contributed greatly to the success of the company. Mr. A. Polin, the superintendent, is likewise an old employee, and has rendered valuable service in the conduct of his department.

EARLY TIMES DISTILLERY CO.

OFFICE: LOUISVILLE, KY.   DISTILLERY: NELSON COUNTY, KY.

SAMUEL BROTHERS & CO., Sole Agents for the Pacific Slope,

Nos. 132 AND 134 FIRST STREET, SAN FRANCISCO, CAL.

"Early Times" Distillery, Nelson County, Kentucky. Bonded Warehouses on the premises not shown in this sketch.

This brand of whiskey has been made in what is now Nelson County, Fifth District of Kentucky, ever since the earliest settlement of the state, hence the brand "Early Times." It was first made by the grandfather of J. H. Beam, the present distiller, and thus it has passed from father to son, a crop having been made every year since that early period by one family of distillers, and it is made now as it was then, on the old primitive plan, handmade sour-mash fire copper over open wood fires, which has given Kentucky whiskies their great reputation for purity and fine flavor. We have added to the distillery only such modern improvements as will facilitate the mashing of the grain, without changing the old style of distillation.

The grain used in the manufacture of this whiskey is the very best corn, rye and barley; and using no patent yeast to force excessive yield, none but absolutely pure old-fashion whiskey is produced, which we bottle expressly for hotels, clubs, druggists, and family use. There are many spurious imitations of this whiskey on the market, therefore we call the attention of those desiring to use the genuine "Early Times" to the fac-simile of our trade mark, (as above,) which is burnt in the head of every barrel, is on the bottom of every bottle, and on the cap, and "Early Times" burnt in the cork, none other being genuine.

H. GOTTBRATH,
DEALER IN
Groceries, Liquors & Tobaccos,
Cor. Eighth and Market Sts.

OLD AND RARE WHISKIES A SPECIALTY
MICHAELBERG BEER ON DRAUGHT
IMPORTED AND DOMESTIC CIGARS
MIN STEW .... PICKLES
Blue Grass Exchange,
—————
GOTTBRATH

LOUIS KORB,
DEALER IN
Wall Paper and Window Shades,
1708 Market Street, between 17th and 18th.

Practical Paper Hanging a Specialty.

D. B. DOLL,
WOOLEN MILLS AGENT,
505 WEST MAIN STREET.

Louisville Coffin Company,
MANUFACTURERS OF
Burial Cases, Caskets,
Shrouds, Linings,
and Funeral Supplies.

Corner Eleventh and Madison Streets.

JOSEPH FIHE
—DEALER IN—
GROCERIES,
PROVISIONS,
Meats & Vegetables,
Cor. Preston and Walnut Sts.

KILLGORE & STILTZ,
MANUFACTURERS OF
PLATFORM AND ELLIPTIC
SPRING WAGONS.
217 TO 223 FIRST STREET.

Ladies', Misses' and Children's
Fine Shoes.
S. BRUNN,
BOOTS AND SHOES,
126 and 128 W. Market St. opp Musr Hall

OHMANN BROS.,
—DEALERS IN—
Staple and Fancy Groceries,
Produce, Fresh Meats, Vegetables, Etc.,
FEED, LIME AND CEMENT.
Choice Sample Room in Rear. Cor. Eighteenth and Kentucky Sts.

WM. TINGLEY.
WAGON BUILDER,
231 To 235 EAST MAIN STREET.

West Louisville Brewery,
GOTTLIEB LAUFFER, Proprietor,
BREWER OF THE CELEBRATED
CREAM BEER.
OFFICE AND BREWERY.
West Market Street, Corner 34th St.
All orders for Beer have Prompt Attention.

JULIUS SUES,
The Oldest House in the City.
230 Fourth Avenue.
Toys, Games,
Rubber Goods,
Children's Carriages, Etc.

THOS. BANNON,
—DEALER IN—
GROCERIES,
Produce, Vegetables,
DRY GOODS, NOTIONS, &c.
Corner Thirty-fourth and Rudd Avenue.

C. BOESWALD.
Groceries and Provisions,
1535 WEST WALNUT STREET.

B. S. HAGGARD & CO.,
WHOLESALE
COMMISSION MERCHANTS
—IN—
HAY, GRAIN, APPLES, POTATOES, ONIONS.
TELEPHONE 2261.
NO. 109 THIRD STREET.
REFERENCES:
AMERICAN NATIONAL BANK, BANKING-SNYDER HARDWARE CO.

E. R. BASSETT,
Fine Paper Hangings
642 FOURTH AVENUE.

E. P. MARTIN,
COMMISSION MERCHANT,
SPECIAL ATTENTION GIVEN TO
TAN-BARK, HOOP-POLES, STAVES,
LUMBER, ETC., ETC.,
827 Broadway bet. Eighth and Ninth.
E. P. MARTIN,
Jefferson Co.

www.ingramcontent.com/pod-product-compliance
Lightning Source LLC
Chambersburg PA
CBHW031618170426
43195CB00037B/983